Helping Teachers Teach

Helping Teachers Teach

A School Library Media Specialist's Role

THIRD EDITION

Philip M. Turner
Ann Marlow Riedling

LIBRARIES UNLIMITED

A Member of the Greenwood Publishing Group

Westport, Connecticut • London

Library of Congress Cataloging-in-Publication Data

Turner, Philip M., 1948–
    Helping teachers teach : a school library media specialist's role / by Philip M.
Turner and Ann Marlow Riedling.—3rd ed.
        p. cm.
    Includes bibliographical references and index.
    ISBN 1–59158–020–X (alk. paper)
    1. School libraries—United States. 2. Media programs (Education)—United
States. 3. Curriculum planning—United States. 4. Instructional materials centers—United States. 5. Libraries and teachers—United States. 6. Libraries and
education—United States. I. Riedling, Ann Marlow, 1952– II. Title.
Z675.S3T88   2003
027.8'0973—dc21   2003047582

British Library Cataloguing in Publication Data is available.

Library of Congress Catalog Card Number: 2003047582
ISBN: 1–59158–020–X

First published in 2003

Libraries Unlimited, Inc., 88 Post Road West, Westport, CT 06881
A Member of the Greenwood Publishing Group, Inc.
www.lu.com

Printed in the United States of America

The paper used in this book complies with the
Permanent Paper Standard issued by the National
Information Standards Organization (Z39.48-1984).

10 9 8 7 6 5 4 3 2 1

CONTENTS

Appendixes

PREFACE

The preface to the second edition of *Helping Teachers Teach* begins with the premise that the school library media specialist is in a position to make a significant positive impact on the children and young adults in our schools. Nine years later, we stand by that premise and can point to many examples of school library media specialists having fundamentally and positively affected the entire educational enterprise of a school. We also are aware of failures, of school library media specialists with good intentions and solid skills who were worn down by a system in which achievement is not always rewarded. The same fundamental belief is the foundation for this edition: Our children are worth the struggle.

The response to the first two editions was beyond all expectations. There was, and still remains, a strong desire among school library media specialists to make a difference in how teachers teach and students learn. *Helping Teachers Teach* provided—and will continue to provide in some small way, the tools for committed professionals to make a difference.

There have been significant changes in the profession during the past nine years. A new set of guidelines formally recognized the role of instructional consultant (referred to as "instructional partner" in *Information Power*, 1998). Revolutionary breakthroughs in large-scale information storage and retrieval and in local- and wide-area networking have put powerful new tools into the hands of school library media specialists. There is no doubt that new technologies have altered the methods that school library media specialists use to help teachers teach. Developments in cognitive psychology have also altered the field of instructional technology. In addition, the pressure to restructure schools at the local level has increased during the past nine years and now the question seems to be how and how much to change rather than whether to change.

Against this backdrop of change, the goals of this book remain essentially the same: 1) to delineate a realistic role structure for the school library media specialist, 2) to present the role of instructional consultant as obtainable and desirable, and 3) to provide the basic tools for increasing participation in instructional consultation.

The first six chapters define the instructional consultation role and place it within the context of the comprehensive role of the school library media specialist. The reader should emerge from this section of the book with the ability to recognize involvement as an instructional consultant and increase this involvement if such an increase is desired.

Chapters 7 through 14 each cover a step in the instructional design process. Each chapter contains information to assist the school library media specialist in providing varying levels of consultation to teachers.

Each of the first fourteen chapters begins with a list of important topics addressed in the chapter. Each chapter concludes with a Thought Provokers section to allow the reader to immediately use the material presented in the chapter.

The role of a school library media specialist can be one of the most challenging and frustrating that anyone can undertake. It can also be one of the most rewarding. Helping teachers teach and students learn is the foundation of the challenge, frustration, and reward. I hope this book enhances both your desire to help and your ability to do so.

We hope this edition meets your expectations.

I

INSTRUCTIONAL CONSULTATION AND THE SCHOOL LIBRARY MEDIA SPECIALIST

The goal of Part I of this work is to present the role of instructional consultant in a way that is perceived as both desirable and achievable by the reader. Furthermore, this part of the book will present information and strategies that should enable the reader to initiate or increase involvement as an instructional consultant to help teachers teach.

Chapter 1 puts the current state of the school library media profession in a historical perspective in an attempt to explain the causes of some of the problems currently occurring within the profession. The chapter concludes by proposing a three-roles-in-one model of school library media practice.

Chapter 2 discusses why the instructional consultation, or helping-teachers-teach, role has not been more widely implemented. A "levels" approach to instructional consultation is proposed that includes many activities currently performed by school library media specialists and presents a logical pathway for increasing involvement in the teacher assistance process.

Chapter 3 presents a process by which the school library media specialist can identify the level of instructional consultation currently being implemented with a given group of teachers. This chapter also contains strategies for increasing the amount of assistance provided to teachers.

Each of chapters 4 through 6 covers one level of instructional consultation in depth. Strategies for reaching that level and recommended tools are provided.

1

The Roles of the School Library Media Specialist

This chapter provides information to help the reader

- recognize role ambiguity in the school library media profession

- compare the evolution of roles with the development of national standards

- understand the three proposed roles and the importance of each

- identify which role each described task represents

ROLE AMBIGUITY IN THE SCHOOL LIBRARY MEDIA PROFESSION

A colleague once described the typical school library media specialist as "an identity crisis waiting to happen." Although this probably is an overstatement, an uncertainty as to role does seem to pervade the profession. A lack of cohesiveness has resulted in a tremendous variety of school library media programs locally, nationally, and internationally. A library media program at one school might consist entirely of library skills instruction. At a school a few miles away, the school library media specialist might spend the majority of effort teaching the history of folktales. At still another school, the dominant activity might be teaching online searching.

This diversity is reflected in certification standards, preparation programs, and literature. A perusal of resources that prepare future school library media specialists to manage programs leaves one with an uneasy feeling that there is no common agreement on purpose within the field, although major strides are currently attempting to better define the roles and directions of school library media specialists.

There have been attempts to list tasks performed by school library media specialists, such as *Guidance for College/University Faculty Preparing a Curriculum Folio in the Area of School Library Media Education as Part of the Precondition Process for NCATE Accreditation* (American Library Association 2001). It is obvious that states vary in certification standards for school library media specialists. Two examples are the Kentucky Standards for School Library Media Specialists (available online at http://www.kde.state.ky.us/"Beyond Proficiency" [May 7, 2003]) and the Texas Standards (available online at http://www.tea.state.tx.us/technology/libraries/standards.html [May 8, 2003]). Although the core standards are virtually the same, specific standards and requirements vary. The drawback of using a listing of tasks to describe the roles of a profession, however, is that the vast number of tasks makes a synthesis difficult, if not impossible. These lists also have the drawback of tending to intimidate the user more than they elucidate. (One group of school library media specialists, attempting to list all the tasks of the profession, concluded with "Performs miracles.")

THE EVOLUTION OF THE PROFESSION

Why are the purposes of the library media center's programs so often unclear? It is beyond the scope of this work to include a detailed history of the development of the profession, but knowledge of the major events may contribute to an answer. An efficient method of tracing the profession's evolution is to follow the development of the standards that were established to provide guidance in the formulation of programs.

Recognizing that a strong school library would be beneficial to a school's English program, in 1915 the National Council of Teachers of English prompted a study of library services at the high school level. This study led to the formation of a committee that produced *Standard Library Organization and Equipment for Secondary Schools of Different Sizes,* more commonly known as the Certain Report (Coleman 1983). This report was far-reaching in its recommendations and was adopted by the American Library Association (ALA). Many regional accrediting agencies promulgated standards based upon this report. Its standards, however, reflected a narrow print orientation.

School Libraries for Today and Tomorrow, published by the ALA in 1945, recognized the needs of elementary and secondary school libraries. Among the functions of school libraries delineated in this report were the provision of reading and library skills centers and a center for information provision (Rossoff 1971).

The 1960 *Standards for School Library Programs,* published by the American Association of School Librarians (AASL), included an expanded treatment of the use of audiovisual materials but stopped short of recommending that the roles of the educational media specialist and librarian be combined.

In 1969, the AASL and the Department of Audiovisual Instruction of the National Education Association jointly produced *Standards for School Media Programs,* which represented the first attempt to develop national standards calling for a unified media center concept. Using endeavors such as the School Library Manpower Project as models, the authors incorporated audiovisual services into the role of the school library media specialist for the first time (Coleman 1983).

The 1975 ALA standards further expanded that role, emphasizing the place of the library media center in the heart of the school program. School library media specialists were urged to assist in curriculum development and implementation. Quantitative guidelines were formulated, often calling for a staff of several professionals and support personnel (American Library Association 1975).

Thirteen years later, the Association for Educational Communications and Technology (AECT) and the AASL cooperated in the creation of a document describing the optimum school library media program. The authors recognized that the document did not set standards enforced by an accrediting body but rather contained information to guide practice on a voluntary basis. As a result, the document was titled *Information Power: Guidelines for School Library Media Programs* (American Library Association 1988).

A committee formed by the AASL and the AECT once again began to define standards for information literacy in 1995. They developed the new standards by identifying existing statements on information literacy. The standards for information literacy developed by Christina Doyle (1992) were used as foundation material. Doyle used the National Educational Goals as a framework to demonstrate the critical nature of information literacy for attaining selected goals. Although this work assisted in developing information literacy standards, its outcomes did not make up the entire focus of student learning. Further documents reinforced this view and led to the development of two other categories, independent learning and social responsibility. Taken together, these categories and their standards describe the content and process that students must master to be considered information literate. This can be seen in the current version of *Information*

Power: Building Partnerships for Learning (American Library Association 1998). Although the mission of the school library media center, "to ensure that students and staff are effective users of ideas and information," remains the same as in the 1988 version, the techniques for accomplishing this have altered. The standards provide a broad conceptual framework to describe an information-literate student. The indicators provide examples of how this framework is built.

The 1998 *Information Power* differed from its predecessor in that it did not contain detailed quantitative descriptions of a standard library media program. The new guidelines did formalize roles and responsibilities for the school library media specialist, who is to serve as an information specialist, teacher, and instructional consultant.

In general, as each new standard was formulated, the role of the librarian, and later of the school library media specialist, was expanded. As each new area was added, however, there was no corresponding deletion of responsibilities.

The publication of *Information Power* was a significant step in clarifying the functions of the school library media program. With the tremendous competition for limited resources today, further consideration must be given in each school as to the appropriate functions of the library media program. Without this consideration, there is a real danger that the legacy of a profession built in layers of responsibilities will be continued identity crisis and burnout.

PROPOSED FUNCTIONS OF THE SCHOOL LIBRARY MEDIA PROGRAM

There are no doubt many ways in which the myriad products and services of a school library media program can be assembled and labeled. The very task of identifying unifying concepts should be beneficial to those interested in the future of the profession. As well as facilitating planning within the library media center, a clear grasp of purpose would help in the promotion of the program to students, teachers, parents, and administrators.

Let's stop here and work through an exercise to determine our own view of the purposes of the school library media program. Imagine that you are serving on a committee to set the funding priorities for your school system for the next five years. Of course you would say that the library media program should have a high priority. Suppose a senior administrator who is a member of the committee turns to you and says, "Well, what can the library media program do?" (i.e., what are its purposes?). Now list at least three purposes of the library media program. See figure 1.1.

1. _____

2. _____

3. _____

In a group of school library media specialists, the responses to such a question naturally vary. Many respondents list activities that enable the program to fulfill its purposes rather than the purposes themselves. A very common response is "A purpose of the library media program is to process materials so that students will have access to them." Processing materials is an essential activity in support of library media programs, but it is not a program purpose. The same might be said for maintaining AV equipment, installing a USB port, or connecting the library media center to the Internet. The means toward an end is too often confused with the goal itself.

In the second edition of this book, a simple model consisting of three primary program areas or purposes was proposed. The positive response this model received validated its creation. Based on an analysis of the day-to-day activities of school library media specialists, procedures described in the literature, and the coursework in preparation programs, three primary program areas or purposes become apparent:

Fig. 1.1. The school library media specialist "in the spotlight"

1. Promoting reading, viewing, and listening by children and young adults. This purpose is listed in *Information Power* as Principle 6 under "Teaching and Learning in Information Power: Building Partnerships for Learning" (American Library Association 1998, 58): "The library media program encourages and engages students in reading viewing and listening for understanding and enjoyment." Now, more than ever, it is a vital part of the school library media specialist's job to encourage reading. We have seen recreational reading lose in competition with other media too often. School library media specialists must also help their students widen their range of experience through reading and viewing. Especially in this age of increasing emphasis on the basics, competency testing, and technology literacy, there needs to be a haven in the school where children and young adults can expand their imaginations outside the bounds of the formal curriculum.

2. Providing information skills. This purpose is described in two principles of "Teaching and Learning" in *Information Power* (58): Principle 5, "Access to the full range of information resources and services through the library media program is fundamental to learning," and Principle 9, "The library media program integrates the uses of technology for learning and teaching." Information technology is experiencing exponential growth in the capacity to provide information to end users. Local and wide-area networks connected to fiber optic backbones provide the power to share sophisticated information resources. A revolution in storage capacity, including erasable magneto-optical and ultra-high-density magnetic storage devices, makes it possible for individual schools to accumulate vast databases on-site. Children and young adults are bombarded with increasing amounts of information; the technology of assisting them to understand the information and use it to create knowledge lags far behind. Students must be provided with the skills to access, obtain, understand, use, and evaluate information that is stored in a variety of media both locally and in remote locations.

In carrying out this program purpose of the school library media program, the school library media specialist may perform many of the roles delineated in *Information Power*. The school library media specialist creates the appropriate technological environment and provides instruction in the use of tools, methods of information classification, care of materials, and other topics. This instruction can be formal, using planned lessons, or informal, as the result of spontaneous requests. Likewise, reference service can both provide information directly and instruct the student in how to obtain information—teaching students to be information literate, lifelong learners.

3. Helping teachers in the design, implementation, and evaluation of resources and instruction. This can be seen in two principles in *Information Power* (58): Principle 3, "The library media program models and promotes collaborative planning and curriculum development," and Principle 4, "The library media program models and promotes creative, effective, and collaborative teaching." There are probably few teachers who believe that they could not improve in this area. Certainly, as *A Nation at Risk* (National Commission on Excellence in Education 1983) pointed out, a great number of teachers are in need of assistance. One purpose of the school library media program can be to provide a wide range of assistance, from building a professional collection to conducting in-service training. This role is especially important for schools using site-based management. In 2001, the National Board for Professional Teaching Standards (NBPTS) released *Library Media Standards*. These standards are organized around three areas: 1) what accomplished school library media specialists *know*; 2) what accomplished school library media specialists *do*; and 3) how accomplished school library media specialists *grow* professionally. These standards are intended to raise awareness of the professionalism and expertise of accomplished school library media specialists and pave the way for greater professional respect and opportunity for the teaching community at large. Standard IV, Integrating Instruction in the NBPTS Library Media Standards, states that "accomplished library media specialists lead by partnering with teachers to create, implement and evaluate learning experiences. . . . As full instructional partners with teachers, library media specialists share responsibility for fulfilling the curriculum goals of the school. Accomplished library media specialists therefore collaborate with teachers to plan and develop units of study that integrate multimedia, research, and information literacy skills into classroom instruction. . . . Collaboration between teachers and library media specialists also helps ensure that the information skills taught reflect students' skills and classroom teaching. By applying collaborative strategies, accomplished library media specialists oversee programs essential to the interdisciplinary learning process at the heart of the school" (19).

In addition, the National Council for Accreditation of Teacher Education Programs (National Council for Accreditation of Teacher Education Programs 1993) developed *Program Standards for the School Library Media Specialist*. These were prepared by the ALA and the AASL. As stated in these standards, "School library media specialists are information providers who can help guarantee a rich flow of resources to the instructional program. School library media specialists are instructional consultants, and they can assist teachers in designing instruction and producing resources to meet the needs of students. School library media specialists can provide leadership in developing and implementing a program to integrate learning and information skills into the curriculum" (2).

THE IMPORTANCE OF THE HELPING-TEACHERS-TEACH FUNCTION

If the activities of the average school library media specialist are studied, the vast majority of those activities can be seen to support one or more of the three program purposes. However, the three program purposes delineated previously seldom receive *equal* emphasis. Some school library media specialists perform activities that fall within the purpose of helping teachers teach, but this purpose tends to be the most neglected. Several studies show this to be true. McIntosh (1994) reviewed library media and education literature and found a foundation for the three roles of the school library media specialist as stated in *Information Power*—information specialist, teacher, and instructional consultant. In addition, McIntosh studied the present role of the K–12 public school library media specialist in two Kentucky counties. It was discovered that all three roles were being practiced at all three school levels. The role of information specialist was the most prominent, followed by teacher and then instructional consultant. A study conducted by Schon, Helmstadter, and Robinson (1991) found that both principals and school library media specialists ranked the instructional consultant role low in importance. Another study of school library media specialists in southern Illinois found that the school library media specialists did not perceive the instructional consultant role as highly important and that they were not practicing tasks representative of the instructional design and consultant role. Unfortunately, this is true despite the advocacy for this role in the literature and the provision by preparation programs of at least the basic skills in instructional design. See figure 1.2.

Chapter 2 of this book contains a discussion of the reasons that helping teachers teach is slighted both in attitude and performance. For now, let's concentrate on why the activities in this area should be increased.

There have been periodic upwellings of discontent regarding American education as far back as anyone cares to remember. This discontent increased during the past decade and was at least partially due to a perceived erosion in U.S. economic competitiveness. Repeatedly, American students fared poorly in comparison to students from other countries, and this lack of academic competitiveness was linked to economic dysfunctions.

In 1983 a wave of educational reform began that included provisions for longer school days, longer school years, curriculum changes, merit pay for teachers, and smaller classes. Despite the perception that less was being spent on education, the opposite was the case. Although teacher salaries rose only 24 percent during the 1980s, spending on overhead rose 110 percent (Barth 1990).

Fig. 1.2. Functions of the school library media program

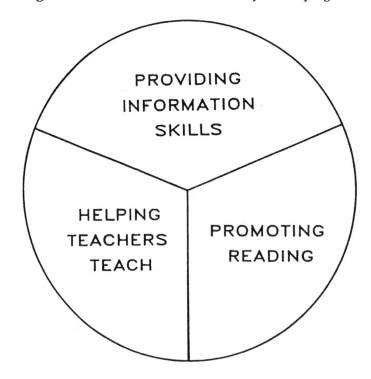

At the close of the 1980s, a view emerged that the answer was not more control from above but less. In the summer of 1989, the president of the United States convened a historic summit with the nation's governors that set six very ambitious goals for American education. The formulation of a specific agenda was important in itself, but even more important was the call for a dramatic restructuring of the school system that emerged in this and subsequent conferences. According to former Secretary of Education Lauro Cavazos, restructuring is not a formula, but a liberation from the dysfunctional mandates that weigh so heavily on principals and teachers (Barth 1990).

It has become obvious that teachers need assistance in designing instruction by school library media specialists; this has definitely increased with the arrival of technologies—in particular, the Internet. Serim (1999) explains that with the arrival of numerous technologies, collaboration with school library media specialists has become even more critical. He states, "As a classroom teacher, when I began to introduce the mind-boggling array of resources that the Internet provided to my students, I quickly found that my professional preparation had neglected crucial concepts and skills. . . . I was forced to rely on intuition and luck in terms of finding, evaluating, managing, organizing and presenting the increasingly small proportion of truly useful information the Internet was shining on my mind. As I began traveling in circles that brought me into contact with . . . others, I saw parallel gaps. It turns out that these very skills are what my colleagues who went to library school had mastered. By communication and collaboration, . . . we can change the world" (10).

As teachers go through the process of building instruction from the ground up, they require much more assistance than if they are simply following a textbook selected by someone else. If teachers are to be held accountable for the success of all students in the school, instruction will have to be tailored to individual learning styles. In short, teachers need help, and the school library media specialist is the logical person to provide it.

Anyone who has worked within a school setting knows that outsiders arrive with two strikes against them in their attempt to implement change. Although some schools are hiring learning specialists to carry out this role, the vast majority of schools have no one other than the school library media specialist prepared to act as the instructional consultant.

In many cases, the principal will welcome with enthusiasm the school library media specialist's involvement with teachers. The principal is nominally the person primarily responsible for improving instruction, but the avalanche of bureaucratic duties, from dealing with bus schedules to placating parents, leaves little time for attention to the curriculum.

Collaboration with educators can enhance the functions of the school library media program (Van Epps 1999). As the school library media specialist works in the design of a unit, information skills and reading promotion can be woven into the design. The bond that is established between the school library media specialist, acting as an instructional consultant, and the teacher serves to further understanding and appreciation of the total library media program.

From a more ominous viewpoint, the school library media program has to be considered part of education overhead. In this era of fiscal stress and increased accountability, each part of this overhead will be scrutinized carefully to determine whether it is contributing sufficiently to the instructional program. In at least one state, there is a strong possibility that school library media specialists will no longer have to be certified as teachers before practicing. In calling for this lowering of standards, a member of the state board reportedly asked, "Why would someone need this preparation to check out books?"

The library media center is still far from being at the heart of the instructional process, although we are gaining ground rapidly in the twenty-first century. However, each step forward goes a long way toward helping teachers teach and toward giving all students a chance to reach their potential.

THOUGHT PROVOKERS

1. Relax, close your eyes, and imagine a school library media specialist in action. Write down the first five activities you visualize this person doing. Now classify each according to the proposed program purposes described in the chapter. In performing the activity, was the school library media specialist promoting reading, viewing, or listening? Providing information skills? Helping teachers teach? Does the particular activity not fit under any of the proposed program purposes? Does it fit under more than one?

2. Go back to the three purposes that you listed for the exercise earlier in this chapter. Is there a significant congruence with the three-purpose model proposed in the chapter? Spend some time rethinking your model. Should it be expanded? Should one or more of the purposes be replaced?

(See appendix A for answers.)

REFERENCES

American Library Association. 1975. *Media Programs: District and School*. Chicago: American Library Association.

———. 1988. *Information Power: Guidelines for School Library Media Programs*. Chicago: American Library Association.

———. 1998. *Information Power: Building Partnerships for Learning*. Chicago: American Library Association and Association for Educational Communications and Technology.

———. 2001. *Guidelines for College/University Faculty Preparing a Curriculum Folio in the Area of School Library Media Education as Part of the Precondition Process for NCATE Accreditation*. Chicago: American Library Association.

Barth, R. S. 1990. *Improving Schools from Within: Teachers, Parents, and Principals Can Make the Difference*. San Francisco: Jossey-Bass.

Cobb, Nina. 1994. *The Future of Education: Perspectives on National Standards in America*. New York: College Entrance Examination Board.

Coleman, J. G., Jr. 1983. The Development of Library Media Services in the Secondary Schools: A Brief History. *Baylor Educator* 8 (2): 18–25.

Doyle, Christina A. 1992. *Final Report to the National Forum on Information Literacy*. Syracuse, N.Y.: ERIC Clearinghouse on Information Resources, ED 351033.

McIntosh, Christine. 1994. *The Evolution of the Role of the K-12 Public School Library Media Specialist*. Thesis (D. Ed.) Spaulding University. Microfiche. Ann Arbor, MI: University Microfilms International.

Naisbitt, J. 1982. *Megatrends: Ten New Directions Transforming Our Lives*. New York: Warner Books.

National Board for Professionals Teaching Standards. 1975. *Media Programs: District and School.* Chicago: American Library Association.

———. 2001. *Library Media Standards.* Arlington, VA: National Board for Professional Teaching Standards.

National Commission on Excellence in Education, U.S. Department of Education. 1983. *A Nation at Risk: The Imperative for Educational Reform.* Washington, D.C.: U.S. Government Printing Office.

National Council for Accreditation of Teacher Education Programs. 1993. *Program Standards for the School Library Media Specialist.* Washington, D.C.: National Council for Accreditation of Teacher Education Programs.

Rossoff, M. 1971. *The School Library and Educational Change.* Littleton, Colo.: Libraries Unlimited.

Schon, Isabel, Gerald C. Helmstadter, and Dan Robinson. 1991. The Role of the School Library Media Specialists. *School Library Media Quarterly* 19 (22): 8–33.

Serim, Ferdi. 1999. How Library/Media Specialists and Teachers Can Change the World. *Multimedia Schools* 6 (4): 10.

Turner, P. M. 1984. ID and the LMS: Past, Present, and Future. In *Instructional Development: The State of the Art, II,* ed. R. K. Bass and C. R. Dills, 501–10. Dubuque, Iowa: Kendall-Hunt.

Van Epps, Sharyn. 1999. Vision to Reality: Transforming the School Library into the Information Technology Hub of the School. *Multimedia Schools* 6 (2): 32–35.

ADDITIONAL READINGS

Cleaver, B. P., and W. D. Taylor. 1989. *The Instructional Consultant Role of the School Library Media Specialist.* Chicago: American Library Association.

Hartzel, Gary. 1997. The Invisible School Librarian: Why Other Educators Are Blind to Your Value. *School Library Journal* 43 (11): 24–29.

Hopkins, Dianne McAfee, and Douglas L. Zweizig. 1999. Power to the Media Center (And to the People, Too). *School Library Journal* 45 (5): 25–27.

Lance, Keith Curry, and David Loertscher. 2001. *Powering Achievement: School Library Media Programs Make a Difference—The Evidence.* San Jose, Calif.: Hi Willow Publishing Company.

Lance, Keith Curry, Marcia Rodney, and Christine Hamilton-Pennell. 2000. *How School Librarians Help Kids Achieve Standards: The Second Colorado Study.* San Jose, Calif.: Hi Willow Publishing Company.

McCracken, A. 2001. School Library Media Specialists Perceptions of Practice and Importance of Roles Described in *Information Power. School Library Media Research.* (4) http://www.ala.org/Content/NavigationMenu/AASL/Publications_and_Journals/School_Library_Media_Research/Contents1/Volume_4_(2001)/McCracken.htm.

National Board for Professional Teaching Standards. 2001. *Library Media Standards.* Arlington, Va.: National Board for Professional Teaching Standards.

Pappas, M., and A. Tepe. Preparing the Information Educator for the Future. *School Library Media Annual* 13: 37–44.

Power of Libraries, The. 2001. *Reading Today* 19 (2): 24–32.

Riedling, Ann. 2001. Role of the School Library Media Specialist in the 21st Century. *Teacher Librarian* 29 (1): 30–33.

Turner, P.M. 1996. What Help Do Teachers Want, and What Will They Do to Get It? *School Library Media Quarterly* 24(4): 208–212.

2
A Levels Approach to Helping Teachers Teach

This chapter provides information to help the reader

- understand the reasons why the instructional design consultation process has not been more widely practiced by school library media specialists

- consider arguments for and against the use of a systematic instructional design process

- learn the eight steps in the instructional design process

- understand the different factors that influence how a teacher plans, implements, and evaluates instruction

- learn the four levels of assistance the school library media specialist can provide at each step

- identify the step and level represented by a particular instructional consultation activity

With the publishing and widespread implementation of the 1960 AASL standards, the school library media program became essentially what it is today. School library media centers with adequate collections of print and non-print materials became the rule rather than the exception. The impact of the 1960 standards was great and helped engender what Loertscher (1980) rightly called a revolution in the field.

The impact of the 1975 ALA standards on the actual practice in the field was not comparable to that of the 1960 standards. The 1975 standards did, however, place a greater emphasis on the role of the school library media specialist in assisting in the planning, implementation, and evaluation of instruction. The 1988 and 1998 ALA guidelines formally designated one of the roles of the school library media specialist as instructional consultant (called "instructional partner" in *Information Power*, 1998).

The emphasis on the role of instructional consultant had some effect on the literature. Professional preparation programs were also affected, though to a lesser degree. A few programs incorporated entirely new courses that prepared students for this role. Others touched on the essentials in courses devoted to other topics.

RESISTANCE TO THE ROLE OF INSTRUCTIONAL CONSULTANT

With the development of the instructional design process, there emerged the role of *instructional design consultant*, a person who assisted teachers in all of the steps in the process. As discussed earlier, school library media specialists, for a number of reasons, have not taken on the role of working with all of their teachers through all of the steps in the instructional design process. The thesis of this book is that school library media specialists can help their teachers teach by serving as an instructional consultant at different levels.

The term *instructional consultant* incorporates any activity of the school library media specialist that helps one or more teachers plan, implement, and evaluate instruction. Instructional design consultation is a subset of instructional consultation in which the school library media specialist uses instructional design tools to help the teacher.

A much-cited Delphi study by Jetter (1972) concluded that the implementation of the instructional consultant role would be the single greatest change in the field for the next decade. Why, then, has a development that began with such enthusiasm and promise not been fully realized? The answer can be found by looking at how the role came to be assigned to the school library media specialist.

Paul Saettler (1990) traced the technology of instruction over 2,000 years. Widespread usage of technology, incorporating general systems theory, came about only with the tremendous demand for mass instruction and training that occurred during World War II. General systems theory incorporating technology posits a holistic, rather than reductionist, approach to problem solving in education. Based also upon systems analysis, step-by-step procedures for the design, implementation, and evaluation of projects were formulated. (See Bertalanffy 1968; Hayman 1974; and Hug and King 1984 for more in-depth discussions of this evolution.)

The application of general systems theory to education, also known as instructional design, had a significant impact on training in the military and in industry. An initial impact was also made in higher education. At the K–12 level, components of instructional design were incorporated into teacher training programs. There was, however, resistance among many teachers to implementing instructional design to its fullest. This resistance stemmed in part from

- a view of the instructional design process as being too rigid, as denying the teachable moment. "What happens," some asked, "when a robin lands on the windowsill, but your lesson involves the solar system?"

- a view of instructional design as being too behavioristic, as lacking in warmth.

- a lack of time to carry out the process adequately. Instructional design is a "front-end loading" process. Although resource savings are often realized in the long run, larger amounts of time are required in the planning stage.

The resistance to the process was even greater among school library media practitioners. School library media specialists were not only supposed to use instructional design components in their own projects but were to be instructional design consultants for the faculty as well, helping them design their instruction. Kerr (1977) found that practicing school library media specialists had less positive attitudes toward working with teachers in this area than did the teachers and administrators. Coleman (1982), in surveying attitudes of school library media specialists toward the 1975 standards, received the least positive responses to the section of the standards that delineated this new role. Staples (1981) found that school library media specialists, in ranking sixty competencies, ranked those that could be termed instructional design as very low. Kvalness and LaCroix (1990) found that school library media specialists in their populations also ranked this competency as low. Johnson (1993) studied school library media specialists in southern Illinois rural public schools and found that they did not perceive the instructional consultant role as highly important and that they were not practicing the tasks representative of the instructional design and consultant role.

Why has there been resistance by school library media specialists to the instructional design consultant role? The primary reason is that the concept arrived at the K–12 level from the military, from industry, and from higher education virtually unchanged in terms of both expectations and terminology.

Instructional design projects at higher levels are often very detailed, consuming large amounts of resources. Furthermore, instructional design incorporates terminology from systems theory building and from psychology. This terminology is necessary for research and theory, but it has proven to be a hindrance to the library media practitioner. Most school library media specialists have been presented with a set of expectations and a terminology that are unfamiliar and often intimidating. One has only to experience the complexity of the models designed for the practitioner to feel the frustration described by Stripling (1984) and Loertscher (1980).

The instructional design consultant role could perhaps have been adopted intact if the school library media profession had been a vacuum waiting to be filled. School library media specialists, however, were not sitting around in their centers with great amounts of time waiting for inspiration (see figure 2.1). Taking on large-scale projects would have involved discontinuing many other activities involving the other functions described in chapter 1.

The tension, therefore, between a proposed role and existing activities was too great. A choice was forced upon school library media specialists, and most often the instructional design consultant role as presented in the literature lost. Once the choice was made, a devaluation of the role could be predicted.

THE VALUE OF INSTRUCTIONAL DESIGN

Despite the lack of complete diffusion of the instructional design process throughout the educational arena, this process remains the single most powerful tool for improving the quality of education today. During the past decade, a second generation of instructional design has emerged that incorporates developments in cognitive psychology. An understanding of how learners construct their perceptions of the environment is a significant addition to the instructional designer's repertoire (Merrill, Li, and Jones 1990). Though almost everyone is aware of one or two "natural" teachers who can hold their students spellbound without any preparation, in general, instruction that has been systematically designed and implemented will be more effective than unplanned, accidental, or coercive instruction.

Instructional design provides for each learner to be accounted for in terms of achievement and the best learning environment. Rather than taking the caring out of instruction, this process provides caring teachers with powerful tools. A systematically designed lesson should not deny the "teachable moment." Instructional design provides for effective instruction between those unplanned experiences. It can accommodate an intermission when the robin arrives.

The advent of new technologies, such as the Internet and hypermedia, has brought about not only technological innovations, but also coupled these with new ways of approaching learning and instruction. Therefore, good instructional design is now, more than ever before, imperative. Every teacher has the tools to create instruction tailored to their students. Bosco (2001) states that certain elements are necessary for technology to be used effectively in classroom. One of the elements is the capability of teachers to use technology. Teachers need to know how to harness the instructional resources that technology provides to really add value to teaching and learning in their classroom. Instructional design consultation has become more vital than ever before.

Given the potential power of the instructional design process and the benefits of participation by the school library media specialist, what can be done to promote a greater fulfillment of the role of instructional design consultant? Two initial tasks must be accomplished:

1. Instructional design consultation by the school library media specialist must be recognized as differing in implementation from instructional design consultation in the military and in industry, where the process first emerged. The theoretical basis is the same, but limited resources and training dictate that the school library media specialist's intervention will commonly be of a less drastic nature.

2. Levels of instructional design consultation must be formulated to provide a logical continuum along which this role may develop.

Fig. 2.1. To ID or Not to ID: A Mid-Semester's Night Dream

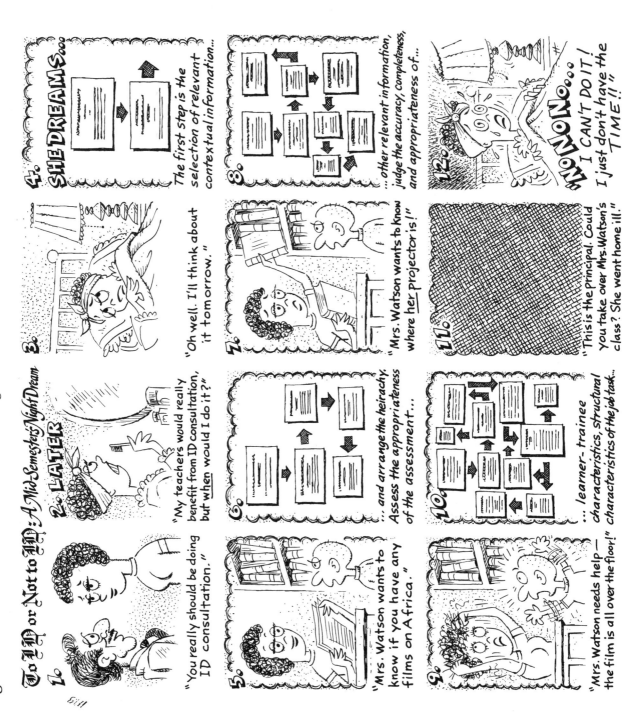

STEPS IN INSTRUCTIONAL DESIGN CONSULTATION

How teachers plan, implement, and evaluate instruction is largely determined by their "practical theory" of education (Handal and Lauvas 1987). A practical theory is a teacher's system of knowledge, experience, and values, and is relevant to teaching practice at a particular time. This practical theory is unique to each teacher and is constantly changing based upon personal experience, reading, conversations, inculcation of new value systems, and other stimuli to growth. Each teacher brings this system of knowledge, experience, and values to the design, implementation, and evaluation of instruction.

Although each teacher brings a unique practical theory to the instructional arena, successful teachers have certain attributes in common. They

- derive the content for their courses from more than one source

- know their students

- know what they expect from their students

- construct effective means of assessing their students

- select a variety of effective instructional strategies, materials, and activities

- use effective learning management techniques

- revise their approach based upon results

Even good teachers can improve, and many teachers can improve significantly. The instructional design approach takes what many good teachers do intuitively and provides a map for teachers to follow. Following the instructional design map increases the probability that effective instruction will occur.

There are many instructional design models that delineate the steps in the process. Figure 2.2 presents a model that formalizes the process of designing, implementing, and evaluating instruction followed by a good teacher.

Figure 2.3 depicts three dimensions across which the instructional consultation provided by the school library media specialists can vary. The level of the instructional consultation can be determined based on the place of the interaction in each dimension.

Amount of Interaction

The school library media specialist might not interact with a teacher or teachers at all in providing instructional assistance. The assistance rendered might simply be purchasing and maintaining an item of instructional equipment. In another case, the interaction might be very informal and minimal. The contact between school library media specialist and teacher might take place in the hallway and might last thirty seconds. The teacher might, for example, mention the topic of the next day's instruction, and the school library media specialist might suggest instructional materials. At the extreme of this dimension, the interaction might involve weeks or months of contact in which the school library media specialist serves as a member of an instructional design team.

Fig. 2.2. Instructional design model

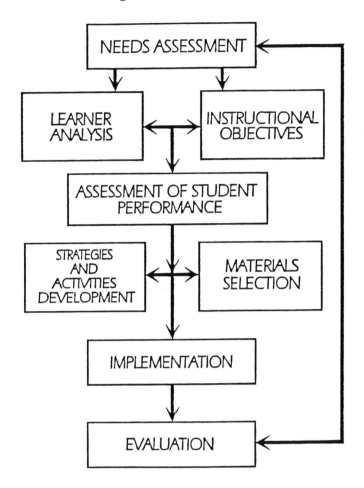

Purpose of Interaction

The amount of change sought in the teacher's practical theory (knowledge, experience, and values) can also vary. The purpose of the instructional consultation might be to provide logistical support only. At the other end of the dimension, the goal of instructional consultation might be the extensive training of one or more teachers to effect a significant alteration in each teacher's practical theory.

Number of Steps Involved

In our consideration of the breadth of instructional consultation, we must recognize that a school library media specialist may not work with a particular teacher in *any* of the steps in the instructional design process. This "no involvement" with some teachers will be a fact of life in even the best library media programs. For most teachers, the library media program will be a source of assistance in several of the steps in the design, implementation, and evaluation of their instruction. At the extreme of this dimension, instructional consultation is provided at every step in the process.

Fig. 2.3. Dimensions of instructional consultation

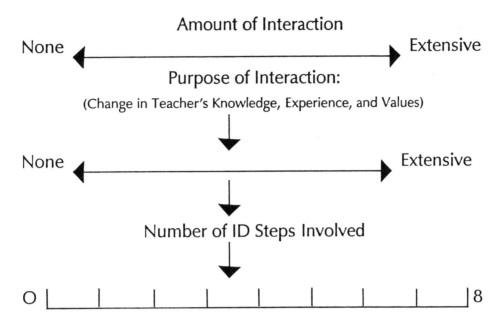

LEVELS OF INSTRUCTIONAL CONSULTATION

Based on where the instructional consultation falls in each of the three dimensions shown in figure 2.3, four levels of instructional consultation are proposed.

No Involvement

For a number of reasons, there may be no involvement by the school library media specialist in helping a particular teacher be more effective. Perhaps no assistance was requested or the school library media specialist was unable or unwilling to provide it.

The Initial Level

At the initial level of instructional consultation, there is little or no interaction between the school library media specialist and the faculty member. The school library media specialist selects and maintains materials, equipment, and facilities that assist the faculty in their teaching. Teachers are virtually left on their own to use the resources in carrying out or improving their teaching.

The Moderate Level

The moderate level of instructional consultation involves more extensive interaction between the school library media specialist and the teacher. This interaction is not as a member of a formal team but usually occurs for a limited duration as the parties cross paths. Often, the interaction will encompass a limited number of the steps in the instructional design process. At the moderate level, changes in teachers' knowledge, experience, and values can occur, but if it does, it is a result of teachers' following up on their own the recommendations of the school library media specialist.

The In-Depth Level

This level of intervention by the school library media specialist most closely resembles formal instructional design consultation as described in the industrial training literature. There is extensive interaction between the school library media specialist and one or more teachers in which all of the steps in the instructional design process can be addressed. An important purpose of this level of intervention is to provide considerable guidance to one or more teachers seeking to increase their abilities to perform particular steps in the future. Accordingly, activities at this level might include serving as a member of an instructional team or presenting an in-service—for example, one regarding new educational software or the methods of properly evaluating Internet sites.

This levels approach to instructional consultation recognizes that each teacher brings a unique background to the instructional encounter. School library media specialists can assist the teacher by providing logistical support or by providing varying degrees of guidance to assist in enhancing the teacher's background of knowledge, experience, and values. As can be seen in figure 2.4, consultation and assistance can be directed at one or more of the steps in the instructional design process.

The implications of this levels approach to instructional consultation by the school library media specialist are significant. The approach defines instructional consultation to include all of

Fig. 2.4. The school library media specialist as consultant

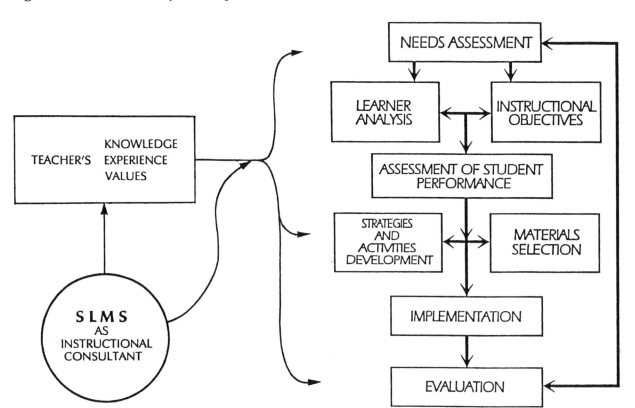

the levels beyond no involvement. Many of the tasks performed by school library media specialists fall within this realm, as well as the more esoteric instructional design consulting activities.

For example, a school library media specialist who processes a CD-ROM for use by teachers is involved in instructional consultation through intervention at the initial level in the materials selection step. A school library media specialist who builds a collection of units on a particular topic so that teachers may refer to it when deciding on instructional content is again involved in instructional consultation at the initial level. This time the needs-assessment step is addressed.

For each of the eight steps in the instructional design process delineated in the instructional design model presented in figure 2.2, the school library media specialist can be involved with a given teacher at one of three levels. Sometimes, when instructional consultation activities by the school library media specialist are analyzed, it might be difficult to place a certain activity at a particular level. Each level represents a combination of three dimensions of instructional consultation. It is important to realize that the levels are not intended to represent discrete categories into which all activities can easily be placed. Rather, they represent gradations of involvement intended to allow the school library media specialist to map a path to higher involvement, if such involvement is desired.

The levels approach to instructional consultation was formulated to ease the tension between instructional design consultation, often perceived as a formidable and impossible-to-implement technique, and the real world of school library media practice. When we incorporate instructional design consultation within the much broader arena of instructional consultation, a logical continuum is established, providing a pathway for increased involvement by the school library media specialist. This increased involvement as an instructional consultant should result in more effective teaching and enhanced learning.

THOUGHT PROVOKERS

1. The following school library media specialist activities represent levels of instructional consultation. Which step and level are represented for each activity?

    a. Mr. Baker requested that a VCR be sent to his room during sixth period for use in his "Sources of Energy" lecture. Paul Johnson, the school library media specialist, arranged to have the equipment delivered.

    b. Pamela Kalyoncu, the school library media specialist, gave an in-service for the social studies faculty on selecting instructional computer software.

    c. Barbara Bryan, the head of the Mathematics Department, requested that the school library media specialist work with mathematics teachers in designing a unit on fractions for the slow-learner group. She said that they were especially interested in input regarding modifying the courseware they had been using with regular groups so that the courseware could be used with these students.

    d. The school library media specialist purchased *Courseware in the Classroom: Selecting, Organizing and Using Educational Software* for the professional collection.

    e. During a coffee break, the third-grade teacher remarked to Paula Hardy, the school library media specialist, "Paula, I'm planning the unit on community helpers, and I just don't know what should be covered anymore." Paula had heard of a teacher at a nearby elementary school who had developed an excellent unit on this topic. Paula offered to call and see if a copy could be obtained.

2. Create an activity that falls to the far left of the first two dimensions in figure 2.3. Now rewrite the activity so that it would fall to the far right of the first two dimensions.

Compare these activities as to resources and training required for the school library media specialist to carry them out. What would the successful completion of the activities do for the image of the library media program?

(See appendix A for answers.)

REFERENCES

American Library Association. 1998. *Information Power: Building Partnerships for Learning.* Chicago: American Library Association.

Bertalanffy, L. V. 1968. *General Systems Theory: Foundations, Development, Applications.* New York: George Braziller.

Bosco, Jim. 2001. School Library Media Specialists and School Administrators as Allies! *Multimedia Schools* 8 (4): 4.

Coleman, J. G., Jr. 1982. Perceptions of the "Guiding Principles" in Media Programs: District and School. Ed.D. dissertation, University of Virginia.

Handal, G., and P. Lauvas. 1987. *Promoting Reflective Teaching: Supervision in Action.* Philadelphia: Society for Research into Higher Education and Open University Press.

Hayman, J. L. 1974. The Systems Approach and Education. *Educational Forum* May: 493–501.

Hug, W. E., and J. E. King. 1984. Educational Interpretations of General Systems Theory. In *Instructional Development: The State of the Art, II,* ed. R. K. Bass and C. R. Dills, 18–28. Dubuque, Iowa: Kendall-Hunt.

Jetter, M. A. 1972. The Roles of the School Library Media Specialist in the Future: A Delphi Study. Ph.D. dissertation, Michigan State University.

Johnson, Julia A. 1993. The School Library Media Specialist as Instructional Consultant. Ph.D. dissertation, Southern Illinois University.

Kerr, S. T. 1977. Are There Instructional Developers in the Schools? A Sociological Look at the Development of a Profession. *A V Communications Review* 25 (7): 243–68.

Kvalness, L., and P. LaCroix. 1990. Levels of Involvement in the Consultant Role of the School Library Media Specialist. Paper delivered at the American Association of School Librarians Research Forum, Chicago.

Lathrop, Ann. 1983. *Courseware in the Classroom: Selecting, Organizing and Using Educational Software.* New York: Addison-Wesley.

Loertscher, D. V. 1980. The School Library Media Center: A New Force in American Education. *Arkansas Libraries* 37 (3): 8–12.

Merrill, M. D., Z. Li, and M. K. Jones. 1990. Second Generation Instructional Design. *Educational Technology* 30: 7–14.

Saettler, P. 1990. *The Evolution of American Educational Technology.* Englewood, Colo.: Libraries Unlimited. (Originally published as *A History of Instructional Technology.* New York: McGraw-Hill, 1968)

Staples, S. E. 1981. Sixty Competency Ratings for School Media Specialists. *Instructional Innovator* 26 (November): 19–23.

Stripling, B. 1984. What Price ID? A Practical Approach to a Personal Dilemma. *School Library Media Quarterly* 12: 290–96.

ADDITIONAL READINGS

Cleaver, B. P., and W. D. Taylor. 1989. *The Instructional Consultant Role of the School Library Media Specialist.* Chicago: American Library Association.

Cohen, S. S., et al. 1997. Meeting the Challenge of Consultation and Collaboration: Developing Interactive Teams. *Journal of Learning Disabilities* 30 (4): 427–32.

Dick, Walter. 1995. Instructional Design and Creativity: A Response to the Critics. *Educational Technology* 35 (4): 5–11.

Dills, Charles R., and Alexander J. Romiszowski, ed. 1997. *Instructional Development Paradigms.* Englewood Cliffs, N.J.: Educational Technology Publications.

Eisenberg, M. B., and R. E. Berkowitz. 1988. *Curriculum Initiative: An Agenda and Strategy for Library Media Programs.* Norwood, N.J.: Ablex.

Fitzpatrick, Kathleen, ed. 2000. *Evaluating the School Library Media Center: Analysis Techniques and Research Practices.* Englewood, Colo.: Libraries Unlimited.

Kemp, Jerrold E., Gary R. Morrison, and Steven M. Ross. 1998. *Designing Effective Instruction.* 2nd ed. Columbus, Ohio: Merrill.

Loertscher, D. V. 1988. *Taxonomies of the School Library Media Program.* Englewood, Colo.: Libraries Unlimited.

Newby, T., et al. 1996. *Instructional Technology for Teaching and Learning.* Englewood Cliffs, N.J.: Prentice-Hall.

Seels, B., and Z. Glasgow. 1998. *Making Instructional Design Decisions.* Columbus, Ohio: Merrill.

Sullivan, J. S. 1980. Initiating Instructional Design into School Media Programs. *School Media Quarterly* 8: 252–58.

Winer, Laura R., and Jesus Vaquez-Abad. 1995. The Present and Future of ID Practice. *Performance Improvement Quarterly* 8 (3): 55–67.

3

Finding Out Where You Are and Where You Want to Go

This chapter contains information to help the reader

- use the instructional consultation assessment chart (ICAC) to evaluate past instructional design consultation activities

- identify possible instructional consultation target areas from a completed ICAC

- devise an instructional consultation action plan for a given step and level

- discuss the importance of creating and sharing a vision of the school library media program

In chapter 2, an approach to instructional consultation was offered, a broad approach that included many activities currently performed by practicing school library media specialists. Such an extension of the concept of instructional design would be of limited value if its only function were to permit a degree of self-congratulation and allow the school library media specialist to don the mantle of instructional consultant. The true value of establishing an instructional consultation continuum is for this continuum to serve as a tool in increasing awareness of and participation in this role. This is of particular importance with the inclusion of the role of instructional consultant in *Information Power: Building Partnerships for Learning.*

USING THE ICAC

The ICAC as a Current-Assessment Device

The first step in increasing your involvement in instructional consultation is charting a record of past instructional consultation activities. The ICAC is a simple, useful instrument that will enable a school library media specialist to do just that (see fig. 3.1). The ICAC graphically represents the steps in the process of planning, teaching, and evaluating instruction and the possible levels of intervention by the school library media specialist.

The steps in using the ICAC are:

1. Identify the teachers for whom you provided instructional consultation. You could consider one teacher, a department, a grade level, or some other combination. (To obtain an initial, general idea of involvement in instructional consultation, it is best to consider the entire faculty of the school as a unit.)

Fig. 3.1. Instructional consultation assessment chart

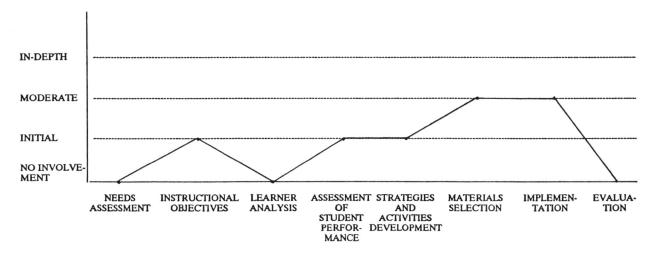

2. Select the unit of time for which the instructional consultation activities will be analyzed. This could be the past week, the past month, or any other reasonable time span. (For the initial analysis, choose a period of at least several months.)

3. For each step in the process of planning, teaching, and evaluating instruction, mark the level that best represents the degree and purpose of interaction with the identified teacher(s) during the identified time period. Connect each of the marks to complete the graph. (Appendix B contains an ICAC form with instructions.)

The instructional consultation activity indicated by the graph in figure 3.1 is probably representative of the overall activity of the typical school library media specialist. In this hypothetical case, few if any professional materials on needs assessment, learner analysis, or evaluation are available in the library media center (thus, the no involvement level). According to this graph, the school library media specialist's highest level of involvement in the instructional objectives, assessment of student performance, and strategies and activities development steps was providing professional collection materials and other resources (initial level). For the remaining steps, materials selection and implementation, the library media program fulfilled specific requests by the teachers (moderate level).

The exact level marked for each step will, of course, involve a subjective judgment by the school library media specialist. But the ICAC is only intended to give a general picture of instructional consultation activities, thereby providing a basis for planning and measuring improvement. It should be used with care as a report card for the library media program.

A question that arises when school library media specialists begin using the ICAC is, How much activity must occur at a particular level before it can be confirmed that the program is operating at that level? If a school library media specialist is attempting to enter a level at a particular step for the first time, a minimum amount of activity should allow the level to be "checked off." If, as in the example portrayed in figure 3.1, the library media program simply maintained an equipment pool with no delivery, the program would be considered to be at the initial level for the implementation step. If in the next year, with a new program for delivery of equipment, 25 percent of the faculty requested and obtained equipment delivery, this certainly should qualify for the moderate level of the implementation step. As involvement in the instructional consultation process increases, or when smaller groups of teachers are considered, threshold percentages might vary.

Are there cases in which the in-depth level but none of the lower levels have been reached for a particular step? Such cases should be rare if not nonexistent. Implementation of higher levels almost always requires that of lower levels also. For example, why would a school library media specialist implement a workshop on selecting instructional materials (in-depth) but not assist individual faculty with titles when requested (moderate) and not maintain a collection of instructional materials (initial)? The lower levels of involvement are providing the infrastructure for instruction. Without this infrastructure in place, it is not logical for more advanced activities to take place.

One important point: The initial use of the ICAC should be value-free. The ICAC is a tool for improvement and should not be construed as being a measure of the value of a library media program. At this stage of the development of the school library media profession, there is no minimum amount of involvement considered acceptable. The ICAC simply illustrates what exists and indicates areas for possible improvement.

Few school library media specialists would graph their instructional consultation activities as a horizontal line along the no involvement level. Anyone who was that inactive could not remain employed for any length of time. Few professionals, however, can accurately graph their activities as a horizontal line along the in-depth level either. Evidence gained from research indicates too strongly that the resources and attitudes required for such a widespread implementation are not yet to be found in the field.

The ICAC as a Planning Device

If a school library media specialist chooses to become more involved in instructional consultation, the ICAC can be used as a planning tool. After the initial graphing of activities, the next move is to choose a target step and level. For the school library media specialist's program represented in figure 3.1, there are eight possible target areas, as the highest level was not reached at any step. Specifically, these targets include

- moving to the initial level for assisting at the needs assessment, learner analysis, or evaluation steps

- increasing involvement to the moderate level at the instructional objectives, assessment of student performance, or strategies and activities development steps

- becoming involved at the in-depth level for the materials selection or implementation steps

Following the selection of the target step and level, a plan of action can be formulated that can be as detailed as desired. Such a plan could include

- a goal statement that describes in one's own words what is to be accomplished

- objectives statements detailing the criteria that must be met

- a list of things that must be done in order to accomplish the objectives, and an accompanying timeline

- resources required and budgetary implications

A Sample Instructional Consultation Action Plan

As depicted in figure 3.1, one target area for our school library media specialist is the in-depth level for the materials selection step. In our hypothetical case, the school library media specialist is currently functioning at the moderate level; an adequate collection of instructional materials exists along with a selection policy and procedure and preview facilities. Professional tools, including those to increase selection skills, as well as selection tools, are also available. A production area with supplies exists for use by teachers. The production area includes a workstation with desktop publishing and hypertext software, a scanner, a digital camera, and a color laser printer. Furthermore, the library media center regularly obtains instructional materials through purchase, loan, or production for faculty, given a title or description of the desired items.

The school library media specialist in our example has selected this level and step as a target area due to the amount of instructional material that had been purchased by teachers and used only once. Although this problem is characteristic of the entire collection, eight computers have recently been installed along with a projection device, and the problems with purchasing materials that are underused is especially apparent with computer software. The principal is concerned that budgets are being cut, and the underutilization of some of these materials makes the library media budget a prime target. Finally, a survey of the faculty at the start of the year indicated that instructional material selection was highly rated as a possible in-service topic. A plan of action follows.

I. Goal statement. Design and implement a workshop or workshops on the selection of instructional materials, particularly computer software. Increase teachers' abilities to select usable materials.

II. Objective statements

A. At least 40 percent of the faculty will attend the entire workshop on a voluntary basis.

B. There will be a noticeable decrease in the percentage of items purchased and used only once.

C. Students and teachers will adopt noticeably more positive attitudes toward the computer software used.

III. Things to do

A. Initially publicize the workshop and talk to faculty about topics to be covered. (9/20)

B. Obtain samples of other workshops on this topic. (9/20)

C. Obtain release from sixth-period study hall for November and December to plan and prepare for workshop.

D. Determine final goals and objectives for the workshop. (10/5)

E. Prepare/obtain materials. (12/10)

F. Finalize activities, schedule workshop, and publicize it again. (12/18)

G. Implement. (Initially scheduled for teachers' in-service day, 1/20)

H. Evaluate. (Ongoing)

IV. Resources required

A. From fifteen to thirty hours of planning time, depending on availability of suitable commercial materials on this topic.

B. Ninety dollars for materials and supplies.

The next step is to communicate the plan. Explain the ICAC to the school library media supervisor if one exists, to teachers and students, and especially to the principal.

A SCENARIO

In this scenario, Arlene Wofford, the school library media specialist, is discussing plans for a workshop for the teachers to be held in January. Paula Zowikowski, the principal, has been told previously that this step and level is a target area for the new year.

LMS: Mrs. Zowikowski, I appreciate your taking time to talk about my idea for a January in-service.

Principal: Well, Arlene, I appreciate how much your program helps our teachers. What do you have in mind?

LMS: When we talked during the preservice day this year, I told you that I was considering getting involved at a higher level with the faculty regarding selection of materials. Since then, I have surveyed the faculty, both informally and formally, and found that most of them would like this also.

Principal: Yes, several teachers have spoken to me about it.

LMS: I'm concerned about the amount of instructional materials that are underutilized. This is especially true of the computer software. On numerous occasions, teachers have told me that when they used some item, it just didn't work, and they would hesitate to use it again.

Principal: We don't want teachers using materials that don't work. It would certainly be cost-effective to select serviceable materials in the first place. We have spent a lot of money recently on computers and projection equipment. What will your workshop accomplish in this regard?

LMS: I hope to provide the teachers who participate with a step-by-step procedure for evaluating any instructional material, including a handout. I'd like to concentrate on questions that are unique to computer materials and that should be answered before purchase.

Principal: Sounds fine. When will the workshop be?

LMS: Tentatively, during the teachers' in-service day in January. I'll probably need about ninety dollars for materials and supplies. I'll rent materials if I can locate them, but I might have to produce some. I'd also like to be relieved from my sixth-period study hall so I will have time to plan and prepare.

Principal: The ninety dollars is not a problem, especially since the district has increased our in-service budget. However, I don't see how I can find a replacement for the study hall. As you know, Personnel hasn't acted on my request to replace the aide we lost last year.

LMS: I had hoped that something could be arranged. The real benefit from this workshop will be for the students, once they are exposed to better materials. I think the workshop will be cost justified, since we'll try to buy only materials we will use to full advantage. Also, as you know, the district often pays consultants' fees for presenting an in-service. Not only will our workshop be very low cost, it could be used for other teachers and maybe even other districts!

Principal: Okay, I'm sold. I'll get on Personnel to see if we can't at least get the aide back part time to give you a month of release time. Would that do?

LMS: Thank you. I'll turn in a more detailed proposal when I turn in my goals for the entire library media program.

Suggestions for Proceeding

At this point, many readers might feel overwhelmed and a bit skeptical. "The in-depth level is so far from my reality!" might be your reaction. Following are a few suggestions for coping.

CREATE A VISION

What should a vision be for a school library media specialist, and why is it important to have one? A vision is a kind of moral imagination that gives one the ability to see the school and one's place in it not as they are but as they might be. A vision offers a clear, sometimes extraordinary, sense of direction. Mattessich and Monsey (1992) explain that in order to develop trust, partners must develop mutually agreed upon goals and a shared vision for the work. Task completion also depends on shared participation.

Barth (1990) makes an observation regarding the importance of creating and communicating a personal vision, one that is especially germane for any school library media specialist who has been assigned the yearbook or cheerleading sponsorship or overseeing fieldtrips. He observes, "Another good reason for school people to formulate and articulate their vision of the ways schools ought to be is that by *not* doing so, they invite random prescription from the outside" (prescriptions such as bus duty and study hall monitoring).

INVOLVE OTHERS

As a general rule, find out the attitudes of the principal, supervisor, teachers, and students toward the involvement of the library media program at any given step and level. Dorian (1993) states that the dynamics and the nature of collaboration between teacher and school library media specialist is the "cornerstone of the school library media program." Bosco (2001) explains, "If you investigate why [collaboration] is working in a particular school district, you will usually find that the way the principals, superintendent, or other school [personnel] are functioning has a lot to do with the success." Emphasize involvement in steps and levels when such involvement will be most welcomed and educate principals and others to increase positive perceptions of the other possible targets.

Show them the target step and levels and ask for feedback. Better yet, choose the target in cooperation with these groups! Explain the plan of action, emphasizing the benefits to be achieved for the resources expended.

At the end of the year, use the ICAC as a tool for illustrating the progress made in increasing the involvement of the library media program in instructional consultation. Publicize gains to groups both inside and outside of your school.

INCREASE YOUR SKILLS

For most school library media programs, progress through the levels will be gradual and often erratic. Acceptance of the levels approach and a willingness to attempt to advance to the next level are essential but not sufficient. Many school library media specialists have graduated from programs that did not provide the strategies and competencies necessary to increase involvement in instructional consultation. Chapters 4 through 14 contain information to help the school library media specialist begin to obtain the essential skills.

BE PATIENT AND PERSISTENT

Virtually every school library media management text calls for the formulation of goals for the media program. The acceptance of a continuum of involvement in helping teachers teach and in the increased use of the ICAC will facilitate both goal setting and progress monitoring.

Even the most dedicated and skilled school library media specialists will encounter factors beyond their control that prevent progress. The important thing to remember is that although achieving the highest level at all steps is an ideal, implementing the next level at any step is of great value. Increased learning by children and young adults is the true goal. Think of the contribution that every school library media program moving up one level at one step would make toward reaching this goal.

There is a wonderful story in *It Was on Fire When I Lay Down on It* (Fulghum 1989, 74) that illustrates the attitude school library media specialists must try to achieve and maintain as they face the formidable tasks that confront them. The story can be paraphrased as follows:

> In fifteenth-century France, a scholar had traveled several days to visit the site of the construction of the famous cathedral at Chartres. The construction had been under way for fifty years, and the cathedral was only half finished. He arrived in the late afternoon as the sunlight was fading. As the visitor stepped inside, he spotted a man planing a beautiful piece of oak. The visitor asked the man, "What are you doing?" The workman replied, "I am building a brace for a confessional." The visitor walked on a little farther in the building and spotted a man working on a multicolored piece of glass. "What are you doing?" the visitor asked. This workman replied, "I am smoothing out this window pane so that it will keep out the rain and snow." As the visitor's eyes adjusted to the fading light, he spotted a very old woman sweeping up bits of wood and glass. Chuckling, the visitor asked, "Old woman, what are you doing?" "I am building a cathedral," she replied.

THOUGHT PROVOKERS

1. Using a copy of the ICAC shown in appendix B, chart your instructional consultation activities over the past year in reference to your entire faculty. If you are not currently practicing, interview a school library media specialist, explain the ICAC, and chart his or her activities. Remember, the purpose of the ICAC is not to make a value judgment!

2. On the basis of the completed ICAC, what are the possible target areas for increased involvement?

3. Devise an instructional consultation action plan at the initial level for the needs assessment step.

4. Suppose your school has a new principal or you are interviewing for a new school library media position. The principal asks you, "What is your vision for the school library media program, especially concerning the improvement of teaching with regard to new technologies?" What would you reply?

(See appendix A for answers.)

REFERENCES

Barth, R. S. 1990. *Improving Schools from Within: Teachers, Parents, and Principals Can Make the Difference.* San Francisco: Jossey-Bass.

Bosco, Jim. 2001. School Library Media Specialists and School Administrators as Allies! *Multimedia Schools* 8 (4): 48–51.

Dorian, R. 1993. Curriculum Encounters of the Third Kind: Teachers and Teacher-Librarians Exploring Curriculum Potential. In *Foundations for Effective School Library Media Programs*, ed. K. Haycock, 155–66. Englewood, Colo.: Libraries Unlimited.

Fulghum, R. 1989. *It Was on Fire When I Lay Down on It.* New York: Villard Books.

Mattessich, P. W., and B. R. Monsey. 1992. *Collaboration: What Makes It Work: A Review of Research Literature on Factors Influencing Successful Collaboration.* St. Paul, Minn.: Amherst H. Wilder Foundation.

ADDITIONAL READINGS

Friend, M.. and L. Cook. 1996. *Interactions: Collaboration Skills for School Professionals.* 2nd ed. New York: Longman.

March, Judith K., and Karen H. Peters. 2002. Curriculum Development and Instructional Design in the Effective Schools Process. *Phi Delta Kappan* 83 (5): 379–80.

Wolcott, L. L. 1994. Understanding How Teachers Plan: Strategies for Successful Instructional Partnerships. *School Library Media Quarterly* 22 (3): 161–65.

4

The Initial Level

This chapter provides information to help the reader

- define the initial level of involvement

- understand the resources the school library media specialist can make available at the initial level

- design and implement strategies for building a professional collection

- locate sources of professional collection materials

We have been told that we are to be an action, not a reaction, profession. The image of the school librarian carefully dusting off a collection of seldom-used books has been used to represent all that is wrong with the profession. Therefore, designating the initial level of instructional consultation as establishing and maintaining collections of things might seem to be heretical or at least regressive.

We know that there are many ways in which we can help teachers teach. We also know that instructional consultation is a continuum of activity and that each level rests firmly on the one below it. Before a school library media specialist attempts to enter into the higher levels, the initial level must be solidly in place.

As discussed in previous chapters, instructional design consultation, strictly defined, has not been practiced by many school library media specialists. The broadened definition proposed in this book represents a significant increase in participation; many school library media specialists are still at the no-involvement level for many of the steps in the instructional consultation process. Participation at the initial level of instructional consultation marks a positive change from no participation at all. This chapter introduces this level in more depth and begins to provide information that will help practitioners who are not involved begin to help their teachers teach.

WHAT IS THE INITIAL LEVEL?

As figure 2.1 shows, a teacher who is following an instructional design approach to planning, implementing, and evaluating instruction goes through a series of steps that help to increase the probability that the right content gets taught effectively and efficiently. A teacher will take some or all of the following actions.

Step 1   Decide what is to be taught.

Step 2   Determine characteristics of the students that might influence the materials, strategies, and activities used to teach the content selected.

Step 3   Decide what the students should be able to do as a result of the instruction.

Step 4   Design a process by which to assess students before and after instruction.

Step 5   Design student activities and groupings, as well as instructional strategies, based upon steps 1 through 3.

Step 6   Obtain (purchase, rent, borrow, produce, etc.) instructional materials, based upon steps 1 through 3.

Step 7   Implement the instruction. The style of implementation can vary from totally teacher-controlled (the teacher as the dominant medium) to totally individualized (the teacher as a strategist using a wide array of media).

Step 8   Evaluate the entire procedure, based upon the results of pretests, posttests, and other information. This evaluation might involve repeating one or more of the steps.

In practicing instructional consultation, the school library media specialist helps the teacher teach by assisting at any or all of these steps. At the initial level, this assistance does not involve a great deal of interaction between the teacher and the school library media specialist. Rather, the library can be thought of as a storefront with the teacher as a consumer.

Following are sample activities that illustrate the initial level, one activity for each step in the previous instructional design process.

Step 1   The school library media specialist obtains a variety of earth science textbooks to be used as resources by the teachers of earth science who are designing a new series of units on this topic. Such textbooks will assist these teachers by providing them with a wide range of possible content.

Step 2   The school library media specialist obtains a microcomputer program that will grade and analyze the results of a learning styles instrument.

Step 3   The school library media specialist obtains a work on writing usable instructional objectives.

Step 4   The school library media specialist obtains an article on using portfolios for assessing student performance.

Step 5   The school library media specialist purchases a book on individualizing instruction in the language arts.

Step 6   The principal has been selecting all non-print instructional materials, which have been sent, uncataloged, directly to the classroom. The school library media specialist begins a program of purchasing a range of materials on the basis of reviews in *School Library Journal*, which are then processed and distributed through the library media center.

Step 7   The school library media specialist maintains a pool of equipment, which the teachers come to the library media center to borrow and return.

Step 8   The school library media specialist purchases a videotape on evaluating teaching effectiveness.

These are only a few of the ways in which the library media program can assist teachers at the initial level. In each case, materials, facilities, or equipment were made available for use by teachers.

RESOURCES THE LIBRARY
MEDIA CENTER CAN PROVIDE

In helping the teacher perform the steps more effectively, the library media center could provide professional collection materials for faculty development in order for the teacher to perform a particular step in the instructional design process more effectively and efficiently; samples of materials to use as resources; instructional tools; equipment; and facilities.

Building a Professional Collection

The professional collection materials we are concerned about in this book are those whose purpose is to prepare teachers to better carry out each step in the planning, teaching, and evaluating process—that is, to better design, implement, and evaluate instruction. A typical initial-level activity at all of the steps in the instructional consultation process is obtaining, processing, and disseminating these materials.

If one of the purposes of the library media center is to support the teaching process, one would assume that there would be significant emphasis in professional publications on building a collection of materials to assist teachers. Standards published over thirty years ago suggested 200 to 1,000 titles of books and 40 to 50 professional periodicals (American Library Association 1969), but the practice of building professional collections has never met this standard. The term *professional collection* is not indexed in some of the major library media administration and collection development works and is covered briefly in Van Orden (1998) and Woolls (1999).

Of the fifteen school and library media center acquisition policies and procedures in Taylor's 1981 work, only two contain sections on professional collection development. The *longer* of these reads: "The school IMC must provide materials for teachers and administrators. This collection should represent all areas of instruction and be both practical and innovative" (75). *Information Power: Building Partnerships for Learning* (ALA 1998) does not include information regarding professional collections.

There is also a dearth of articles on this topic. A search of ERIC and several online databases, combining each of the descriptors "faculty development," "teacher improvement," and "instructional improvement" with "selecting library materials," yielded very little information.

Obviously, the professional collection does not often have a high priority in either the literature or in practice. A quality professional collection can be a powerful tool and is especially important in building the necessary infrastructure to move to higher levels of instructional consultation. Following are suggestions for making the impact greater.

Include a strong statement for the professional collection in your policy and procedures statement. Include in your center's philosophy that part of the library media program's role is to improve instruction through the provision of these materials.

Target specific steps in the instructional design process and obtain materials that support this step. As an example, if the school population is changing, targeting the learner analysis step might be beneficial. Find out which teachers are interested in this topic. Some might be taking a related course, and you could put these teachers on your library committee.

Select the materials carefully so that they will be used and useful. Know your faculty. Most teachers will not often use a lengthy work that demands plowing through a lot of jumble to reach what they perceive as useful. Match your materials to your faculty's motivation and needs. Try to provide a range of materials and make materials available in both traditional and newer formats (see figures 4.1 and 4.2). If possible, label the material as to the instructional design step or steps covered. (An example: "This material provides examples of activities for use with students with various learning styles.") Be sure that your collection contains materials that can be read or viewed in less than forty-five minutes. If you have access to electronic information services, either on CD-

ROM or online, consider doing searches on topics you believe would be useful to your teachers. Routing the abstracts via the LAN to your teachers and making copies of the documents available can be considered.

See if specific items that deal with the topics selected can be obtained on extended loan from the district center. Look into borrowing from other schools, and from local colleges and universities. Call on the faculty at these institutions for assistance in selection.

Search for alternative funding. Selecting a particular step in the instructional design process is very helpful in justifying a grant. Improvement of instruction is a high priority with many funding agencies. Local businesses and civic groups are good funding sources for small collection-development grants.

Fig. 4.1. Professional collection in traditional . . .

Fig. 4.2. . . . and newer formats.

Fig 4.3. Traveling Professional Collection

Make the collection accessible and visible. In practice, even the best faculty development materials shelved inconspicuously in the library media center are not often used. Make the materials easy to find and use. For example, start a traveling professional collection that stops often in the teacher's lounge. Establish a "cubbyhole" for teachers in the center. Provide coffee and maybe some easy listening music with headphones. Regularly feature in your promotions materials on certain steps in the instructional design process. (See figure 4.3 for an example.)

Another effective way to increase your program's visibility is to give a book talk. School library media specialists have the ability to make a work sound interesting and useful and should use this ability to make their teachers aware of an item in the professional collection that can be of special help. Ask the principal for one or two minutes at a faculty meeting or the department head for time at a departmental meeting. Keep the talk short.

In this scenario, the school library media specialist has requested to speak to the teachers during a faculty meeting.

A SCENARIO

I want you to imagine that you are about to attend a lecture entitled "Effects of Semantic Integration Training on the Recall of Pictograph Sentences by Children in Kindergarten and First Grade." Whew. Unless you are an expert in this area, you would need to do some preparation before the lecture begins. In preparing for the lecture, you might translate the topic into something you are more familiar with, like, "Does teaching young children to read picture stories have any effect on their understanding of the stories?" In doing this "translation," you would use a critical thinking skill, one of many covered in Heiman and Slomianko's useful little book, *Critical Thinking Skills*. This work is intended to provide teachers with a practical guide to introducing critical thinking skills into the classroom. It will be in our HAVE YOU SEEN THIS? section of the professional collection for your use. Thanks for your attention.

Fig. 4.4. Book-talking the professional collection

Finding sources of titles of professional collection materials is a challenging task. There are really no current sources that detail "opening day" professional collections. There are many useful materials, and it is up to school library media specialists to develop collections on their own to match the unique needs of the professionals in their school.

Following is a list of specific sources:

Van Orden, P. 1995. *The Collection Program in Schools.* Englewood, Colo.: Libraries Unlimited.

Homa, L., ed. 2001. *The Elementary School Collection.* 23rd ed. Williamsport, Pa.: Bodart.

Woolls, B. 1999. *The School Library Media Manager.* 2nd ed. Englewood, Colo.: Libraries Unlimited.

The following publishers routinely disseminate titles that should be considered when building a professional collection:

ABC-CLIO, Inc.
130 Cremona Drive
Santa Barbara, CA 93117

ACE-Educational
5670 West Sample Rd.
Margate, FL 33073

American Federation of Teachers
555 New Jersey Avenue N.W.
Washington, DC 20001

Association for Educational Communications and Technology
1800 North Stonelake Dr. Suite 2
Bloomington, IN 47404

Association for Supervision and Curriculum Development
1703 North Beauregard St.
Alexandria, VA 22311

D.O.K. Publishers
P.O. Box 605
East Aurora, NY 14052

Educational Resources Information Center (ERIC)
4483-A Forbes Blvd.
Lanham, MD 20706

Educational Technology Publications, Inc.
700 Palisade Avenue
Englewood Cliffs, NJ 07632–0564

Grolier Publishers, Inc.
90 Sherman Turnpike
Danbury, CT 06816

Gryphon House, Inc.
P.O. Box 207
Beltsville, MD 20704

Heinemann, Inc.
88 Post Road West
P.O. Box 5007
Westport, CT 06881

Holt, Rinehart & Winston, Inc.
8217–33 Sunspring Circle
Orlando, FL 32825

Inspiring Teachers
2510 Meadowridge Drive
Garland, TX 75044

International Reading Association
800 Barksdale Rd.
P.O. Box 8139
Newark, DE 19714–8139

Libraries Unlimited, Inc.
P.O. Box 6633
Englewood, CO 80155–6633

Linworth Publishing, Inc.
480 East Wilson Bridge Rd. Suite L
Worthington, OH 43085

Macmillan Publishing Co.
866 Third Avenue
New York, NY 10022

McGraw-Hill Publishing Co.
1221 Avenue of the Americas
New York, NY 10020

Merrill Education/Prentice Hall
445 Hutchinson Avenue
Columbus, OH 43235–5677

National Association of Secondary School Principals
1904 Association Drive
Reston, VA 22091

National Council for the Social Studies
1904 Association Drive
Reston, VA 20191–1537

National Council of Teachers of English
1111 Kenyon Road
Urbana, IL 61801–1096

National Council of Teachers of Mathematics
1906 Association Drive
Reston, VA 20191–1502

NEA Professional Library
P.O. Box 2035
Annapolis Junction, MD 20701–2035

Neal-Schuman Publishers, Inc.
100 Variet Street
New York, NY 10013

Nystrom Publishing, Inc.
3333 Elston Avenue
Chicago, IL 60618

Phi Delta Kappa
408 N. Union Street
P.O. Box 789
Bloomington, IN 47402–0789

Random House, Inc.
280 Park Avenue
New York, NY 10017

Rowman and Littlefield Publishing Group
4720 Boston Way
Lanham, MD 20706

St. Martin's Press
175 Fifth Avenue
New York, NY 10010

Scholastic, Inc.
557 Broadway
New York, NY 10012

Scott, Foresman
1900 East Lake Avenue
Glenview, IL 60025

Teachers College Press
Columbia University
1234 Amsterdam Avenue
New York, NY 10027

Zephyr Press
P.O. Box 13448
Tucson, AZ 85732–3448

A Sample Materials Collection

Moving up to the initial level for several of the steps in the instructional design process can involve obtaining and making available examples of developed materials for faculty use. Instructional design involves a lot of theory, and a few good examples go a long way toward enabling teachers to put the theory into practice. Following are two ideas for starting a collection of these materials.

- Gather a textbook collection including as many teacher editions as possible. Textbooks can often be obtained at very reasonable cost. They are great sources for content, activities, and test items.

- Set up a unit exchange. Planning a good unit or lesson takes a lot of time and effort. The school library media specialist can manage an exchange program within a school system in which teachers voluntarily pool samples. These can be samples of entire units or of portions of units such as test items, objectives, or activities.

An Instructional Tools Collection

Attempting to establish a universe of instructional tools without extensive interaction with the faculty is not the best method. The high cost of instructional materials prohibits guessing which should be purchased. Obtaining instructional materials as part of a process of systematically designing instruction is the method in which the materials obtained will have the greatest likelihood of use and effectiveness.

At the initial level of instructional consultation, the school library media specialist has not built the depth of relationship with the faculty where instructional materials are selected as the result of instructional design efforts or even through informal interaction with the faculty. An interesting approach to collection development that uses a map of what the teacher is doing in the classroom is called curriculum mapping. Curriculum is a merging of educational techniques, course content, learning outcomes, educational experiences, and assessment of the student's environment and learning style. Curriculum mapping displays these key elements of the curriculum and the relationships between them, which will help both teachers and students. The essence of mapping is to give a broad picture of the taught curriculum—a road map. Curriculum mapping is about representing the different components of the curriculum so that the whole picture and the relationships and connections between the parts can be easily identified. This tool will be further discussed in chapter 7.

There are cases when the school library media specialist will be selecting instructional materials in virtual isolation from the classroom action. Although this is probably not an efficient use of funds, there are materials to assist the school library media specialist in developing a collection. In most cases, the titles that are recommended here have been reviewed. (See chapter 12 for more information on obtaining instructional materials.)

Equipment Selection and Maintenance

Ashland Independent School District. http://www.ashland.k12.ky.us/technology/tips.htm [May 7, 2003].

Mike's Home Computer Service. http://www.mikescomputerservice.com/mikestips.html [May 8, 2003].

PC Tips. http://brigada.org/today/articles/pctips.html [May 7, 2003].

Prostano, E. T., and Prostano, J. S. 1999. *The School Library Media Center.* 5th ed. Englewood, Colo.: Libraries Unlimited.

Santa Clara County Office of Education, Library Services. 2001. *Where Do I Start? A School Library Handbook.* Worthington, Ohio: Linworth Publishing.

Stein, B. L. 1992. *Running a School Library Media Center: A How-To-Do-It Manual.* New York: Neal-Schuman Publications.

Tips and Tricks. http://www.isc-unlimited.com/tiptrick/default.htm [May 8, 2003].

Woolls, B. 1999. *The School Library Media Manager.* 2nd ed. Englewood, Colo.: Libraries Unlimited.

Facilities

As part of creating the infrastructure necessary to carry out an instructional consultation role in which the school library media specialist helps the teachers in the school, effort is often required to maintain, if not create, instructional facilities. As computers have proliferated in the school, the school library media specialist has often been called upon to make recommendations in the design of computer use areas. This is in addition to the continuing expectation of expertise in designing audiovisual production and projection areas. These tasks often seem daunting, but there are sources of information that can be of assistance, some of which are listed here:

American School and University. 2002. Unique School with Neighborhood Design. 74 (6): 16.

Baule, S. M. 1999. *Facilities Planning for School Library Media and Technology Centers.* Worthington, Ohio: Linworth Publishing.

Baule, S. M. 1999. First Steps in Planning for Facilities Renovation. *Library Talk* 12 (5): 6.

Cochran, S. and Gisolfi, P. 1997. Renovate It and They Will Come. *School Library Journal* 43 (2): 25.

Media and Methods. 2001. School Furniture Update: An Assessment Survey. 37 (7): 14.

Walters, D. 2001. Media Center Makeovers. *Book Report* 20 (1): 54–56.

NETWORKING

One of the most significant tasks facing school library media specialists who want to help their teachers is to push for access to electronic information networks. Through these networks, teachers can link up with others and with various databases. At a minimum, the library media program should provide a modem for access. The school library media specialist should be in the forefront in pushing for access to the Internet. Contact through the Internet to information sources, both formal and informal, will play an increasingly important role for teachers who want to improve their instruction.

CONCLUSION

The initial level of involvement in the instructional consultation process accomplishes two important tasks. First, it provides teachers and administrators with the resources to carry out their job better and, in the end, positively affects the students in the school. Second, involvement at the initial level creates the necessary infrastructure to move up to higher levels of instructional consultation.

Many school library media specialists will have already reached the initial level for several of the steps in the instructional design process. We hope that the information provided in this chapter will help them enhance this involvement. For those steps where the initial level has not been reached, the information in the chapter can assist in the targeting of steps and the design of an instructional consultation action plan.

Chapters 7 through 14 of this book contain reference sources and action ideas for each of the steps in the process. Keep in mind that although the initial level is the lowest level of involvement, it is still important and necessary for involvement at higher levels. The provision of materials, as well as facilities and equipment, does help teachers teach and students learn.

THOUGHT PROVOKERS

1. Design a poster for display in the teachers' lounge to accompany selected faculty-development materials that you will rotate from the center.

2. Select any publication you believe would help members of the faculty perform one or more of the instructional design steps. Design an accompanying sheet that states the purpose of the publication and indexes the most important parts. Finally, write the start of a book talk that you would deliver during a faculty meeting (total talk time 30 to 180 seconds).

(See appendix A for answers.)

REFERENCES

American Library Association. 1969. *Standards for School Media Centers*. Chicago: American Library Association.

———. 1998. *Information Power: Building Partnerships for Learning*. Chicago: American Library Association and Association for Educational Communications and Technology.

Taylor, M. M. 1981. *School Library and Media Center Acquisitions Policies and Procedures.* Phoenix, Ariz.: Oryx Press.

Van Orden, P. 1998. *The Collection Program in Schools: Concepts, Practices, and Information Sources.* Englewood, Colo.: Libraries Unlimited.

Woolls, B. 1999. (2nd ed.). *The School Library Media Manager.* Englewood, Colo.: Libraries Unlimited.

ADDITIONAL READINGS

Andronik, C.M., ed. 1998. *School Library Management.* 4th ed. Worthington, Ohio: Linworth Publishing.

Buzzeo, T. 2002. *Collaborating to Meet Standards: Teacher/Librarian Relationships for K-6.* Worthington, Ohio: Linworth Publishing.

Farmer, L.S.J. 1999. *Partnerships for Lifelong Learning.* 2nd ed. Worthington, Ohio: Linworth Publishing.

———. 2001. Managing the Hard Stuff: Technology. *Library Talk* 14 (4): 6–7.

Haycock, K. 2001. Role of Clarification and Role Dilemmas: New Challenges for Teacher-Librarians? *School Libraries in Canada* 21 (2): 3–4.

Ishizuka, K., Minkel, W., and Evan S. L. 2002. 5 Biggest Challenges for 2002. *School Library Journal* 48 (1): 50–51.

Palma, L. 2001. Going It Together. *Independent School* 61 (1): 26–30.

School Library Journal. (2001). Elementary School Collection Publishes Its Last Edition. 47 (7): 16.

CHAPTER

5

The Moderate Level

This chapter contains information to help the reader

- define the moderate level of involvement and discuss its importance

- identify moderate-level activities for each step in the instructional design process

- identify the personal characteristics necessary to move to the moderate level

- acquire effective communication skills for interaction with teacher clients

- create procedures for increasing teachers' awareness of moderate-level services of the library media center

- target the instructional design step that provides the greatest probability of success

- design and implement an instructional consultation action plan for the moderate level

WHAT IS THE MODERATE LEVEL?

The moderate level of instructional consultation is the sum of the informal interactions between the school library media specialist and the teachers in the planning, implementation, and evaluation of instruction. The moderate level is different from, but based upon, the initial level. In the initial level, materials, facilities, and equipment are obtained and arranged for use by teachers. The moderate level of consultation adds value to these through interactions between the teacher and the school library media specialist. Often, this interaction takes the form of an informal dialogue resulting in the offering of advice or information by the school library media specialist. The teacher has asked for assistance and is enabled to better perform a step in the instructional process.

The moderate level of instructional consultation usually stops short of systematic consultation with teams of teachers and the performance of in-service activities, which is the point where the in-depth level begins. Moderate-level activities also differ from in-depth level activities in that increasing the teacher's instructional design skills is not usually the explicit reason for the interaction. Another distinction is that at the moderate level, usually only one step in the instructional design process is involved.

Following are sample moderate-level scenarios for each step in the instructional design process.

STEP 1: NEEDS ASSESSMENT

While setting up chairs for the PTA meeting, Layton, the sixth-grade math and science teacher, remarked to Paul Pratwell, the school library media specialist, "Paul, I'll be teaching my unit on space next month, and I am concerned that there have been so many developments recently that I might be missing something important which should be covered."

Paul offered to contact the university library and obtain NASA publications detailing the most recent explorations.

STEP 2: LEARNER ANALYSIS

Bill Carson (math teacher) and Paula Bracken (school library media specialist) are talking over coffee.

Paula: Well, Bill, you look worn out.

Bill: I am worn out. It's the constant hassle to reach the same few kids every time that's worn me out. You know, they are really not behavioral problems, they just get as frustrated as I do sometimes.

Paula: Most of the other students . . . they seem to catch on?

Bill: Yes. Of course everyone has an off day, but some have a lot more than others.

Paula: Well, there's been a lot of progress recently in defining learning styles. Some kids just learn in different ways from the majority. Why don't I bring some material on learning styles to you during your planning period tomorrow? Maybe it will help.

STEP 3: INSTRUCTIONAL OBJECTIVES

While visiting the library media center, Bob Thompson remarked that writing instructional objectives for language arts was certainly a lot more difficult than for mathematics. The school library media specialist offered to obtain samples of objectives she had located through the Internet.

STEP 4: ASSESSMENT OF STUDENT PERFORMANCE

Laura Imhotep (school library media specialist) meets Bill Martin (history teacher) after school.

Bill: Laura, I just read on a Web site that the NEA has come out in favor of using authentic assessment for testing rather than standardized tests. What does this mean?

Laura: I saw the same story yesterday and I put a message on my library media LISTSERVE. This morning, there were several messages that provided some good sources on alternative techniques for assessment. I am ordering several of these. They should help us both to learn about authentic assessment and other ideas.

STEP 5: TEACHING STRATEGIES AND ACTIVITIES DEVELOPMENT

A teacher who had heard from a colleague about role playing in language classes asks the school library media specialist for information on this topic. The information is provided.

STEP 6: MATERIALS SELECTION AND PRODUCTION

Nancy Smith (fourth-grade teacher) and Patricia Renson (school library media specialist) are at lunch.

Nancy: These twenty-minute lunch periods make it almost impossible to eat and talk, but I have to try.

Patricia: What's up?

Nancy: Well, we got the achievement tests back yesterday, and about ten of the fourth-graders out of the three classes missed a lot of the competencies that they should have gotten in third grade.

Patricia: Sounds like remedial time.

Nancy: I could really use your help in getting some good materials. I'll send the competency descriptions to you.

Patricia: Tell me a little about these students and the type of material you're looking for.

Nancy: Well, they're slow learners. They need the material presented in small chunks with lots of feedback and reward. And, of course, their reading level is an obstacle. I need to continue moving on with the other students, so these materials should be for individual use if possible.

Patricia: When I get the competencies, I'll collect what we have and give you a preview session.

STEP 7: IMPLEMENTATION (A CONTINUATION OF THE PREVIOUS SCENARIO, SEVERAL DAYS LATER.)

Nancy: I appreciate your finding these materials for me. Where did they come from?

Patricia: The videotape is ours, and the multimedia program and the programmed instruction booklet are from the central office. The multimedia program is on preview. We just lucked out on that one.

Nancy: On preview? That's the one I believe would do the job best. Can we keep it?

Patricia: I think we have enough left in the budget. I agree that it is well done and have shown it to several other teachers. Let me see what I can do.

Nancy: Should the computer be sent to my room?

Patricia: Since there are only ten students involved, and the material is self-contained, let's set up a schedule to send them two at a time to the center. I have helpers trained to assist on the computer.

STEP 8: EVALUATION

The social studies department has recently completed a unit on urban America that the teachers developed and taught as a team. The department head requests the school library media specialist to provide some information on evaluation. The specialist sends two books and a CD-ROM.

The previous scenarios represent only a sample of the many ways the school library media specialist can interact with the teacher to assist in the instructional process. School library media specialists acting at the initial level provide the foundation for instruction. When functioning at the moderate level, they act as resource people who, through interacting with the teachers, heighten the impact of the library media center on teaching and learning in the school.

MOVING UP TO THE MODERATE LEVEL

There are steps in the instructional consultation process in which many school library media specialists have reached the moderate level. Probably the majority of specialists have not reached this level for many of the steps. This should certainly not be construed as a failure of the profession but rather as a logical result of the realities of professional practice. Lack of time, funds, clerical assistance, and a clear perception of role have all contributed to restrict the sophistication of instructional consultation achieved.

It is important to keep in mind that enhancing involvement in instructional consultation can be a gradual process accomplished in small increments. This involvement, if planned and executed properly, should bring both extrinsic and intrinsic rewards. Breaking into the moderate level is especially important because it is at this level where bonds are established with individual teachers and administrators. It is at this level where the question posed by Boardman (1988), "Are we integral or supplementary?", begins to be answered in a positive manner. Once a school library media specialist decides to increase involvement in instructional consultation to include the moderate level, specific actions need to be taken. These are targeting the step, assessing and increasing instructional consultation capabilities, assessing and increasing positive personal characteristics and communication skills, and publicizing—that is, letting the faculty know of the instructional consultation services.

Targeting the Step

Through the use of the ICAC (see chapter 3), the school library media specialist can determine which of the steps in the instructional design process have been reached at the initial level but not yet at the moderate level. Once these steps have been identified, one or more can be selected and an action plan formulated.

Following are questions to consider when targeting a step:

- Does the faculty seem to require assistance at a particular step? Perhaps the school system has recently mandated that teachers submit instructional objectives to the principal and this has raised interest in that step. Perhaps re-districting has recently brought an influx of students with a variety of learning styles into the school. Perhaps a new type of instructional equipment has become available and interest in purchasing materials has increased. Sometimes a need is merely intuited by the school library media specialist; sometimes it is recognized on the basis of comments made by several teachers.

- What are the teachers' attitudes toward the involvement of the library media program at this particular step? Sometimes, for a variety of reasons, the faculty is disposed to ask for assistance on some steps more than others. Often, school library media specialists are seen as simply the providers of teaching resources. The school library media specialist should discuss this issue with teachers to obtain their views. Teachers will be more disposed to seek assistance at steps where they believe the school library media specialist has a role. Given a choice between attempting an increase in involvement at a negatively and a positively regarded step, with all else being equal, the latter should be chosen.

- What is the principal's attitude toward increased involvement at a particular step? The principal's support is often vital to success, particularly at the higher levels of involvement. His or her input should be obtained at the planning stage.

- What are the resources required for increased involvement at each step? Some steps (materials selection and implementation, for example) require more resources than do others. All else being equal, the step requiring the least resources to increase involvement should be chosen.

- What is your preference? What step in the instructional design process especially interests you? The instructional consultation role has gained increasing acceptance, and many school library media specialists feel pressure to increase their involvement. Moving up to the moderate level is especially intimidating because interaction with faculty is involved. If a teacher fails to use the professional collection, this is not as bruising to the school library media specialist's ego as is an unsuccessful interaction. Interest by the school library media specialist by itself does not ensure success, but it helps to carry one through the inevitable trials and tribulations of initiating interactions with teachers.

Assessing and Increasing Instructional Consultation Capabilities

Knowing their own capabilities to assist at any particular step is certainly part of the process of school library media specialists targeting steps for increased involvement. Nothing kills an attempt to increase involvement at a particular step more quickly than creating but not meeting expectations. Credibility is a very fragile commodity. Teachers, as Baker (1984) pointed out, tend to be conservative. They are also usually pressed for time and can be unforgiving of those who waste what little is available to them. In any consultant-client relationship, the client's most valuable resource is attention. Most often, a client will give you that resource once, and you must earn it after that. Before advertising that the library media program is available to assist teachers at a particular step, specialists should make sure that they possess the requisite competencies to perform the services advertised.

Of course, the school library media specialist should not nor cannot wait until all of the competencies for a particular step are obtained before increasing levels of involvement. Few consultants in any field enter a situation in which they are 100 percent comfortable. As Dalbotten and Wallin (1990) point out, school library media specialists must be risk-takers who are willing to sometimes "fly by the seat of their pants" in order to assist in classroom instructional design. The school library media specialist needs to be aware of competencies within each step and emphasize strengths.

For example, because of increased interest by many teachers in learning styles, the school library media specialist might be willing to locate materials and resource persons to assist the teachers. However, the same specialist might not be competent at explaining and recommending a particular diagnostic instrument. School library media specialists must be careful to emphasize areas in which they are comfortable and competent and not create unrealistic expectations.

Many school library media specialists received little or no preparation in instructional design tools as part of their professional training. Even if they did, that field has changed significantly in the past few years. Therefore, in order to serve as instructional consultants, they need continuing education. The school library media specialist can obtain or increase instructional design skills in certain steps through reading, in-services, and formal courses.

Assessing and Increasing Positive Personal Characteristics and Communication Skills

Moving up to the moderate level involves interacting with teachers, and the success of this interaction is influenced by personal characteristics projected by the school library media specialist and by the communication skills that the school library media specialist possesses. The following are two of the most critical of these.

CONFIDENCE AND BELIEF IN THE ROLE

A sense of confidence is of major importance to a school library media specialist's success in cooperative planning. It takes fortitude and a good self-image to survive rejection in approaching a teacher.

A strong sense of confidence will enable the school library media specialist to take the risk attendant with offering one's services. This risk-taking will be easier if one truly believes in the role of instructional consultant. Remember that the children and young adults in your school need and deserve the best educational experience possible. You have it in your power to act as a catalyst for change for the better. Also, remember that there are levels of instructional consultation. Select the level at which you are most comfortable. This comfort will be reflected in the confidence you display.

TRUST

Trust is the cornerstone upon which relationships between school library media specialists and teachers is built. In the absence of trust, very little communication will take place because the risk is often perceived as too great. It is certainly not easy to engender a feeling of trust in teachers in your role as an instructional consultant, especially if this is a first attempt to implement this role above the initial level.

Two significant components of trust are empathy and acceptance (Hewlett 1983). Another crucial factor is a continual flow of accurate information between parties. Misunderstanding can quickly destroy trust. In the hectic world of the school, there are ample opportunities for miscommunication and accompanying recrimination and loss of credibility. A successful library media center is usually in a state of controlled chaos and provides plenty of opportunities for distracting your attention from the teacher-client.

How does a consultant begin to develop a trusting relationship with clients? How are empathy, acceptance, and accurate communications ensured? The first step is to continually attempt to see the world through the eyes of the client. For the school library media specialist, this means understanding the teacher-client's "practical theory." The consultation process has as its goal the modification of a teacher's practical theory, and the consultation must originate in the teacher's practical theory.

There are communication skills that can assist the school library media specialist to enter the client's world and demonstrate empathy and acceptance. In addition, these skills increase the probability that the communication is accurate. The following suggestions are based upon the microcounseling technique developed by Allen Ivey (see Ivey 1971 and Ivey and Authier 1978) and augmented by the work of Hewlett (1983) and Griffin and Lamb (1987). For the very limited time that this approach takes, it is very effective.

Using the Attending Skills

In face-to-face meetings with teachers, they will both see you and hear you. Information critical to the success of the communication will be derived from your nonverbal and verbal behavior.

Fig. 5.1. Too busy to help?

PHYSICAL ATTENDING SKILLS

1. *Eye contact.* Maintain eye contact with the client (teacher). This does not have to continue 100 percent of the time, but contact should be made the majority of the time.

2. *Posture.* Face the client. Lean toward the client. Nod occasionally. Project a positive attitude.

3. *Relax!* Be in the present, not in the past or future. Focus your energy on the client. Arrange supervision for any students in the center if needed.

These skills should be used so long as both you and the client remain comfortable. Your own comfort will increase with practice.

VERBAL ATTENDING SKILLS

1. *Minimize closed questions:* those that can be answered in one word. Examples:

   a. Are you having problems teaching the equations unit?

   b. Do you have several types of learners in your class?

   c. Have you thought about a motivational activity for this lesson?

As you can see, this type of question does not facilitate good communication between the school library media specialist and the teacher.

2. *Use open questions:* Encourage answers in complete sentences. Examples:

   a. What are some difficulties you have encountered in teaching the equations unit?

   b. What makes one learner different from another in your class?

   c. What would be some ways to get the students motivated for this lesson?

3. *Use confirming responses:* these include agreeing, clarifying, and supporting statements versus irrelevant, incoherent, or negative responses. Examples:

   a. Yes, a field trip to the museum would certainly provide many opportunities to see a variety of the dinosaurs that they have been studying.

   b. When you said that the electronic index wasn't effective, was it because it was difficult to use or did it just not contain the topics that your students needed?

   c. You certainly know a lot about Chaucer!

4. *Paraphrase:* Restate in your own words the important information given by the teacher. Example:

Teacher:	I sure don't know about that textbook I'm supposed to use to teach the remedial math class. Sets, intersections, the universe! Wow!
LMS:	Your students need to learn basic math skills, and the textbook is not appropriate?

5. *Summarize:* At the end of the communication, recap the main points and any agreed-upon actions. Example (at the conclusion of the conversation):

Teacher: Yes, I suppose I could do that by then.

LMS: Great. Now, let me make sure that I have it clear in my mind what we're going to do. Since the textbook you're using really doesn't cover what you believe it needs to, you are going to develop your own materials, at least for the decimals unit. We'll both be collecting materials on decimals and will meet next Tuesday, same time, to see what we have gathered.

Nonverbal communications assist the school library media specialist to be approachable and interact positively with others. Verbal skills are often more difficult to isolate and master. Once a verbal skill is learned it should be reviewed and refined if one is to communicate more effectively. Skillful communication takes practice. Here are some pointers:

- Be aware of your posture.

- Think about the gestures you make.

- Consider your facial expression.

- Be cognizant of your tone of voice.

- Maintain appropriate eye contact.

- Make positive (respectful) responses.

- Speak motivational words (encourage).

- Reflect on what has been said.

- React positively.

- Avoid premature answers, diagnoses, or opinions.

- Restate or paraphrase content.

- Remember.

- Ask open questions.

- Reach closure.

The attending and communication skills, if properly employed, will make the teachers feel welcome and respected, and communication will be more precise.

Publicizing

The defining component in moderate-level activity is interaction with a teacher or teachers. Recognition by a teacher that help is needed at a particular step in the instructional design process is necessary but not sufficient. The teacher must realize that the library media center can fulfill that need. Publicizing available resources would increase the effectiveness of initial-level activities. Letting the faculty know what the school library media specialist can do is crucial for moving to the moderate level. In short, initial-level activities can be performed in isolation; activities at the moderate level cannot.

There is a wide variety of ways in which the school library media specialist can make the faculty aware of the assistance available in the process of planning, implementing, and evaluating instruction. When school library media specialists communicate information about instructional consultation services, they should distinguish between features and benefits and concentrate on benefits. The social studies teacher might be fascinated by a description of the speed of locating information on the local-area network (LAN). More likely, interest will be raised by pointing out that the same information gathered in a manual search of newspapers can be acquired in a fraction of the time by using a database available on the LAN. Following are some suggestions for enhancing faculty awareness.

- Use your library media services manual to describe the assistance available to teachers for each step in the instructional design process. Be sure to specify any constraints that might exist in the rendering of the assistance.

- Post notices on the library media center's faculty bulletin board. Best located in high teacher traffic areas, the board can be a good vehicle for letting faculty members know what assistance can be given them. Keep announcements simple and to the point. Remember to specify what the teacher must do, as well as what you can do. For example, if the center will produce a transparency if given a master, specify this. If the center can design transparency masters, this should be made clear. (Of course, such notices do not have to be restricted to a bulletin board but can be located in any high-traffic area.)

- Include notices in the library media center's newsletter or on the library media center's homepage. Once again, to avoid later difficulties, be as specific as possible. (See appendix D.)

- Target new teachers. (See appendix D.)

- Make presentations where teachers gather, for example at faculty meetings, department or grade meetings, coffees, and in-services. You can plug a special service. Keep your remarks short and to the point.

- Encourage the gathering of teachers. Consider establishing a place in your center where teachers can buy coffee, tea, or soft drinks and share goodies. Add a supply of best sellers and discarded magazines. A relaxed and happy teacher is a prime target for instructional consultation. If your personality and interests point in this direction, organize a photography group, a boat or raft trip, or a weekly volleyball game. A leadership role in any area can build trust and respect and facilitate the consultation role.

- Have an open-door policy in the center after school. If there is room, encourage grade or department meetings in the center.

- Place articles with routing slips in teachers' mailboxes.

- Be seen and accessible. Never tell a teacher you are too busy without first setting a time to meet.

- Publicize in a variety of ways that you have a role to help teachers teach. (See figures 5.2 and 5.3 for examples.)

Fig. 5.2. Publicizing the instructional consultant role

Use word of mouth. The best way to persuade a teacher to request assistance is through the recommendation of another teacher. The best way to make this happen is to sell the right person or persons and to do an outstanding job. A teacher whose use of the center's assistance has resulted in better, more efficient teaching will be the best advertisement.

Sample Instructional Consultation Action Plan

At this hypothetical library media center, the moderate level of the learner analysis step was one of eight target areas. This area was selected for the following reasons:

- The school (grades 7–9) groups students according to ability rather than grade. Five teachers are assigned to teach the lowest-ability students. In the past three years, there have been twelve different teachers for these students. Achievement test results have been disappointing, and there have been numerous behavior problems.

- The homogeneity of the classes makes expenditures of resources for instructional design cost-effective.

- The teachers are new and motivated to innovate.

- The administration has expressed concern and asked the school library media specialist for ideas.

- The school library media specialist is interested in this area.

Fig. 5.3. A sample bulletin board notice

The following is a sample plan for moving up to the moderate level at the learner analysis step.

I. Goal statement: Encourage teachers to request assistance from the library media program in order to increase their abilities to design instruction tailored to the characteristics of each student.

II. Objective statements

   A. At least 20 percent of the teachers will use professional collection materials or request information on the topic.

   B. At least 10 percent of the teachers will report that they have incorporated some form of learner-analysis procedure into their teaching. (Both objectives will be measured over a twelve-month period.)

III. Things to do

   A. Review materials on this topic in the professional collection.

   B. Read and review to upgrade own competencies and to locate and acquire more information, if required.

   C. Discuss the program with the principal and finalize the services the library media program will offer in this area.

   D. Prepare grant proposal to System Professional Development Fund.

   E. Publicize materials and services.

      1. Prepare an announcement for bulletin board and other areas.

      2. Put notice in newsletter for at least three issues.

      3. Meet with the teachers of the low-ability students during their regular meeting and explain materials and services available.

      4. Target two teachers who seem to need the service and would be receptive. Visit informally at least twice.

      5. Make further presentations if requested.

   F. Answer questions and obtain materials.

IV. Resources required

   A. One to two hundred dollars for additional professional collection materials, excluding instruments.

   B. Four to six hundred dollars for instruments and scoring, depending upon amount and type used.

   C. Fifteen hours per month for two months. Zero to ten hours per month for remainder of year depending upon demand.

   D. Five to fifteen hours clerical time.

PUTTING IT INTO PERSPECTIVE

No matter how well you plan and how fantastic the benefits are that you offer your teachers, there will be some teachers who do not respond. Given the limited resources of most school library media specialists, this might not be a bad thing. Especially when embarking on a program to begin moderate-level consultation at a particular step, you would be better off doing well with one or two teachers than doing a poor job because of trying to work with too many.

An interesting and useful way to deal with the frustration generated by recalcitrant teachers is to think of instructional consultation by the school library media specialist as an innovation much the same as compact disc players or home electronic information services. Harries (1972) has identified certain personality types that correlate with receptivity to adopting an innovation:

- The innovator is ready and eager to try an innovation and will do so without evidence of its effectiveness.

- The middle adopter will try an innovation if evidence exists that it will increase effectiveness or efficiency.

- The late adopter will not try an innovation even if overwhelming evidence exists that it is beneficial. If this type does adopt an innovation, it will be because of social pressure (everyone else is doing it) and not because of the benefits of the innovation.

The secret to raising instructional consultation above the initial level is to sell the innovators and middle adopters and forget the late adopters. This does not mean that the school library media specialist should not try to work with all teachers, but rebuffs and failures should not be viewed as devastating. Instructional consultation at higher levels is not possible with every teacher.

CONCLUSION

Effective implementation of moderate-level instructional consultation is not simple. Planning, publicity, and communication skills are required.

This level can be reached by targeting a single step in the planning, teaching, and evaluating process over an extended period of time. A school library media program operating at the moderate level provides some benefits that cannot be obtained at a lower level, no matter how many materials, facilities, and items of equipment are obtained. At the moderate level the school library media specialist becomes *visible* to the teacher, and through the teacher to the administration. More important, instructional consultation at a heightened level helps teachers teach better and students learn more—a good reason, by itself, to try.

THOUGHT PROVOKERS

1. What are some questions that should be answered before a particular step is targeted for the moderate level?

2. Assume that you are a school library media specialist who has targeted the materials-selection step. Design a poster (11 by 14 inches) that will inform the teachers of some or all of the services you are offering.

3. Find a partner and explain the physical attending skills. Carry on a conversation, intentionally not using the skills. How did it make you and your partner feel? How effective was the communication? Now try the same conversational topic while using the skills. Answer the same questions.

4. Change the following closed question into an open one: "Are you satisfied with the video-tape on Africa?"

5. Create a confirming response for the following teacher statement: "I worked all weekend on the lesson plan for today's class, and it still didn't go as well as I had hoped."

6. Paraphrase the following teacher statement: "The kit was just beautiful! I have never seen such great photography. I would like to have several of those pictures hanging on my wall. I don't know why those students did so poorly on the test."

7. Read the following interaction and write a final statement that the school library media specialist might make to accurately summarize the stated problem and express the actions he or she intends to take.

LMS:	It's good to see you in the center. Jack. What can we do for you today?
Teacher:	Well, I saw the sign on the board—you know, the one in the lounge, about transparencies. I use a lot of diagrams in my lectures, and I usually draw them on the board.
LMS: (nodding)	Uh-huh . . .
Teacher:	I don't mind drawing them, and they have worked in the past. The problem is that now that I'm a "wandering" teacher and teach in three different rooms, I don't have the time to draw the same one three times.
LMS:	You're not dissatisfied with the effects of drawing diagrams on the board, it's drawing the same ones repeatedly that's the problem? How detailed are these diagrams, and are different colors involved?
Teacher:	They're not overly complex, but they're not simple either. I suppose color might help, but I've never used any. That colored chalk doesn't erase well, you know.
LMS:	It can be a real mess. . . . You know, I'd like to see a few of these diagrams. What kind of sketches do you have of them?
Teacher:	I probably have a sketch of each diagram, but there's only one copy of each.
LMS:	Losing them would create a problem. How difficult would it be to make a copy of, say, three that are representative of the rest?
Teacher:	Not very. I'll send copies to you this afternoon.
LMS:	Great. Give me a few days, and I'll get back to you with a few ideas.
Teacher: (getting up to leave)	Okay. I sure hate the wandering around. Wish I had my classroom back.
LMS:	I'll bet trying to teach and run is a real drain.

(See appendix A for answers.)

REFERENCES

Baker, D. P. 1984. *The Library Media Program and the School.* Englewood, Colo.: Libraries Unlimited.

Boardman, E. M. 1988. Positioning the School Library: Are We Integral or Supplementary? *Book Report* 7 (1): 11–17.

Dalbotten, M., and J. Wallin. 1990. *Classroom Instructional Design: Tools for Teacher/Media Specialist Interaction.* St. Paul, Minn.: Minnesota Department of Education.

Griffin, D. J., and J. A. Lamb. 1987. Positive Relationships Produce Positive Results. *School Library Journal* 34 (3): 27–29.

Harries, T. E. 1972. *The Applications of General Systems Theory to Instructional Development.* Washington, D.C.: National Special Media Institute.

Hewlett, B. 1983. Communication Skills and Strategies for Teacher-Librarians. *Emergency Librarian* 11 (1): 14–19.

Ivey, A. E. 1971. *Microcounseling.* Springfield, Ill.: Charles C. Thomas.

Ivey, A. E., and J. Authier. 1978. *Microcounseling: Innovations in Interviewing, Counseling, Psychotherapy, and Psychoeducation.* 2nd ed. Springfield, Ill.: Charles C. Thomas.

Riedling, A. 2000. *Reference Skills for the School Library Media Specialist: Tools and Tips.* Worthington, Ohio: Linworth Publishing.

ADDITIONAL READINGS

Farmer, L.S.J. 2001. *Teaming with Opportunity: Media Programs, Constituencies, and Technology.* Englewood, Colo.: Libraries Unlimited.

Flowers, H. F. 1998. *Public Relations for School Library Media Programs: 500 Ways to Influence People and Win Friends for Your School Library Media Center.* New York: Neal-Schuman Publications.

Gallagher-Hayashi, D. 2001. The Professional Collection: The Teachers' Professional Collection Materials: Stimulating Use. *Teacher Librarian* 28 (5): 13–17.

Hartzell, G. 1994. *Building Influence for the School Library.* Worthington, Ohio: Linworth Publishing.

Hawthorne, K., and J. E. Gibson. 1999. *Bulleting Boards and 3-D Showcases That Capture Them with Pizzazz.* Englewood, Colo.: Libraries Unlimited.

LaRocque, L., and D. Oberg. 1991. The Principal's Role in a Successful Library Program. *The Canadian School Executive* 11 (4): 17–21.

Maxymuk, J. 1997. *Using Desktop Publishing to Create Newsletters, Library Guides and Web Pages: A How-To-Do-It Manual.* New York: Neal-Schuman Publications.

Minkel, W., and G. Junion-Metz. 2002. No More Boring Boards. *School Library Journal* 48 (4): 37.

Snyder, T. 2000. *Getting Lead-Bottomed Administrators Excited about School Library Media Centers.* Englewood, Colo.: Libraries Unlimited.

Wolfe, L. A. 1997. *Library Public Relations, Promotions, and Communications: A How-To-Do-It Manual.* New York: Neal-Schuman Publications.

6

The In-Depth Level

This chapter contains information to help the reader

- define the in-depth level of instructional consultation

- understand in-depth-level activities

- increase the probability of participating on an instructional consultation team

- plan and implement a successful in-service

WHAT IS THE IN-DEPTH LEVEL?

Instructional consultation at all levels has as a goal the promotion of faculty growth and renewal, resulting in the ability to better design, implement, and evaluate instruction and thus resulting in greater achievement by students. At each succeeding level of instructional consultation, larger-scale projects and more sustained efforts are usually involved. Many of the activities found at the in-depth level are consistent with the traditionally held concept of instructional design. Activities at this level generally fall within two categories: 1) the instructional consultation team, and 2) in-service programs.

MOVING UP TO THE IN-DEPTH LEVEL WITH INSTRUCTIONAL CONSULTATION TEAM PARTICIPATION

The moderate level of instructional consultation consists of interaction with a teacher in order to fulfill some request for assistance. Most often, this interaction can be characterized as informal; it is spontaneous and of limited duration. Most important, this assistance usually involves only a single step in the instructional design process.

If the process is extended to include more carefully planned interactions that are of longer duration, are often instigated by the school library media specialist, or cover several steps in the instructional design process, the in-depth level has been reached. The teacher or teachers involved, along with the school library media specialist, are an instructional consultation team. As the process continues, others may become part of the team—the guidance counselor, curriculum consultant, reading expert, principal, or an outside content expert. Several specific steps should be taken to initiate involvement at the in-depth level.

Targeting the Step

With few exceptions, before a school library media specialist targets particular steps in the instructional design process at the in-depth level, the moderate level should have been achieved. To attempt the in-depth work that characterizes the in-depth level without the practice (and advertising) successful moderate-level work provides is to ask for disappointment.

Once particular steps are identified for consideration, the school library media specialist must also consider:

- *Competencies required.* As a member of an instructional consultation team, the school library media specialist should have a high level of competency. An instructional design consultant should never be reluctant to say "I don't know" and offer to find the information, but too many such responses might hinder progress. Reading and viewing, formal courses, and contact with experts (including other school library media specialists) are a few of the ways to increase competency.

- *Needs of teachers and students.* Do particular teachers seem in need of in-depth assistance? Do standardized test scores indicate a need? Has there been a recent change in school demographics? Are units or courses scheduled for revision?

Publicizing

An important ingredient for success at the moderate level is advertising. This is true to an even greater extent at the in-depth level, but the range of channels is usually narrower. Unless the situation at a particular school is exceptional and instructional consultation is widespread and at consistently high levels, methods such as notices on bulletin boards and announcements at faculty meetings will not work. Instructional consultation at the in-depth level is still too new to be readily adopted through such methods.

As with the moderate level, the best publicity is through word of mouth. Membership on instructional consultation teams should be a part of the written policy of the library media program, but nothing will beat successful work with a team to obtain places on other teams. When the time seems right, a likely teacher can be approached and membership on a team (maybe only a team of two!) can be requested.

Maximizing the Climate for Success

The relationship between the instructional consultant and the client or clients is critical to the success of the project. Some models of instructional consultation portray the instructional consultant as a leader and the subject-matter expert as simply a provider of information (Armstrong and Sherman 1988). Others use the physician-patient relationship as a model (Bratton 1983). The authors believe that neither of these approaches is appropriate for a relationship involving school library media specialists and teachers.

Although teachers might be attracted by the idea of obtaining help in their teaching, they are often reluctant to surrender the concept of the totally self-contained classroom where decisions are not questioned. In addition, teachers who work with a school library media specialist are often faced with someone who has little knowledge about their areas of expertise. They may question whether an outside consultant is really needed. The best role for a school library media specialist acting as a member of an instructional consultation team is that of a helper. The members of the team are equals, but the teacher has the ultimate responsibility and, therefore, the authority to make final decisions. School library media specialists will gain authority by demonstrating their worth to the team.

Choosing the Initial Team

Because future opportunities at the in-depth level depend largely on initial success, the school library media specialist should try to maximize the probability that the first attempt at service on an instructional consultation team meets with success.

A friend on the team is helpful but not necessary. More important are team members who are outgoing and excited about teaching. They should be flexible and able to stick to a commitment. Once in-depth-level activities have been firmly established as part of the school library media specialist's repertoire, more challenging teachers can be approached.

Getting Off to a Good Start

Armstrong and Sherman (1988, 16) emphasize the importance of establishing a strong foundation for the project and recommend a written contract. Although this might be a bit extreme for K–12 instructional consultation, the issues they recommend including in the contract provide guidance for topics to be covered in initial conversations among team members:

- *Time constraints.* When will the lesson or unit be taught? Is there a fallback time?

- *Meeting frequency.* How often can and should the team meet? Are there alternatives to face-to-face meetings, such as electronic mail?

- *Possible stress situations.* Initial discussions should clarify the roles and responsibilities of the team members.

- *Goals.* What does the team want to accomplish? These can be stated in very general terms at this point, but it is important to discuss why you have decided to work together.

- *Costs.* Often, teachers will enter a consulting relationship not realizing the effort that must be expended to design instruction. There are real costs involved in time and effort. If the school library media specialist senses that the teacher expects significant results but is not willing to spend the time necessary to achieve them, now is the time to discuss this issue.

- *Benefits.* Closely tied to costs are benefits. What does the teacher gain from leaving the self-contained classroom and participating on a team? If this is the initial cooperative venture at this level, the school library media specialist may want to emphasize the more familiar role and point out assistance that can be rendered in the area of materials selection and activities development.

Using Appropriate Communications Skills

School library media specialists can increase the chances of success by letting teachers know that they care and by using good communication procedures. The communication skills detailed in chapter 5 should be incorporated into everyday behavior.

Following are two scenarios illustrating first steps toward participation on an instructional consultation team at the in-depth level.

SCENARIO 1

Brenda Mathers, the school library media specialist at Wilkinson Elementary, has for the past two years targeted the moderate level at the needs-assessment, instructional-objectives, learner-analysis, and materials-selection steps. On numerous occasions she has provided materials and advice to several teachers on these steps. She has noticed that the fourth-grade teachers have been by far the most frequent users of her services in these areas.

This year, because of her success with this group of teachers, the competencies she has gained in these areas, and the fact that the school system is making release time available for team planning, Brenda has chosen to target the in-depth level. She approaches Polly Wallison, the informal leader of the fourth-grade teachers and a good friend, with a proposal.

Brenda: Polly, are the fourth-grade teachers planning to revise any units this year, or create new ones?

Polly: Well, we talked last year about doing a unit on the history of our city. It would fit into the social studies competencies plan and should be fun to do. Did you know that there was a settlement called New Town that predated Millidgeville and disappeared mysteriously?

Brenda: Wow! No, I never heard of that.

Polly: We could bring in a lot of important skills in this unit. The only problem is lack of time to plan. We are all so busy, and you are, too. You sure have helped us in the past.

Brenda: And I want to in the future. That brings me to why I brought up the subject. I'd like to try working with a group of you right from the start of the unit planning. I think we would all benefit. We could apply for some of the release-time money, so we could have an opportunity to plan as a team.

Polly: Sounds good. Let me mention it to the others, and we can all get together for a bit after school today or tomorrow. I want to talk to you about the book-character parade also.

SCENARIO 2

The New Hope Consolidated School District has changed drastically in the past decade. What was once a fairly homogeneous student population has evolved into one that includes a wide variety of backgrounds, home environments, and aspirations. Most of the teachers at Woodrow Wilson High School have been there for more than ten years. Although discipline has been maintained, achievement test scores have fallen steadily. Dropout statistics have approached the alarm point.

The mathematics department is probably the best illustration of these problems. Winners of state competitions are still produced among the students, but there are signs that all is not well. Teacher morale is at an all-time low. Several teachers have indicated dissatisfaction with student achievement. The lecture method is used the vast majority of the time.

Jim Carson, the school library media specialist, targeted the moderate level at the learner-analysis step the previous year. Several teachers requested information and assistance in obtaining materials and interpreting results. Two teachers actually developed alternative learning centers that targeted specific learning styles. However, the mathematics department seemed untouched by Jim's attempt.

Buzz Williams, the head of the mathematics department, is a good friend of one of the teachers who developed the alternative learning centers. One day, Buzz appears in the library media center.

Jim: Hey Buzz, what can we do you for?

Buzz: Well, I just thought I'd drop in and see what you do here. We don't get much call to use the library as math teachers, you know.

Jim: What you do up there doesn't require our services much. About the only time I see you is at faculty meetings or at ball games. You'd be surprised, I bet, at some of the things we're doing down here.

Buzz: I suppose I would, but some of the things you're doing I do know about. Paula Bradford and I carpool, and she told me about her work with learning styles. It really seemed to work for her.

Jim: Yes, Paula did a fine job of designing some centers for both remedial and advanced work. I'm glad you had a chance to talk to her about them.

Buzz: We sure have a variety of students in our math classes. You just can't teach them all the same.

Jim: What works for trigonometry might not go over too well in basic math. Sometimes, even within the same class, kids need different approaches. There's been a lot of research in this area in the past few years.

Buzz: Well, some of the teachers in the department would like to know more about this. What have you got on the topic?

Jim: I have a lot of materials. I also would be willing to work with one or more of your teachers if they decide to try to use some of the instruments.

Buzz: I don't know. A teacher's time is so limited, you know.

Jim: I know how busy you all are. I believe, though, that if you're really seriously considering designing instruction to fit your students' learning styles, I could save you time by telling you as a group what I know. Perhaps Paula could also help.

Buzz: I'll send you the dates of our next departmental meetings. If you could let me know the date of the earliest one you could attend, I'll clear the agenda.

Jim: Great. As soon as I get the list of dates from you, I'll put some materials on reserve in your department. Thanks for stopping in.

MOVING UP TO THE IN-DEPTH LEVEL WITH IN-SERVICE PROGRAMS

The second category of in-depth-level activities is in-service programs. With the in-service category, the goal is to train the faculty. A successful in-service should result in increased probability of instructional consultation team membership for the school library media specialist as well as activity at lower levels of involvement. In-service can be defined as "a series of planned instructional programs made available to a specified group(s) of professional staff members for purposes of promoting growth and increased job competence" (Rogus 1983, 9). What distinguishes in-service from all other instructional consultation activities is that formal instruction is involved.

Drawbacks of In-Service Activities

Attempting to begin an in-service program for one or more of the steps in the instructional design model can be a harrowing experience that sends the bravest of school library media specialists back to the lower levels of involvement. In-service education does not have a glorious history within the educational establishment. Indeed, it has been categorized as "the slum of American education" (Davies 1967). Skeele (1999) makes this observation: "Teachers often get a pained expression on their faces at the mention of in-service or professional development.... far too often professional development is a dreaded term that bring to mind boring and irrelevant..." (20). Sharma (1982) brought some of the frustrations of teachers to light in her article "Inservicing the Teachers." She compared the teachers' experiences to those of a cow on her grandfather's farm: "I felt really sorry for poor old Flossie. She didn't have any fun. It just happened to her. And if it happened to her four times and she didn't take, it was off to the butcher with her" (403).

One of the greatest challenges of trying to create and implement a formal program to assist teachers in designing, implementing, and evaluating instruction is that the instructional enterprise cannot be halted while it occurs. As Randell and Bitzer point out, it is often like "servicing an airplane in flight" (Randell and Bitzer 1998).

Benefits of In-Service Activities

In-service is the most direct approach to increasing the instructional design skills of teachers. The in-service audience usually consists of several teachers, which reduces the per-person cost.

Furthermore, virtually all of the contact time can be spent in instruction, a situation rarely found in other instructional consultation activities. And despite the failures of in-service education, there have been successes. Effective in-service programs can be carried out. The potential benefit they hold for enhancing instructional design tools should ensure their consideration.

Designing a Successful In-Service

Several authors have prescribed practices to increase the probability of success for an in-service program (see the References and Additional Readings sections at the end of this chapter for a listing). What is interesting about their recommendations, taken as a whole, is that they can be summed up in the statement: An in-service program that follows the steps in the instructional design process will have the most chance of success! Following are some of these prescriptions.

1. *Assess yourself and the audience.* Think about your attitude toward the topic and in-services in general. Are you confident in your abilities and grasp of the topic? If not, take some time to gain that confidence. Smith-Westberry and Job (1986) recommend taking stock of one's public speaking and communications skills. (See the Communication Skills section in chapter 5.)

   Perform a needs assessment. An in-service that does not include topics perceived as valuable by the teachers in the audience will not succeed. The school library media specialist should determine whether an in-service planning committee exists for the district or school. If so, an attempt should be made to become part of this group.

   Before targeting a step in the instructional design process as an in-service topic, the school library media specialist should receive teacher input, both formally and informally. Ideally, the teachers should be asked to rank several possible topics in order of preference. If there is a wide divergence in expertise in the topic(s) to be covered among the teachers, special care should be taken to ensure that the most competent teachers facilitate rather than impede the learning process for others.

2. *Analyze the learner.* Adults are special learners with special needs and styles of learning (Bents and Howey 1981). The characteristics of the teachers in the potential audience should be considered. Anderson (2000) provides several tips for making an in-service relevant and useful to the learner:

   - Know your audience's level of expertise so that you can tailor the presentation to known needs and ability levels.

   - Focus on the specifics of that learning experience.

   - Remember that a few hours of focused and committed time provides huge benefits.

   - Meaningful in-service programs work best with administrative support.

3. *Select instructional objectives.* Know what the teachers should be able to do if the workshop is successful. Skeele (1999) believes that the school library media specialist conducting the in-service should state what the teacher should know at the end of the session.

4. *Provide incentives.* Increased effectiveness as a teacher, the product of a successful in-service, is a powerful intrinsic motivation for attendance and output of effort. However, extrinsic

motivation is sometimes required to overcome teachers' initial reluctance. The school library media specialist should work with the principal in determining what incentives are possible. These might include release time during the school day, in-service requirement credit, recognition in the local news media, and awarding of certificates.

5. *Plan materials and activities in relation to audience and objectives.* Following are some techniques Skeele (1999) uses successfully:

   - Make it practical—something teachers can use as soon as they leave.

   - Conduct small sessions rather than large ones (have several small ones if necessary).

   - Provide worksheets with specific questions.

   - Construct groups ahead of time to come up with a good mix of teachers and abilities.

   - Print an agenda.

   - Provide a "tip sheet" as well as an instructional guide with your name, phone number, and e-mail address.

   - If possible, have assistants (students typically love to assist).

   - Use humor and give prizes.

   - Be flexible—change your plans if necessary.

   - Use equipment that you are familiar with—and practice, practice, practice.

   - Keep it simple.

   - Make them laugh.

6. *Use guided practice* (Smith-Westberry and Job 1986). Allow the participants to use the new knowledge while the instructors are present. This reinforces the learning and provides an opportunity to diagnose the need for further instruction, more practice, or moving ahead.

7. *Try to involve small groups rather than large ones.* Avoid required attendance unless you know everyone is interested. Nothing will destroy an in-service more quickly than the presence of someone who really wants to be somewhere else.

8. *Evaluate the in-service.* At the close of the in-service, the presenter will often be exhausted and faces the many tasks that were put aside in order for the workshop to be possible. Despite the temptation to put the in-service out of mind, an effort should be made to evaluate the effectiveness. A simple feedback form can provide the basis for this evaluation. Notes jotted down while giving the workshop can be organized. Making a brief list of things to add or delete the next time can significantly add to the effectiveness of future workshops.

9. *Continue to be available to faculty after the in-service.*

Evaluating the Inservice

Robinson (1998) identifies five levels of goals for an inservice and key measurements for each. These are:

1. Reaction

    - Satisfaction with the event

    - Perceptions of the relevance and value of the inservice

2. Learning

    - Changes in specific knowledge, skills, and attitudes

3. Change in work performance

    - Improvements in the individual's work behavior

4. Change in the department or peer group

    - Improvements in the procedures and achievements of the working teams

5. Impact on the organizational goals

    - Achievements of some overall goal of the organization (might include a change in values or culture)

CONCLUSION

In-depth-level activities provide the opportunity for the school library media specialist to make the greatest impact on the instructional program. However, for many school library media specialists, the probability of reaching this level in the near future is slight. Rather than becoming discouraged, these professionals should realize that in-depth-level activities are at one end of a continuum with the other end anchored by no activity at all. Activity between these anchor points is also instructional consultation and is valuable.

The philosophy offered in this book includes the belief that the instructional consultation role should be considered by each school library media specialist. Each specialist should determine the level of instructional consultation activity currently being performed and make an honest assessment of whether an increase in involvement is desired. This decision is personal and involves perceptions of self-needs as well as the needs of teachers and students. Another tenet of this philosophy is that moving from no involvement to the initial level and moving from the moderate to the in-depth level are both valuable. Both improvements are helping teachers to teach and students to learn.

For those who decide to increase involvement, the levels approach provides the tools for mapping the strategy to implement this increase. Involvement as an instructional consultant, if approached in a sane, deliberate, and nonjudgmental manner, can be a real force for excellence in the education of our children and young adults.

THOUGHT PROVOKERS

1. Several viewpoints of the optimum instructional consultant-teacher relationship were presented in this chapter (expert/passive client, physician/patient, and helper/partner). Take some time to think about your personal style of interaction with others. Which of these matches your vision of the instructional consultant-teacher relationship?

2. You are working with three third-grade teachers to select materials for a unit on forming plurals. The following dialogue takes place:

   Teacher 1: I saw some titles of computer software in the Sunburst catalog. Let's plan on using them.

   Teacher 2: I think that we shouldn't plan on using anything until we have looked at it.

   Teacher 3: What do you think?
   (turning to
   SLMS)

   How would you respond?

3. Interview a K–12 teacher. Ask him or her to describe the last in-service he or she attended. What were the three best things about the in-service? The three worst things?

4. Based on the results from the interview in question 3, what actions would you take in designing an in-service to replicate the good factors and avoid the bad?

5. What are some methods of publicizing an in-service?

6. You have just acquired some strong competency in WebCT, a web learning platform and have demonstrated it to the principal. The principal is very impressed and says, "Let's have an in-service after school for all the teachers. Those social studies faculty can really use some of this technology. It would be good to separate them from their chalk!" What are some potential responses to the principal? What are possible pitfalls in each response?

(See appendix A for answers.)

REFERENCES

Anderson, M. A. 2000. Staff Development: Your Most Important Role. *Multimedia Schools* 7 (1): 24–27.

Armstrong, J. B., and T. M. Sherman. 1988. Caveat Emptor: How SME's Can Ensure Good ID. *Performance and Instruction* 27 (4):13–18.

Bents, R. H., and K. R. Howey. 1981. Staff Development-Change in the Individual. In *Staff Development/Organization Development*, ed. B. Dillon-Peterson, 11–36. Alexandria, Va.: Association for Supervision and Curriculum Development.

Bratton, B. 1983. The Instructional Design Specialist-Subject Matter Expert Relationship. *Educational Technology* 23 (6): 13–16.

Davies, D. April, 1967. Notes and working papers prepared for the Senate Committee on Education.

Randell, C., and E. Bitzer. 1998. Staff Development in Support of Effective Student Learning in South African Distance Education. In *Staff Development in Open and Flexible Learning*, eds. C. Latchem and F. Lockwood. New York: Rutledge.

Robinson, R. 1998. A Strategic Perspective of Staff Development for Open and Distance Learning. In *Staff Development in Open and Flexible Learning*, eds. C. Latchem and F. Lockwood. New York: Rutledge.

Rogus, J. R. 1983. Building an Effective Staff Development Program: A Principal's Checklist. *NAASP Bulletin* 67 (March): 8–16.

Sharma. T. 1982. Inservicing the Teachers. *Phi Delta Kappan* 63: 403.

Skeele, L. 1999. Professional Development That They Will Cheer For! *Book Report* 17 (4): 20–23.

Smith-Westberry, J., and R. L. Job. 1986. How to Be a Prophet in Your Own Land: Providing Gifted Program Inservice for the Local District. *Gifted Child Quarterly* 30 (3): 135–37.

ADDITIONAL READINGS

Callison, D. 1999. Keywords in Instruction: Collaboration. *School Library Media Activities Monthly* 15 (5): 38–40.

Hartzell, G. 2002. Principals of Success. *School Library Journal* 48 (4): 41.

Lincoln, M. 2001. Internet Inservice: The Unit Design Approach. *Book Report* 19 (4): 37–39.

Medley, K. P. 2002. Would You Like to Collaborate? *Library Talk* 15 (1): 16–18.

Miller, S. 1999. Professional Development for the Library Media Specialist. *Book Report* 17 (5): 20–22.

Muronago, K., and V. Harada. 1999. Building Teacher Partnerships: The Art of Collaboration. *Teacher Librarian* 27 (1): 9–14.

Wolcott, L. 1996. Planning with Teachers: Practical Approaches to Collaboration. *Emergency Librarian* 23 (3): 8.

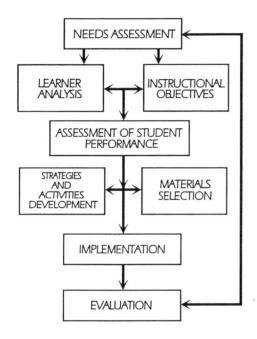

THE STEPS IN THE INSTRUCTIONAL DESIGN PROCESS

One method of solving problems in the instructional arena is to identify and improve the systems involved. A system is the sum of the parts that work together to achieve an outcome (Kaufman 1972). An example of a system is a classroom filled with students, materials, and a teacher. In addition, all that is contained in the administrative suite, the cafeteria, and the library media center are a part of a system. A system can be improved through a problem-solving approach known as the systems approach, which is both a tool for solving problems and a philosophy. Looking at how systems really work can be enlightening—or a wake-up call (Zemke 2001).

EVOLUTION OF THE SYSTEMS APPROACH

Prior to World War II, the predominant method of problem solving was through reducing a problem to its smallest parts and analyzing each part. Thus, scientists searched for smaller and smaller parts of matter. Organizations splintered into departments, each with its own function.

The large-scale projects involved in World War II required a new method of solving problems. In this method, a problem was approached by studying the relationship between a system and its components. Although the individual part remained important, the importance of the relationship of the part to other parts and to the entire group of parts was recognized.

The problem-solving tool that characterizes the systems approach involves the following steps (Kaufman 1972):

1. identification of problem based upon needs

2. identification of requirements of solution

3. determination of alternative strategies

4. selection of specific strategy

5. implementation of strategy

6. determination of performance effectiveness

7. implementation of required revisions

More recent versions of this approach have been developed by other scholars, such as Ethan Sanders (1999) and Carol M. Story (1998). Sanders describes these steps as: Analysis, Design, Develop, Deliver, and Evaluate. Story condenses them into three functions: 1) identifying the outcomes of the instruction, 2) developing the instruction, and 3) evaluating the effectiveness of instruction. (See References and Additional Readings for more sources.) Regardless of the names of the steps, it should be noted that specific problem-solving methodologies were designed in many fields on the basis of the systems approach. In education, the instructional design process is derived from this approach.

THE PURPOSE OF THE INSTRUCTIONAL DESIGN PROCESS

The rationale behind the systems approach in instructional design is that logical, careful, and systematic planning will result in greater probability of success. Teaching involves, and always will, a certain amount of artistry, and sometimes the outcome is influenced significantly by luck. Proponents of the instructional design process do not purport to make the teacher solely a technician or to remove all of the art from teaching. But the instructional design process, properly applied, goes a long way toward substituting for good luck.

There are many models representing the instructional design process, each differing slightly in nomenclature or the inclusion or exclusion of certain steps. (See Gustafson (1981) for a variety of these models and Tennyson (2000) for the "fourth generation" model.) Because all can be traced back to the original problem-solving sequence delineated in the systems approach, their commonalities exceed their differences.

The instructional design model used in this book was selected for its relative simplicity. Other models would be more applicable in large-scale projects or when used by highly trained developers.

Our instructional design model is pictured with each step connected to a previous and a subsequent step. This is done to emphasize the dependence of one step on another. If any step is poorly implemented, the performance of subsequent steps will be impaired. It is also important to note that in practice, a step is not completed and never thought of again. The classroom environment is ever changing, and a good instructional consultant will be sensitive to the implications of the changes in the classroom for revisions of prior steps in the model. Indeed, one of the major properties of the systems approach is its nonlinearity (Hug and King 1984). Diane M. Gayeski (1998) further explains the importance of nonlinear performance models for instructional systems design. Chapters 7 through 14 in this book each present a step in the model, introducing the step and providing school library media specialists with skills and information to begin instructional design consultation at steps and levels where they are not currently active. This is not intended to be an all-inclusive instructional design text, and the reader is encouraged to refer to the titles listed in the References and Additional Readings section to increase competencies in this area.

REFERENCES AND ADDITIONAL READINGS

Boger, Stephanie (e.). 2001. Instructional Design [SITE 2001 Section]. 12th Orlando, FL, March 5–10.

Dewald, Nancy, et al. 2000. Information Literacy at a Distance: Instructional Design Issues. *Journal of Academic Librarianship* 26 (1): 33.

Dick, Walter, et al. 2000. *The Systematic Design of Instruction.* 5th ed. Boston: Addison-Wesley.

Gayeski, D. M. 1998. Out-of-the-Box Instructional Design. *Training and Development* 52 (3): 36–40.

Gustafson, K. L. 1981. *Survey of Instructional Development Models.* Syracuse, N.Y.: ERIC Clearinghouse on Information Resources.

Hug, W. E., and J. E. King. 1984. Educational Interpretations of General Systems Theory. In *Instructional Development: The State of the Art, II,* ed. R. K. Bass and C. R. Dills. Dubuque, Iowa: Kendall-Hunt.

Kaufman, R. A. 1972. *Educational System Planning.* Englewood Cliffs, N.J.: Prentice-Hall.

Lee, William, and Diana Owens. 2000. *Multimedia-Based Instructional Design: Computer-Based Training, Web-Based Training and Distance Learning.* San Francisco: Jossey-Bass.

Macbeth, Douglas. 2002. A Commentary on Instructional Design. *Journal of the Learning Sciences* 11 (2/3): 373.

March, Judith K., and Peters, Karen H. 2002. Curriculum Development and Instructional Design in the Effective Schools Process. *Phi Delta Kappan* 83 (5): 379.

Pitkurich, George. 2000. *Rapid Instructional Design: Learning ID Fast and Right.* San Francisco: Jossey Bass.

Sanders, E. 1999. Where Learning Technologies and ISD Meet. *Technical Training* 10: 36–38.

Schott, F., et al. 2001. What Kind of Instructional Theory Do We Need for Instructional Technology in the 21st Century? *Journal of Structural Learning and Intelligent Systems* 14 (4): 371.

Serim, Ferdi. 2000. New Tools for Learning in a New Millennium. *Multimedia Schools* 7 (1): 6.

Smith, Patricia, and Tillman Ragan. 1999. *Instructional Design.* 2nd ed. San Francisco: John Wiley and Sons Software.

Solomon, Gwen. 1999. Collaborative Learning with Technology. *Technology and Learning* 19 (5): 511.

Story, C. M. 1998. What Instructional Designers Need to Know about Advance Organizers. *International Journal of Instructional Media* 25: 253.

Sulaiman, Jelani, and Francis Dwyer. 2002. The Effect of Varied Instructional Text Design Strategies on the Achievement of Different Educational Objectives. *International Journal of Instructional Media* 29 (2): 215.

Tennyson, R. D. 2000. Fourth Generation Instructional Systems Development: A Problem Solving Approach. *Journal of Structural Learning and Intelligent Systems* 14: 229–53.

Thomas, Karen Jarrett. 1999. Teaching via ITV: Taking Instructional Design to the Next Level. *T.H.E. Journal* 26 (9): 60.

Zhang, Jian X. 2001. Cultural Diversity in Instructional Design. *International Journal of Instructional Media* 28 (3): 299.

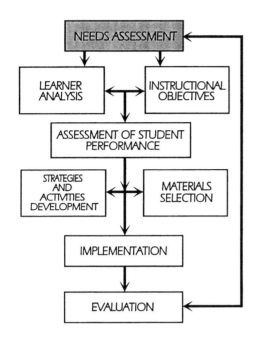

7

Needs Assessment

This chapter provides information to help the reader

- understand the purpose of the needs assessment step

- define a need

- differentiate between content determination and needs assessment

- state five sources of information for needs assessments and provide an example for each

- perform a small-scale needs assessment

THE PURPOSE OF THE NEEDS ASSESSMENT STEP

The needs assessment step is the first step in the instructional design process. The purpose of this step is to establish the content around which the instruction is to be designed. Interestingly, the practice of performing a needs assessment comes out of the humanistic tradition rather than the behavioral, which was the more typical breeding ground for the instructional design process (Wulf and Schave 1984).

A few teachers will regularly go through the process of determining from the ground up the content to be taught. Most teachers derive the content they teach from curriculum guides and textbooks. However, as will be discussed later in this chapter, a teacher must make many decisions in the classroom to match mandated content to their students.

What Is a Need?

Labeling the first step in the instructional design process "needs assessment" often causes initial confusion. Why call it needs assessment? If the purpose is to establish content, why not use the term *content determination*. The answer to this question illustrates the importance that the instructional design process puts on enabling all students to move forward from where they are. Let's look at a description of a needs assessment: "A needs assessment is a process that consists of the determination of gaps in results between *what is* and *what should be*" (Kaufman 1983, 54). This description of a needs assessment contains three important points that make the needs assessment process unique, powerful, and different from the more common practices employed in determining content:

- *The needs assessment process concentrates on results rather than on means.* Kaufman distinguishes between "needs," which are gaps in results, and "quasi-needs," which are gaps in resources to achieve those results. Thus, it might be true that a school "needs" an ESL teacher due to an influx of refugees, but the true need is for the students to be able to read and compute.

- *The content that is determined by using the needs assessment procedure is content that has not been mastered by the student.* Teachers involved in the traditional methods of content determination hope that students do not know the material before it is taught, but this is often only an assumption and is sometimes unwarranted. Surely, to expect that all students issued a particular textbook will begin with the same knowledge is naive at best. And yet that is the assumption under which the lock-step textbook content labors, an assumption the needs assessment procedure attempts to avoid.

- *The needs assessment procedure recognizes that a value judgment is involved.* If a teacher is asked, "Who chooses the content to be taught?", the reply is often, "I use a textbook." Who chooses the textbook? The fact is, someone has made a value judgment in saying, "That content should be taught."

In short, a needs assessment procedure is used as the first step in the instructional design process because it is desirable that the content is seen in terms of student learning outcomes, is systematically and carefully selected, and has not been previously mastered.

Affective Needs

Often, when the topic of needs assessment is considered, only intellectual skills are mentioned. Student attitudes are often worthy of consideration and can be the focus of a needs assessment effort.

As pointed out by Martin (1989), the needs assessment processes for ascertaining cognitive and affective needs are very similar. The difference is in the emphasis and the questions asked. Sometimes, in addition to focusing on the content to be mastered, considering the attitude toward the content is important. There are some subject areas in which an assessment of attitudes is especially important. (See Sanna, Lehtinen and Salonen (2000) regarding emotions and cognition.) Math education probably tops the list in terms of the standard curriculum. Martin (1989, 8) points out that sex and drug education are important examples. Others include promoting a litter-free environment and a respect for peoples of other ethnic groups.

An assessment of students' attitudes about themselves as learners is another important area for an assessment of affective needs. This might include an assessment of general self-esteem as well as specific measures such as learning anxiety.

SOURCES OF INFORMATION FOR NEEDS ASSESSMENTS

The needs assessment procedure recognizes that all instruction begins with the determination of what content ought to be mastered and puts this step at the start of the process. What process should be followed to determine what ought to be learned and the extent to which this important content has been mastered? Initially, let us concentrate on the procedure for determining what children and young adults ought to learn during their schooling. What are sources and procedures that will guide us in determining what ought to be taught?

Posner and Rudnitsky (1986) describe three categories of needs that should form the foundation of educational content. These are 1) the needs of the learner, 2) the needs of society, and 3) the intrinsic importance of the subject matter.

Based on Bradshaw (1972) and Burton and Merrill (1977), the following are five sources and procedures for determining what ought to be taught.

1. *Determining what ought to be taught based on established standards.* In this type of need, an established standard determines the "ought to be" known. A need exists, therefore, when someone falls below the criterion.

   The standard can be a particular percentile on a normed achievement test: "All students in Jones Middle School Advanced Math Class will score at or above the 50th percentile on the yearly achievement test." According to this standard, if a student scores at the 45th percentile, then a need for certain math knowledge exists. Results of promotion and retention tests can also serve as standards to generate instructional content needs.

   Formal curriculum guides can be thought of as standards that determine what ought to be known in a particular subject area. Many school systems have created very detailed hierarchies of content to guide teachers. Using a textbook adopted by a statewide committee is another example of determining the content to be mastered according to an established standard.

   Obviously, the use of established standards to determine what needs to be mastered is a quite common practice and can save the instructional designer a great deal of effort. What needs to be kept in mind when using these sources of content is that someone else has made an initial value judgment concerning this content, and the instructional team should consider validating this judgment in light of the needs of the students in question. Examples of "ought to be" based on established standards:

   > (Taken from a school-system curriculum guide) By the end of the 2nd six-weeks session, students in sixth-grade advanced mathematics should be able to solve word problems involving a three-variable formula.

   > (Based on the norms of a yearly nationwide achievement test) Each child at the third-grade level ought to be competent in arithmetic. *Competent* is defined as scoring higher than the 3.0 level on the achievement test administered in the spring of the third-grade year.

2. *Determining what ought to be taught based on what is being taught somewhere else.* This process is initiated when content being taught somewhere else is discovered and determined to be appropriate and of value for the students in question. The advantage of this source of information is that a model exists from which to gather data.
   Example of "ought to be" based on comparison with another curriculum:

   > The Upper Millbury school system curriculum committee decides that the college-bound seniors should take calculus because Lower Millbury students have done this and entered the university ahead of their peers.

3. *Determining what ought to be taught based on what will be needed in the future.* At some point in a long-range planning process, decision makers are often required to predict what will need to be known five to ten years into the future as new technologies emerge and the requirements to obtain productive employment change. Projected changes in admissions requirements announced by one or more universities would create the need for changes in the content to be mastered at the college preparatory level. The identification of anticipated needs has the benefit of making the efficient allocation of resources possible.

Example of "ought to be" based on content that will need to be mastered at a future date:

> The curriculum oversight committee of the Edgeville school system includes this statement in their long-range plans: "All students who complete ninth grade four years from now will be able to perform a basic information search using two online databases and two contained on CD-ROMs.

4. *Determining what ought to be taught based on asking the population to be taught.* This source of information, and the one that will be discussed as number 5, differs from the first three in that the source of the information is not from a higher authority but from the end user. In this case, students are approached and asked what they would like to learn in the lesson, unit, or course. There are many techniques to use in the asking process. These can include questionnaires, interviews, and focus groups. (See Rossett (1987), Zemke and Kramlinger (1982) for detailed descriptions of some of these techniques.)

A potential drawback of this type of process is that students might not know what they really need (see figure 7.1). They might make choices that involve short-range and immediate goals rather than long-range goals with greater benefits.

Example of "ought to be" based on asking students:

> A student is asked, "What would you like to learn this year in geography?" The student replies, "I would like to learn about the countries in the Middle East and where they are located."

Fig. 7.1. A felt needs assessment!

5. *Determining what ought to be based on requests from students.* In this case, students feel strongly enough about needing to learn something that they approach the decision maker and request that the content be taught. An advantage to this source of information is that the sentiment is presumably strong because the students took it upon themselves to ask. The same danger of superficiality exists as in asking the students what they want to learn. Example of "ought to be" based on students' requests:

> Several students come up to the physical education teacher after class and say, "When we get to the dance unit, can we learn (latest dance)?"

THE NEEDS ASSESSMENT PROCEDURE

There are generally four steps in an educational needs assessment procedure, although specific descriptions may differ slightly (Klein 1971 and Kaufman 1972).

1. *Generate goals.* Based on the types of information described earlier, goals are generated with respect to the subject matter that ought to be mastered. These goals can result from studying course syllabi, processing survey results, responding to requests from students, or reviewing many other input categories.

2. *Rank the goals in order of importance.* Whoever is involved (students, faculty, and parents) is asked to rank the "ought to be" statements (goals) as to perceived importance.

3. *Determine the extent to which each goal ("ought to be" statement) is being reached at present.* The result of this determination is a discrepancy statement describing the difference between what ought to be and what is—that is, the need.

4. *Identify in priority order which needs (from step 3) should be addressed.* This entails a process that Okey (1990) describes as a needs analysis. Questions are asked regarding the probability of obtaining a particular goal given the resources available and the existing learning environment. The relative payoff of obtaining particular goals is also considered. The ranking that results from this step might differ greatly from that in step 2. Although a goal might have received high priority in the initial listing, resources required and distance from realization of the goal might result in a lower priority for actual implementation. For example, a high-priority goal might be that all high school students successfully complete physics or chemistry courses. The fact that new teachers would be required and many students lack the prerequisite math courses might lead to a lower priority for this goal.

THE SCOPE OF NEEDS ASSESSMENT

Needs assessments can vary greatly in terms of purpose and complexity. Initially the needs assessment procedure was in large-scale use—for example, creating curriculums for school systems and even entire states. Although there was a great deal of enthusiasm regarding needs assessments, there was a lack of a systematic procedure. Rossett (1982, 28) describes the situation in her article on needs assessments: "Nowhere is the presence of fervor and the absence of prescriptive detail more obvious than in the topic of needs assessment." In the past, the needs-assessment procedure has been modified and applied to the training process. Systematic procedures for determining instructional content for very small units of instruction, sometimes even a single task, have been developed. (For an example, see Rossett, 1987.)

This variety of scopes for needs assessment is reflected in Zais's (1976) categories of educational goals, which include curriculum aims, goals, and objectives. Curriculum aims are described as "life outcomes, targets removed from the school situation to such an extent that their achievement is determined in that part of life well after completion of school" (306). Goals are long range but are realized during the school experience and are attributable directly to this experience. Objectives are specific, relatively short-term outcomes of classroom instruction.

Large-Scale Needs Assessment

On one end of a continuum of complexity of needs assessments would be very large-scale projects that determine the curriculum for large numbers of students. The outcomes of these projects fall within Zais's first two categories. These projects are very involved and often use sophisticated measurement tools and planning techniques. Many works on needs assessment are devoted to this scope of project (see, for example, Stufflebeam et al. 1985).

The ought-to-be statements for this level of needs assessment are often global and very philosophical. Oliva (1982) lists needs of society, of contemporary life, of a community, as well as of specific students as providing the information for a needs assessment. Posner and Rudnitsky (1986) add the students' perceptions of the subject matter to this list.

What can be the role of the school library media specialist in the conduct of large-scale needs assessments? The school library media specialist can play a useful role, but getting the recognition that leads to requests for assistance is often difficult. Because the role of instructional consultant has not been fully understood by many decision makers, it is not likely that school library media specialists will be significantly involved in large-scale needs assessment in the near future.

Small-Scale Needs Assessment

School-level and classroom-level needs assessment seems to be the most promising area for involvement by the school library media specialist. This is due to the presence of the school library media specialist in the school and the ability to maintain continued contact with potential and actual clients. A further appeal of the small-scale needs assessments is that the management tools required for implementation are much less sophisticated and more likely to be in the repertoire of the school library media specialist.

No matter how carefully the curriculum is designed at the state, system, or even the school level, there must be modifications made at the classroom level. Model curricula designed for everybody and nobody create what Wulf and Schave call the "grand fallacy of education" (1984, 23). Although the instructional content taught in a classroom is not often redesigned from the ground up, it should always be modified to match the needs and learning styles of the particular students in the classroom.

What should a classroom-level needs assessment accomplish? It should provide the instructional planners the opportunity to consider a range of content to be learned, to prioritize their content, to determine which content has yet to be mastered, and to select the content to be taught within the constraints of the classroom and school environment.

The following description of the four basic steps in a small-scale needs assessment is based upon the needs assessment procedure delineated by Burton and Merrill (1977). This process provides guidance to the instructional team in the process of identifying the instructional content to be mastered.

> I. Phase 1. An initial list of the content to be mastered is generated. This is often stated as a list of possible goals.
>
>   A. Sources of information

1. Competency-test descriptions

2. Descriptions of norms for the particular subject (local, regional, state, or national)

3. Results of surveys of the students, parents, teachers, etc.

4. Extant course materials (textbooks, curriculum guides, other instructional materials)

5. Results of needs assessments with similar courses and learners

6. Any other materials that might be sources of goals

B. Persons involved (the teacher and at least one of the following)

1. School library media specialist

2. A student who will be in the course

3. A parent

4. A potential employer of students

5. An instructor of a course that is based on the content being selected

6. Any other person who might provide potential goals

C. Actions

1. Persons involved (from B) meet and determine initial logistics (scope of content, meeting times, etc.).

2. A plan to collect information is formulated. This involves some basic philosophical decisions regarding how the content that ought to be mastered is determined. (Should the curriculum be based on authority, on what students want, or both? What is possible in the particular school environment?) If information regarding perceptions is to be collected, how should this be done? (See Rossett (1987) and Zemke and Kramlinger (1982) for detailed procedures for collecting these data.)

3. Information sources (from A) are reviewed based on the decisions made in 2.

4. A wide variety of goals is brainstormed.

5. Similar goals are combined, and goals not stated in terms of the student are eliminated. Goals stated in too complex a manner are simplified.

6. Agreement on the potential goals list is obtained. (For participants to agree to a goal does not mean that they believe that the goal should be reached but rather that the goal is understood. Ranking of the goals is done later.)

D. Output. List the goals that represent a constrained universe of the content that ought to be mastered by the students in question.

Note that at the onset of the needs assessment procedure, it is important to attempt to discriminate which instructional problems are due to deficiencies in knowledge or skills of the students and which are due to environmental or motivational problems. This front-end analysis will help prevent the instructional designer from selecting goals that are not obtainable with instructional methodologies (Okey 1990).

II. Phase 2. Rank goals in order of importance.

    A. Sources of information

        1. List of goals from phase 1

        2. Guides to ranking procedures. Some commonly used ranking procedures include:

            a. Scale rating. The respondent is given a form on which the goals are listed. Beside each goal is a scale from 0 (not important) to 5 (very important). The responses are compiled and averages obtained for each goal. The goals are then ranked by these averages.

            b. Card sorts. In this procedure, each goal is written on a card. The respondents sort the cards into piles that indicate the degree of importance (pile 1, least important; pile 5, most important). The goals are then assigned a numerical value, means are derived, and the goals ranked.

    B. Persons involved

        1. If sophisticated techniques are used, a measurement specialist from the central office or local university might be required. For the simpler techniques, the school library media specialist-teacher(s) team should be able to administer the procedure.

        2. Appropriate persons from B in section I above.

    C. Actions

        1. A procedure for ranking goals is selected. This can involve one of the procedures described in II.A.2 or one of the more complex techniques. In many cases, however, even the simpler techniques may not be possible because of time constraints. Often only one teacher will be involved, thus simplifying the ranking procedure.

        2. Each respondent ranks the goals.

        3. The responses are analyzed and mean rankings are obtained.

    D. Output. List the ranked goals.

III. Phase 3. Determine the extent to which the goals have been reached.

    A. Sources of information

        1. List of ranked goals from II.D

        2. Curriculum map of the school

    B. Persons involved

    1. Teacher(s) on the instructional design team

    2. School library media specialist (if required for assistance)

C. Actions. The purpose of this step is to determine how many students have already reached the goals and the distance the remaining students are from reaching those goals. There are a number of ways in which this determination can be made, including:

    1. Systematic behavioral analysis. Strictly applying a systematic needs-assessment procedure would require a goal analysis to clarify vague goals and an observation of the behavior of all students, or at least a representative sample. This is probably the way that the teacher(s) can be most confident of what the students know and what they need to be taught. In many classrooms such measurement is difficult, if not impossible.

    2. Analysis of the "real," "null," and "hidden" curriculum. Fenwick English (1979) cautions against basing decisions regarding what students are presumed to know on formal curriculum guides. He delineates another type of curriculum, the "real" curriculum, as more important in the determination of the content to be mastered. The real curriculum is what teachers have actually attempted to teach.

        English (1978) describes the process for creating a curriculum map based on a content analysis of the curriculum. Zenger and Zenger (1982) detail a quick assessment procedure that uses a matrix of content, critical skills, and topics taught throughout the school.

        Connelly and Clandinin (1988) add two categories to English's curriculum. They describe a "null" curriculum as content that is deliberately *not* taught. A "hidden" curriculum, according to Connelly and Clandinin, is what is taught even though it was not planned to be taught. Most of their work is devoted to methods by which the teacher can ascertain the hidden curriculum. They advocate using diaries, picturing, being a participant observer, and interviewing to determine what actually happens within a school.

    3. Intuitive approach. The teacher may intuit the discrepancies between the goals and actual student achievement. If the teacher knows the students well enough or if the content is obviously new to the students, then the intuitive approach may suffice. Often, it is the only approach that the teacher will tolerate due to limited time.

        A school library media specialist working as an instructional consultant at the needs assessment step should be careful in promoting the intuitive approach unless it is clear that other techniques are not possible. Teachers' intuitions about their students' needs can be wrong. There are advantages, however, in having the teacher at least think about the discrepancies between stated goals and what the students can actually do prior to instruction.

The instructional design team needs to decide which of these methods should be used to determine the content that has previously been mastered. The method chosen is often based on the resources available to the team.

D. Output. List the needs (the content that the instructional team has determined has not been, and needs to be, mastered).

IV. Phase 4. Prioritize the needs. The purpose of this phase is to decide the order in which the content should be addressed (and what content cannot be taught due to various constraints). This step is also called a needs analysis (Okey 1990) and involves selecting and sorting among identified needs based on budgetary, personnel, environmental, and instructional factors.

A. Information sources

1. List of needs statements from III.D.

2. Information on resource availability (budget, scheduling, etc.).

B. Persons involved: appropriate persons from I.B

C. Actions

1. Rate each need statement according to agreed-upon criteria. Obviously, the first criterion would be the original ranking from phase 2. Other criteria might be cost of implementation, time required, materials required, and number of students who possess the need (have not reached the goal). A possible procedure is to take the most highly ranked goal from phase 2 and ask "Why should and should not this goal be of highest priority?" Possible "should nots" might include high costs, special materials required, or very few students possessing the need for instruction.

2. Obtain consensus on rankings. In the absence of mathematical procedures that relate cost, time, and other requirements, an intuitive ranking might have to suffice.

D. Output. List the need statements in priority order. These need statements are the instructional content for a given topic that has not been taught but that the teacher(s) has decided should be taught.

NEEDS ASSESSMENT FOR INFORMATION SKILLS

As mentioned in chapter 1, playing a role in the imparting of information skills is a very important function of the school library media program. Given this assumption, there exists the need to determine the specific information skills to be mastered. Unfortunately, this determination is often out of the school library media specialist's control. The information skills that are taught may be from a curriculum generated outside of the school with no connection to what is taught in classrooms.

Eisenberg and Berkowitz (1988, 37) contend wisely that "it is not necessary or recommended that each school library media specialist or even district create his or her own scope and sequence of skills. Many reasonable outlines already exist." The authors also contend, "In practical terms, the realization of the goals and objectives of a school is the curriculum as carried out in classrooms. The points of intersection between classroom content and the library curriculum are the optimal teaching opportunities for library and information skills instruction" (5).

How should the information skills be matched to the curriculum as carried out in the classroom? Acting as an instructional consultant provides the best opportunity to make valid decisions regarding which information skills are required. In addition, as instructional consultants assisting the teacher to be more effective, school library media specialists have the leverage to enhance the teaching of information skills in the classroom. The school library media specialist can tailor information skills through instructional consultation to the individual classroom so that the information skills are truly tailored to the student and the instruction.

Types of Information Skills

As much as possible, for *every* unit we need to provide the opportunity to locate, access, comprehend, analyze, synthesize, and create information and knowledge. Students at every level need to be taught the learning skills critical for carrying out these tasks. The school library media program has as a function providing assistance in the teaching of a very important category of learning skills, that of information-processing strategies.

The following seven categories of information skills are based on Eisenberg and Berkowitz's "big six skills." They are divided into two steps. First, there is the process of locating information. This process can be either very simple or very complex and can involve a variety of levels of learning. Second, once the information is found, it needs to be processed. Again, this processing can range from very shallow (recognition of memorized information) to very complex (forming of new information and knowledge).

These steps involve locating the information:

1. *Define the information task.* Sample behaviors: List questions used to describe the information problem, explain the questions used for describing the information problem in terms of the concepts and generalizations involved, and explain the information problem to someone else.

2. *Select the information-seeking strategy.* Sample behaviors: Select the key concepts, construct a combination of concepts using logical operators, describe and explain the range of possible strategies, and select strategy(s).

3. *Locate and access information.* Sample behaviors: List and describe a variety of available resources, select appropriate resources, use resources to identify information sources, and acquire information. (This includes technological skills needed to use whichever medium is involved, e.g., operate a VCR or CD-ROM.)

These steps involve processing and using the information:

4. *Use information.* Sample behaviors: Separate critical information from "noise," rank information as to usefulness, analyze information, create generalizations about information, and transfer information from one medium to another.

5. *Synthesize information.* Integrate information from various sources into a coherent whole. Sample behaviors: Paraphrase information as it is obtained, summarize large blocks of information, and use information from various sources and media to create a summary of an event (given photographs of the Civil War, description of a battle from a text, and artifacts, write an account of the event).

6. *Create new information/knowledge.* Sample behaviors: Form generalizations and solve problems (given environmental and resource data, create a city plan).

7. *Evaluate the process.* Sample behavior: Constantly generate questions to determine the quality of the information-seeking process to that point and determine the efficiency and effectiveness of each action.

Characteristics of the Unit That Influence Information Skills Integration

What are the characteristics of an instructional unit that dictate the types of information skills that need to be integrated into that unit? As Figure 7.2 illustrates, four factors should influence this decision.

In the development of instruction, learner characteristics, number of information sources, the amount of guidance provided, and the level of learning of the instruction should drive the selection of the information skills. Obviously, if the teacher has selected a low-level objective that requires only the recall or recognition of memorized information and insists on maintaining the textbook as the universe of information, there are few information skills that need to be taught (probably limited to textbook reading skills).

Conversely, a teacher who wants students to solve a problem (for example, How do we know which directions glaciers traveled?) and provides no information or learning guidance would require students to be taught or already possess high-level information skills. If these students possess certain characteristics that make it difficult for them to extract information, the teaching of information-gathering skills takes on even more importance.

Students vary in their learning characteristics and these influence the information skills that should be taught. Chapter 8 provides guidance in identifying these characteristics. Teachers also vary in the amount of information and learning guidance they provide to the student. On one end of the continuum is the case where one source of information is provided to the student with complete guidance as to its use. A self-contained CD-ROM–based lesson that serves as the total source of learning is an example of this. As we progress away from one source with total guidance, multiple sources and then no sources are provided. Also, less guidance as to learning strategy is provided. At the end of the continuum is the ultimate in inquiry learning where no materials or strategies are provided. Students are totally on their own to locate and use a variety of sources.

Learning follows a natural progression from the learning of simple associations to the solution of complex problems. (See chapter 9 for a detailed explanation of the levels of learning.) All learning involves information processing to some degree, and Tessmer, Jonassen, and Caverly (1989) describe four levels of strategies that can be required during a learning task. Ranging from simple to complex, these are recall, integration, organization, and elaboration.

In the ideal world, the majority of the instructional experiences provided in our schools would consist of resource-based inquiry learning. (See, for example, *Breaking Away from the Textbook* by Cordero and Kintisch listed in the recommended readings in the Initial Level section of this chapter.) In this situation, we could count on implementing a sequence of increasingly higher-level information skills. In reality, while assisting in the development of units of instruction, we must use our experience and intuition to select the appropriate information skills.

In summary, the school library media specialist can take the following steps to determine the content of the information skills to recommend for inclusion into a particular unit,

1. Use existing lists of information skills to form a resource base.

2. Identify these information skills as to type (for example, locating and accessing information or creating new information/knowledge).

3. While working with the teacher(s) in designing the unit, assess:

   a. learning characteristics of students

   b. number of information sources

Fig. 7.2. Characteristics of unit that influence information skills integration

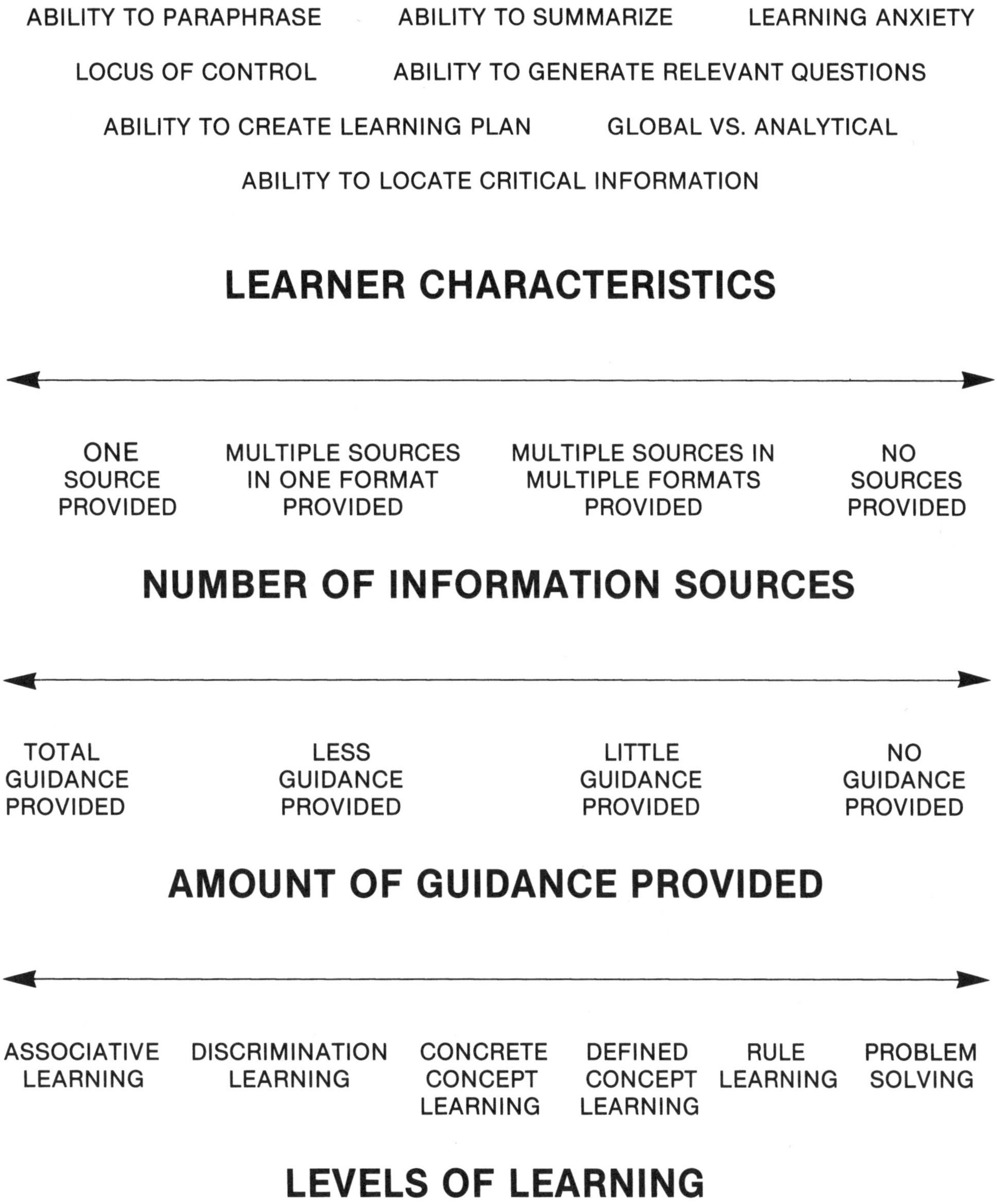

ABILITY TO PARAPHRASE   ABILITY TO SUMMARIZE   LEARNING ANXIETY

LOCUS OF CONTROL   ABILITY TO GENERATE RELEVANT QUESTIONS

ABILITY TO CREATE LEARNING PLAN   GLOBAL VS. ANALYTICAL

ABILITY TO LOCATE CRITICAL INFORMATION

LEARNER CHARACTERISTICS

<--->

| ONE SOURCE PROVIDED | MULTIPLE SOURCES IN ONE FORMAT PROVIDED | MULTIPLE SOURCES IN MULTIPLE FORMATS PROVIDED | NO SOURCES PROVIDED |

NUMBER OF INFORMATION SOURCES

<--->

| TOTAL GUIDANCE PROVIDED | LESS GUIDANCE PROVIDED | LITTLE GUIDANCE PROVIDED | NO GUIDANCE PROVIDED |

AMOUNT OF GUIDANCE PROVIDED

<--->

| ASSOCIATIVE LEARNING | DISCRIMINATION LEARNING | CONCRETE CONCEPT LEARNING | DEFINED CONCEPT LEARNING | RULE LEARNING | PROBLEM SOLVING |

LEVELS OF LEARNING

    c.   amount of guidance provided

    d.   levels of learning

4. Select the appropriate information skills to enhance the instruction for this unit for these students.

5. Use steps 1–4 above as a substitute for phase 1 of a small-scale needs assessment. Take the output from step 4 through phases 2, 3, and 4 to arrive at information skills that are needs.

LEVELS OF INVOLVEMENT BY THE SCHOOL LIBRARY MEDIA SPECIALIST AT THE NEEDS ASSESSMENT STEP

The Initial Level

At the initial level of instructional design consultation, the school library media specialist provides resources to enable the teacher to perform the step more effectively. For the needs assessment step, such resources might include a computer program that would aid in scoring and interpreting results of goal and need rankings, and a meeting room for the planning team.

Of course the library media center itself is a rich source for phase 1 of the needs assessment procedure. In addition to maintaining the general collection, the school library media specialist might focus on developing a collection of materials specifically to provide a foundation for the needs assessment procedure.

Materials might include a collection of state or locally mandated competencies, sample units to use as idea starters, various textbooks, achievement-test norms, curriculum guides, sample rating instruments, standardized goal statements, sample scope and sequences of information skills, and results of previous surveys for a needs assessment. The library media center might also collect the results of previous attempts to obtain feedback from students, teachers, and others as to content that should be covered. Diaries, reports of observations, results of focus-group interviews, and other such information can be kept in a database to provide guidance for future needs assessment efforts.

Professional reading might include any works that would help the teacher perform this step more effectively. The following are recommended titles:

Briggs, L. J., ed. 1977. *Instructional Design: Principles and Applications.* Englewood Cliffs, N.J.: Educational Technology Publications.

Burris, K. G. 2002. Evaluation of Pedagogical Quality in Early Childhood Education: A Cross-National Perspective. *Childhood Education* 78 (12): 189–91.

Cassel, R. N. 2000. The Senior High School Student Rating Scale (SHRS). *Education* 121: 10.

Cordero, W., and S. Kintisch. 1990. *Breaking Away from the Textbook.* Lancaster, Pa.: Technomic.

Eisenberg, M. B., and R. E. Berkowitz. 1988. *Curriculum Initiative: An Agenda and Strategy for Library Media Programs.* Norwood, N.J.: Ablex.

Faiks, A., and Hyland, N. 2000. Gaining User Insight: A Case Study Illustrating the Card Sort Technique. *College and Research Libraries* 61: 349–57.

Garcia, J. G. Coll. 2001. An Instrument to Help Teachers Assess Learners' Attitudes towards Multimedia Instruction. *Education* 122: 94–101.

Gratz, D. B. 2000. High Standards for Whom? *Phi Delta Kappan* 81: 681–89.

Gumpel, M. W., and Shalev, R. 1998. An Item Response Theory Analysis of the Conners Teacher's Rating Scale. *Journal of Learning Disabilities* 60: 525.

———. 1991. *Information Problem Solving: The Big Six Skills Approach to Library and Information Skills Instruction.* Norwood, N.J.: Ablex.

Hunter, B., and E. Lodish. 1989. *Online Searching in the Curriculum.* Santa Barbara, Calif.: ABC-CLIO.

Jweid, R., and M. Rizzo. 1988. *The Library-Classroom Partnership: Teaching Library Media Skills in Middle and Junior High Schools.* Metuchen, N.J.: Scarecrow Press.

———. 1998. *The Library-Classroom Partnership 2: Teaching Library Media Skills in Middle and Junior High Schools.* Metuchen, N.J.: Scarecrow Press.

Kaufman, R. A. 1972. *Educational System Planning.* Englewood Cliffs, N.J.: Prentice-Hall.

Learning Team. (nd). *The Math Finder.* Reston, Va.: National Council of Teachers of Mathematics.

March, J. K., and K. H. Peters. 2002. Effective Schools: Curriculum Development and Instructional Design in the Effective Schools Process. *Phi Delta Kappan* 83: 379–83.

Reiger, R. C. 2000. Graduating Seniors Make Democracy Become Alive by Evaluating the Pleasantville High School Program. *Education* 121: 16.

Rivera, D. B. 1993. Understanding Problems Faced by Classroom Teachers: An Application of Q-Methodology. Paper presented at the Annual Meeting of the Mid-South Educational Research Association, New Orleans, La.

Walker, H. T., and P. K. Montgomery. 1983. *Teaching Library Media Skills.* 2nd ed. Englewood, Colo.: Libraries Unlimited.

Wilkins, L. P., and M. B. White. 2002. Interrater Reliability and Concurrent Validity of the Global Assessment of Relational Functioning (GARF) Scale Using a Card Sort Method: A Pilot Study. *Family Therapy* 28: 157–70.

The Moderate Level

Instructional consultation on the needs assessment step at the moderate level is a cross between merely providing resources and serving as a consultant through the entire process. Generally, moderate-level involvement results from the teacher requesting assistance. For the needs assessment step, this assistance might include obtaining, upon request, samples of goals from other school districts in the form of planned units, textbooks, and other materials. The school library media specialist might be asked for assistance in brainstorming goals, determining rating procedures, or administering sample instruments. The school library media specialist might also serve as a facilitator at a meeting where needs are being prioritized and perhaps provide information on material costs and availability at such a meeting.

The In-Depth Level

IN-SERVICE PROGRAMS

One way the school library media specialist can be involved at the in-depth level is through designing and implementing an in-service, which could present the concept of needs assessment generally, present the small-scale procedure, or be totally devoted to one step in the procedure, such as sources of goals.

INSTRUCTIONAL DESIGN TEAM PARTICIPATION

At this, the highest level of involvement, the school library media specialist can serve as a member of an instructional design team working through the entire process. The following is an example of a small-scale needs assessment procedure involving a teacher of a self-contained third-grade class. The school library media specialist and the teacher agreed to act as a team in the development of a science unit involving animal study. The school library media specialist explained the small-scale needs assessment procedure to the teacher, and they agreed to follow this procedure as closely as possible.

I. Phase 1. Generate a list of possible goals.

    A. Sources of information

        1. *The Alabama Course of Study,* a statewide curriculum guide

        2. *Jefferson County Curriculum Guide,* the county schools' curriculum guide

        3. The textbook that was assigned to this teacher

    B. Persons involved

        1. Teacher

        2. School library media specialist

        3. Students

    C. Actions. The teacher examined the courses of study and the material in the textbook on the topic, and both the school library media specialist and teacher talked to the students asking what they would like to learn about animals. Through these sources and brainstorming on the part of the two professionals, the following goals were selected:

        1. All students should be able to recognize physical differences between animals.

        2. All students should be able to recognize differences between hair, feathers, scales, and skin.

        3. All students should know the difference between lungs and gills.

        4. All students should know the difference between warm-blooded and cold-blooded animals.

5. All students should know the difference between live birth and egg hatching.

II. Phase 2. Rank goals in order of importance.

The teacher and the school library media specialist ranked the goals from phase 1. They did this together informally rather than using an instrument. This informality was chosen because there were only two participants and five goals. The goals were ranked as 1, 2, 3, 5, and 4, respectively.

III. Phase 3. Determine extent to which goals have been reached.

The members of the team decided that, for this grade level, the best method of determining the extent to which the goals had been met was to question informally a sample of students. The teacher did the questioning. Based upon the results of the questions, goals 1 and 2 were judged to have been met; therefore, no need for instruction existed. The remaining three goals were interpreted as in need of instruction.

IV. Phase 4. Prioritize the needs.

The teacher and school library media specialist estimated resources needed for each goal, including time for instruction and selecting instructional materials. Of those needs that remained from the original list, that which had been of highest priority also required the least in resources, so this priority continued. The following list of needs, in priority order, was the result of the needs assessment procedure.

1. All students should know the difference between lungs and gills.

2. All students should recognize the difference between live birth and egg hatching.

3. All students should recognize the difference between warm-blooded and cold-blooded animals.

The team decided to carry all three final goals into the next step of the instructional design process. The school library media specialist also wanted to insert information skills into this unit in order to enhance the students' abilities and experience. The school library media specialist considered the dimensions that would influence the information skills to be taught:

- *Learning characteristics of the students.* Some of these students had a great deal of learning anxiety and would most likely be uneasy about any venture outside of the textbook.

- *Number of information sources and amount of guidance.* Traditionally, this teacher used one source and provided a great deal of learning guidance. The teacher had contacted the school library media specialist with the goal of enriching the lesson, so it was assumed that several sources would be used and that the students would have to do at least some learning on their own.

- *Level of learning of the content.* Though the team had yet to write the instructional objectives for this lesson, the school library media specialist assumed that the teacher would emphasize rather low-level learning—for example, recall by matching labels to pictures.

Then a procedure was formulated and followed:

Phase 1. The school library media specialist discussed the categories of information skills with the teacher. The teacher decided that no more than three sources (video, encyclopedia on CD-ROM, and an illustrated book on reptiles and mammals) outside of the textbook should be used. Guidance would be provided, including walking the students through determining the information tasks (topics to be searched and possible synonyms) and discussing the content of the three sources that could be used. It was decided that the information skills should concentrate on use of the sources.

The team identified the following possible information skills:

1. Operate VCR.

2. Operate a computer/CD-ROM reader.

3. Relate captions to illustrations.

4. Use table of contents and index of textbook.

5. Enter search terms when requested.

Phase 2. Based on a number of factors such as availability of students to assist in equipment operation, the team ranked the skills in order of importance: 3, 4, 5, 2, and 1.

Phase 3. The team knew that the students had considerable experience with the textbook and that use of the table of contents and index had been covered earlier in the year in the library. Many of the students had operated the VCR in second grade and earlier in the year. The team therefore judged the students as having skills 4 and 1 as listed in phase 2.

Phase 4. Because many of the students had not been exposed to a variety of pictorial learning materials in books, the use of captions in guiding the extraction of the important information from illustrations was given a high priority. Even though there was assistance available in the operation of the equipment, the school library media specialist believed that each student should develop the ability to turn on the computer, bring up the CD-ROM, and enter data when requested. The priority of the topics after phase 4 of the needs assessment procedure was 3, 2, and 5.

The needs assessment procedure, like all of the steps in instructional design, can be employed with varying degrees of sophistication. The more sophisticated applications will yield more reliable outcomes but require more resources to implement.

School library media specialists who attempt to move up in the levels of involvement at the needs assessment step should be aware of the tension between sophistication of application and requirement of resources. Compromise is often the only way any progress can be made. In the small-scale needs assessment example just provided, more sources of goals could have been employed, measurement techniques could have relied less on intuition, and the goals could have been more tightly worded. In this case, the school library media specialist realized that the teacher was able to put forth only a limited amount of effort and was venturing out of the textbook for the first time. Rather than have no needs assessment at all, the school library media specialist decided to rely on teacher judgment.

THOUGHT PROVOKERS

1. Write examples of "ought to be" (goals) statements for each type of source listed in the Sources of Information for Needs Assessment section of this chapter.

2. The sources of "ought to be" statements given in this chapter can be placed into two categories. They can be based on sources and situations external to the group for whom the needs are being determined, or they can be determined by studying what the students are doing or what they have requested.

    a.   What would be a benefit and a drawback of using each category?

    b.   Under which category does the small-scale needs assessment procedure described in this chapter fall?

3. Select a content area with which you are familiar. Select a group of students and go through the four phases in the needs assessment procedure. (Much of what you do might be fictitious in this exercise. The point is to get practice working through the procedure.)

4. Using the results from 3, perform a needs assessment to determine the information skills to be taught with this unit. (Again, the important thing at this point is to work through the procedure.)

(See appendix A for answers.)

REFERENCES

Bradshaw, J. 1972. The Concept of Social Need. *New Society*, March 30, 643.

Burton, J. K., and P. F. Merrill. 1977. Needs Assessment: Goals, Needs, and Priorities. In *Instructional Design: Principles and Applications*, ed. L. J. Briggs, 21–48. Englewood Cliffs, N.J.: Educational Technology Publications.

Connelly, F. M., and D. J. Clandinin. 1988. *Teachers as Curriculum Planners.* New York: Teachers College Press.

Davidson, G. V., and P. L. Smith. 1990. Instructional Design Considerations for Learning Strategies Instruction. *International Journal of Instructional Media* 17 (4): 227–45.

Eisenberg, M. B., and R. E. Berkowitz. 1988. *Curriculum Initiative: An Agenda and Strategy for Library Media Programs.* Norwood, N.J.: Ablex.

Eisenberg, M. B., and R. E. Berkowitz. 1999. *Essential Skills for the Information Age: The Big6 in Action.* Video recording. Worthington, Ohio: B6 Media.

English, F. W. 1978. *Quality Control in Curriculum Development.* Arlington, Va.: American Association of School Administrators.

———. 1979. Re-Tooling Curriculum within On-Going School Systems. *Educational Technology* 19 (May): 7–13.

English, F. W., and R. A. Kaufman. 1975. *Needs Assessment: A Focus for Curriculum Development.* Washington, D.C.: Association for Supervision and Curriculum Development.

Kaufman, R. A. 1972. *Educational System Planning.* Englewood Cliffs, N.J.: Prentice-Hall.

———. 1983. Needs Assessment. In *Fundamental Curriculum Decisions*, ed. F. W. English, 53–67. Alexandria, Va.: Association for Supervision and Curriculum Development.

Kaufman, R. A., and S. Thomas. 1980. *Evaluation without Fear.* New York: New Viewpoints.

Klein, S. P. 1971. Choosing Needs for Needs Assessment. *Procedures for Needs Assessment Education.* CSE Report No. 69. Los Angeles: Center for the Study of Evaluation.

Martin, B. L. 1989. A Checklist for Designing Instruction in the Affective Domain. *Educational Technology* 29 (August): 7–15.

Okey, J. R. 1990. Tools of Analysis in Instructional Development. *Educational Technology* 30 (June): 28–32.

Oliva, P. F. 1982. *Developing the Curriculum.* Boston: Little, Brown.

Posner, G. J., and A. N. Rudnitsky. 1986. *Course Design: A Guide to Curriculum Development for Teachers.* New York: Longman.

Rossett, A. 1982. A Typology for Generating Needs Assessments. *Journal of Instructional Development* 6 (Fall): 28–33.

———. 1987. *Training Needs Assessment.* Englewood Cliffs, N.J.: Educational Technology Publications.

Sanna J., Lethinen, E., and Salonen, P. 2000. Socio-emotional Orientation as a Mediating Variable in the Teaching-Learning Interaction: Implications for Instructional Design. *Scandinavian Journal of Educational Research.* 44(3):293–306.

Stufflebeam, D. L., C. H. McCormick, R. O. Brinkerhoff, and C. O. Nelson. 1985. *Conducting Educational Needs Assessments.* Boston: Kluwer-Nijhoff.

Tessmer, M. A., D. P. Jonassen, and D. C. Caverly. 1989. Learning Strategies: A New Instructional Technology. In *World Yearbook of Education for 1988: Education for the New Technologies,* ed. D. Harris, 29–47. London: Evans Bros.

Witkin, B. R. 1977. Needs Assessment Kits, Models, and Tools. *Educational Technology* 22 (November): 5–18.

Wulf, K. M., and B. Schave. 1984. *Curriculum Design.* Glenview, Ill.: Scott, Foresman.

Zais, R. S. 1976. *Curriculum: Principles and Foundations.* New York: Harper & Row.

Zemke, R., and T. Kramlinger. 1982. *Curriculum: Principles and Foundations.* New York: Harper & Row.

Zenger, W. F., and S. K. Zenger. 1982. *Curriculum Planning: A Ten-Step Process.* Palo Alto, Calif.: R & E Associates.

ADDITIONAL READINGS

American Association for the Advancement of Science. 1989. *Science for All Americans.* Washington, D.C.: American Association for the Advancement of Science.

Gable, R. K., R. L. Pecheone, and T. B. Gillung. 1981. A Needs Assessment Model for Establishing Personnel Training Priorities. *Teacher Education and Special Education* 4 (4): 4–14.

Kemp, J. E. 1971. *Instructional Design.* Belmont, Calif.: Fearon.

(See also professional collection materials in The Initial Level section of this chapter.)

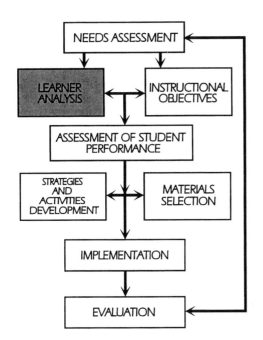

8

Learner Analysis

This chapter provides information to help the reader

- understand the purpose of the learner analysis step

- name and describe three categories of learner characteristics

- understand unidimensional learner analysis procedures

- compare and contrast multidimensional learner analysis procedures

- conduct learner analyses

The learner analysis step is extremely important in the instructional design process. In our model (see figure above), this step is placed at the same level as the instructional objectives step. This is to emphasize that together, these two steps provide the foundation for all that transpires in the instructional process. Once a teacher has determined what successful students are expected to be able to do, and the unique ways in which each student learns, the probability that appropriate materials and activities will be used is greatly enhanced.

WHAT IS THE PURPOSE OF THE LEARNER ANALYSIS STEP?

Learner analysis is the identification of characteristics of the learner that will influence the selection of instructional materials and activities. Again, it is important to note that, together with instructional objectives, the outcomes of learner analysis form the basis for the design of teaching and learning.

Keefe (1982, 44) described these learner characteristics as "cognitive, affective, and physiological traits that serve as relatively stable indicators of how learners perceive, interact with, and respond to the learning environment." Learner characteristics are the result of genetics, development of personality, motivation, and adaption to the environment (Keefe 1988). Furthermore, these characteristics tend to be represented on a continuum in the population of learners as a whole. In other words, for each learner characteristic, some learners will possess it to a high degree, some to a moderate degree, and some not at all. Many, but not all, of these characteristics are what Keefe calls "value-neutral," that is, possession of a particular trait is deemed neither good nor bad. (For additional information regarding learner characteristics, see Additional Readings at the end of this chapter.)

THE EVOLUTION OF LEARNER ANALYSIS

Throughout the history of education there has been a concern for the learner as an individual. Such a concern was a central factor in the progressive education movement (Henson and Borthwick 1984). This concern was demonstrated with the passage of Public Law 94–142, which required school systems to recognize the need for specific types of instruction for students with certain characteristics.

References to learner characteristics, beyond intelligence and physical and emotional disabilities, were present in the literature as early as 1892 (Keefe 1982). Researchers were, however, preoccupied with finding the "ultimate" learner characteristic. After World War II, there was a surge of interest in cognitive learner characteristics. Not until the 1970s were affective characteristics and the less obvious physiological characteristics studied in a methodological manner (Dunn 1984). Interest in learning styles continued throughout the 1980s and into the twenty-first century. An entire issue of *Theory into Practice* was devoted to learning styles, and in the lead article Henson and Borthwick (1984) predicted that learning-style research would eventually change teacher-education programs and the way students are taught.

The path to the point where the average teacher ascertains the student's learning styles and modifies instruction accordingly has not been an easy one, nor has the goal been reached. Two factors impede progress:

1. The concept of learning styles is an appealing one to many, and as a result, the concept has been popularized to such an extent that some approaches were implemented without a strong theoretical or empirical basis. (See Doyle and Rutherford (1984) for a detailed discussion.) In 1982 Gregoric warned that learner analysis was being viewed too often as a panacea and resulted in the raising of impossible expectations with accompanying disappointment.

   The school library media specialist, as instructional consultant, needs to stress that existing learner analysis tools are not foolproof. However, their use can provide a method of more clearly seeing one's students and a foundation of a dialogue between teacher and student regarding what transpires in the instructional setting.

2. Many teachers lack the resources and energy to diversify the instructional process. The goal at the foundation of the learner analysis process is to vary instruction to match the individual learner. If a teacher is confronted with a process in which it is expected that students will have materials and activities tailored to them, most will balk at considering the concept.

   The school library media specialist needs to be very careful to stress that knowing the learning characteristics of each student can be helpful even if the class is taught as a whole group. That group will have certain characteristics in common, and the instruction can be tailored to those. In addition, there are times when instruction can be easily and simply adjusted to match the characteristics of the minority.

Despite the barriers to the implementation of a learning-styles philosophy, progress has been made. The National Association of Secondary School Principals has devoted considerable attention and resources to the concept of learning styles and has published one of the best diagnostic tools. Using learning styles to modify instruction has been demonstrated successfully in the classroom. Several research studies are listed further on in this chapter. Particularly impressive results were obtained by Carol Marshall, working with slower learners (Marshall, 1990).

GENERAL TYPES OF LEARNER CHARACTERISTICS

Physiological Characteristics

Some obvious physiological characteristics a student may possess will influence the materials, strategies, activities, and teaching sequence used to reach a given set of objectives. A student who is blind or deaf, for example, requires certain kinds of materials and activities. This is also the case for a student who has lost the use of arms or legs.

Less obvious are the characteristics of the large proportion of students deemed average. Some learners prefer to work in well-lighted environments and thrive when they do so; the performance of others may suffer under the same conditions (Dunn et al. 1987). Anyone who has ever had their daily schedule of classes rearranged and seen their normally angelic second-period students turn into monsters during sixth period will appreciate that time-of-day preference is a learner characteristic that has research to back it up (Dunn et al. 1985).

Many researchers believe that the teaching-learning process is greatly facilitated when performed in a learner-preferred environment. Is giving in to a student's preference for physical activity or sound stimulus "proper discipline?" Are we spoiling students if we do so?

Garger (1990) provides a compelling basis for tailoring the environment to a student's preference. There exists a threshold of activity that must be present in the cortex in order for a person to be able to select one stimulus from others. If this minimum activity is not present, a student will have real difficulty concentrating on the task because all stimuli are reacted to similarly and the student is in a constant state of response. In the most severe cases, the student may be diagnosed as hyperactive and prescribed a stimulant to raise the cortical tone to a threshold level where concentration is possible. Garger maintains that there are many students whose attention deficit is not severe enough to be treated with medication but for whom some stimulating activity helps to maintain the ability to pay attention. "It seems plausible in less severe cases than those just described, students' needs for mobility, tactile stimulation, intake, kinesthetic learning, and sound in the environment are in effect the body's adaptive strategies for increasing the arousal level of the neural system to make focusing on the task at hand possible. In other words, the stimulation to the cortical nervous system by gum chewing and fidgeting provides the system with a mild jolt, acting like a nonprescription amphetamine to increase the flow of electrical current" (64).

Affective Characteristics

Motivation is one of the most important, if not the most important, factor in successful learning. The combination of factors that motivate a particular student can vary drastically from the factors that motivate their classmates. Anyone who has assigned an independent project to a class knows that the way in which it is approached varies by student. Some students immediately team up with a stronger student. Some prefer to act as a peer tutor, and some prefer to work on their own. There are always those students who repeatedly question the teacher about the assignment so that they know what to do.

Learners are motivated by a variety of things. Some students like to work in groups. Others prefer to work alone. Still others prefer to work with an adult. Some learners are motivated best by being told constantly exactly what to do. Others work best in a nonstructured environment with an open-ended task. These characteristics can be determined and instruction modified to match.

Students can be gently guided into situations that train them to enlarge their universe of preferred learning environments. Keefe (1988) observes that physiological and affective characteristics should be dealt with by both training and matching instructional strategies.

Cognitive Characteristics

Learners are presumed to go through certain processes during the act of learning (Gagne, Briggs, and Wager 1988, 11). A simplified description of these processes follows. Note that the majority of these processes are internal and invisible to the observer. For this discussion, let's suppose that a student is using a multimedia presentation on geometric shapes.

1. *Reception* of stimuli and *registration* of information. (Visual information from a screen and audio information from speakers reach the student.)

2. *Selective perception* of information for storage in short-term memory (STM) takes place. (Student pays attention to the rhombus and to the audio description of it.)

3. *Rehearsal* to maintain information in STM. (Student looks away, visualizes the figure, and repeats the description.)

4. *Semantic encoding* for storage in long-term memory (LTM). (Student associates figure and description of rhombus with other quadrilaterals and begins to merge this experience into an instructional schema, eventually modifying one or more instructional enterprises in long-term memory.)

5. *Retrieval* from LTM to STM. (Subsequently, the student retrieves the modified instructional enterprise from long-term memory during a quiz in which the question "How is a rhombus different from a square?" is posed.)

6. *Response generation.* (Student uses the modified instructional enterprise to form the basis of a response to the question.)

7. *Performance* in the learner's environment. (Student answers the question.)

8. Throughout the seven previous steps, the student utilizes *executive strategies* to *control* the process.

At each of these stages, learners differ in their instructional needs. Cognitive learning characteristics are the internal controls of the information-processing system, which assists the learner in carrying out these steps. Some learners possess the cognitive tools to use fast-paced abstract information, others can only use slow-paced concrete examples. Some learners can use certain information modalities such as aural or tactile much better than others. Some can pick out embedded information easily; others cannot. These abilities are among the many cognitive learner characteristics.

SPECIFIC LEARNER ANALYSIS PROCEDURES

As mentioned earlier, many learner analysis procedures have been developed in recent years. These can be categorized as either *unidimensional* or *multidimensional*. Unidimensional learner analysis procedures deal with a single learner characteristic representing one specific type (physiological, affective, or cognitive). Each procedure purports to quantify a characteristic for individuals in a given population. A multidimensional procedure is used to identify and quantify several learner characteristics. Sometimes these characteristics are not all within the same type of learner characteristic, and collectively the procedure may determine physiological, affective, and cognitive characteristics. Although several unidimensional procedures will be mentioned, the bulk of the remainder of this chapter will be devoted to describing multidimensional tools.

Unidimensional Procedures

- *Time-of-day preference (physiological).* It has always been common sense that some people work better in the morning and others work better at night. Preference for time of day has been advanced as a learner characteristic that can be correlated with success when this preference is matched with appropriate instruction. (See Dunn and Dunn 1978 for a listing of relevant readings on the topic, and also Dunn et al. 1987 for the results of a two-year study on this characteristic.)

  Quantifying instrument: *Questionnaire on Time* by Rita Dunn, Center for the Study of Learning and Teaching Styles, St. John's University, Grand Central & Utopia Pkwys., Jamaica Plains, NY 11439.

- *Locus of control (affective).* This procedure is based on the theory that learners vary in their source of reinforcement and structure. On one end of a continuum are learners who constantly look to others for reinforcement and direction (external). At the other pole are learners who generate reinforcement and direction from within (internal). It is thought that if instruction is designed to match the learner's style, increased learning will take place (Crandall, Katkovsky, and Crandall 1965; contains instrument).

- *Field dependence/independence (cognitive).* According to the theory upon which this learner analysis procedure rests, a normally distributed group of learners would fall between two poles defined by the ability to locate information embedded in a background (Witkin et al. 1971). This information may be visual, aural, tactile, or a mixture of several modes. Learners who are field dependent will need assistance in locating relevant information in a presentation.

  Quantifying instrument: *Group Embedded Figures Test* by Philip K. Oltman, Evelyn Raskin, and Herman A. Witkin, Consulting Psychologists Press, 3803 E. Bayshore Rd., Palo Alto, CA 94303.

- *Learning/testing anxiety (cognitive).* This learner characteristic is potentially a very powerful learner analysis tool. Although it is included here as a unidimensional characteristic, it is thought to impinge on several phases of learning. Specifically, Hockey (1979) predicted that heightened anxiety or arousal will 1) narrow the range of input, 2) reduce working-memory capacity, 3) speed up processing of information, and 4) increase impulsivity in selection of learner responses. Turner (1983, 1985) obtained results consistent with this theory in two studies involving the location of relevant visual information. Highly anxious learners had significantly greater difficulty in locating embedded information.

  Quantifying instrument: *Test Anxiety Inventory* by C. D. Spielberger et al., Consulting Psychologists Press, 3803 E. Bayshore Rd., Palo Alto, CA 94303.

Multidimensional Procedures

Six procedures that purport to quantify more than one learner characteristic are discussed in this section. These six were chosen because they can be obtained at low cost, are simple to use and to interpret, represent a variety of the types of characteristics, or are currently in widespread use.

Furthermore, the school library media specialist, with a minimum of preparation, should be able to assist teachers in the use of these procedures.

LEARNING STYLE INVENTORY

Developed by Dunn, Dunn, and Price (1981), the *Learning Style Inventory* (LSI) is designed to identify preferred learning environments. The learner characteristics identified are primarily affective and physiological types. The authors of this instrument have been in the forefront of research and dissemination concerning learning styles. Enough data have been gathered to provide norms and to establish validity (Price, Dunn, and Dunn 1976).

Four stimulus preference areas are addressed by the instrument:

- immediate environment (sound, heat, light, and design)

- emotionality (motivation, responsibility, persistence, and structure)

- sociological needs (self-oriented, peer-oriented, adult-oriented, or combined)

- physical needs (perceptual preference, time of day, food intake, and mobility)

The model is based on the assumptions that (1) it is possible to identify individual student preferences for learning environments and (2) it is possible to use a variety of instructional procedures and to modify the instructional environment to match the preferences. As a result the student will improve his or her ability to learn. The LSI is offered for grades 3 and 4; grades 5 and above; and "PEPS" for adults. Forms cost $4.00 for one copy, but less as the number ordered increases. For an additional $2.00 (to each individual scoring price) you can receive a narrative individualized interpretive report. For ordering information see http://www.learningstyle.com /order.html, call 1–800-LSI-4441, or write to Price Systems, P.O. Box 1818, Lawrence, KS 66044–8818

Sample Items (answered by true or false):

I study best when it is quiet.

I concentrate best when it is cool.

I have to be reminded often to do something.

I really like to mold things with my hands.

It's hard for me to sit in one place for a long time.

I do better if I know my work is going to be checked.

Nobody really cares if I do well in school.

I study best at a table or desk.

The things I remember best are the things I read.

I try to finish what I start.

I hardly ever finish all my work.

I can ignore most sound when I study.

I like to study by myself.

The things that I remember best are the things that I hear.

I really like to draw, color, or trace things.

When I can, I do my homework in the afternoon.

(Items from the *Learning Style Inventory* (LSI), copyrighted. Reproduced by permission.)

The 104 items in the LSI are combined in the analysis of the data into twenty-two categories that represent the four stimulus preference areas. These twenty-two categories include preference for light, preference for warmth, preference for learning with adults, kinesthetic preferences, and others. The results of the LSI are available in three forms: 1) an individual profile for each student, identifying standard scores in each category; 2) a group summary showing individuals who have a standard score greater than one standard deviation above or below the mean; and 3) a category summary indicating the number and percent of the total group that scored one standard deviation above or below the mean in each learning style category.

The LSI manual provides prescriptive advice to help teachers design activities and materials for learners who score high or low in each of the twenty-two categories. For example, the prescription for students who score high in the "preference for sound" category is "provide soft music, conversation areas, or an open learning environment" (Dunn, Dunn, and Price 1981, 4).

This LSI is a comprehensive learner analysis tool that has norms, reliability, and validity data. Such data are important to teachers who interpret results in order to assist them in the design of classroom environments and learning activities (Curry 1987). The instrument is simple to administer, and the computer scoring and profiling make it very easy to use. This ease of use, however, is obtained at a cost that might preclude its use in programs with little or no funds. Also, the instrument is not strong in the diagnosis of cognitive learner characteristics. However, for educators who are serious about matching learning environments and teaching practices to student needs, the *Learning Style Inventory* should be considered.

STUDENT LEARNING STYLES—A SURVEY

Student Learning Styles—A Survey was developed as a result of a project conducted at the Murdock Teacher Center, Wichita, Kansas (Project CITE 1976). It consists of forty-five items that are posited to represent nine learner-characteristics areas (Friedman and Alley 1984) of the cognitive and affective types. The nine areas are

- *auditory linguistic* (prefers to learn by means of spoken word)

- *visual linguistic* (prefers to see words in order to learn)

- *auditory numerical* (learns easily from hearing numbers and oral explanations)

- *visual numerical* (prefers to see numbers in order to learn)

- *audio-visual-kinesthetic combination* (likes a combination of the three basic modalities)

- *individual learner* (works best alone)

Fig. 8.1. Learning Styles Inventories

In the left side of this page is a *sample* circle. Compare the SIZE of the *sample* with the SIZE of the circle on the right side of the page. Do not measure the circles. mark either *A, B,* or *C* on your answer sheet for each circle.

A. if the circle is *smaller* than the *sample*
B. if the circle is *larger* than the *sample*
C. if the circle is the *same size* as the *sample*

sample

I am bothered by any sound when I am trying to think and study for an exam.

A. Always   B. Usually   C. Sometimes   D. Rarely   E. Never

If I get an answer wrong, I keep trying until I get the right answer.

A. Always   B. Usually   C. Sometimes   D. Rarely   E. Never

Doing homework is easier if I can lie down.

A. Always   B. Usually   C. Sometimes   D. Rarely   E. Never

On your answer sheet, mark A if you see a PICTURE, B if you hear a SOUND, and C if you have a FEELING about the word.

SUMMER   A. Picture   B. Sound   C. Feeling

- *group learner* (likes learning with others)

- *oral expressive* (prefers to share knowledge by telling others)

- *written expressive* (prefers to share knowledge by writing)

Each of the forty-five questions on the instrument is a statement about learning and responding. Using an answer sheet, the student responds to each question on a 1 to 4 scale. Anchors for this scale are (1) "least like me" and (4) "most like me." (See appendix E for the instrument and answer sheet.) Sample item: If I need help in the subject, I will ask a classmate for help. (This item is under the group-learner characteristic.)

It can be inferred from the description of the process provided by Friedman and Alley (1984) that the applicable grade range would be similar to that stipulated for the LSI. Furthermore, the instrument could probably be delivered via tape, orally, or in written form.

After the instrument is completed, it is scored using a very simple worksheet that allows for self-scoring by the student. (See appendix E for worksheet.)

A score of 24 to 32 indicates a minor preference in the characteristic area. A score above 32 indicates a major preference. Recommendations for teaching techniques are provided for learners who have a major preference in a given characteristic area.

We have not been able to locate either norms or validity data for this instrument. Friedman and Alley (1984), however, do provide five case histories that illustrate use of the procedure in situations ranging from an individual classroom to an entire school system.

The strengths of *Student Learning Styles—A Survey* are accurately described by Friedman and Alley (1984). It is a simple instrument that can be quickly administered and scored. Because the instrument was developed with federal monies, it is in the public domain and therefore is very inexpensive to use. This procedure includes cognitive as well as affective characteristics.

The main weakness is lack of validity data. Basically, the instrument provides information on which to base input and output media and grouping decisions. Many important learner characteristics are not covered. With these limitations in mind, this procedure could be recommended for a school library media specialist or teacher who is planning an initial move into learner analysis and who has limited funds.

LEARNING STYLE INVENTORY: PRIMARY

The *Learning Style Inventory: Primary* (LSI:P), as its title suggests, was developed for use with very young children. Developed by Dr. Janet Perrin, it is based on the *Learning Style Inventory* originally created by Dunn, Dunn, and Price mentioned earlier in this chapter. The instrument uses pictorial representations of learners in various situations, and the student indicates which situation is preferred (see figure 8.2). Students are tested individually, and the testing requires about twenty minutes. Prices: $35.00 for an instrument, reproducible answer forms, and a manual. Also available: *A Storybook Explaining Learning Style to Children: K-2* ($8.00). Order from Dr. Janet Perrin, 31 Doncaster Rd., Malverne, NY 11565.

The strength of the LSI:P is that it does not require reading. The vast majority of learner analysis instruments cannot be easily used with prereaders. This instrument is designed specifically for this group. The cost for this instrument is quite reasonable because the charts can be reused and the Individual Student Profile Form can be reproduced.

The LSI:P has reliability and validity data provided. The examiner's manual also includes information on techniques that can be used by the teacher to match the learning characteristics identified by the LSI:P. There is also information regarding the matching of instructional materials to learning-style characteristics.

KOLB LEARNING STYLE INVENTORY

The *Kolb Learning Style Inventory* is a statistically reliable and valid 12-item assessment tool developed by David A. Kolb, Ph.D. Based on Experiential Learning Theory, it identifies preferred learning styles, and explores the opportunities different styles present for problem solving, working in teams, resolving conflict, communicating at work, communicating at home, and considering a career.

Four scores are calculated, one each for: Concrete Experience, Abstract Conceptualization, Reflective Observation, and Active Experimentation. Kolb states that a high score in concrete experience (CE) represents a receptive experience-based approach to learning that relies on feelings-based judgments. High CE people tend to be empathetic. They learn best from specific examples in which they can be involved. These learners tend to relate to peers, not authority. A high score in abstract conceptualization (AC) indicates an analytical, conceptual approach to learning that relies heavily on logical thinking and rational evaluation. High AC people tend to be more oriented toward things and symbols, and less toward other people. They learn best in authority-directed, impersonal learning situations that emphasize theory and systematic analysis. A high score in reflective observation (RO) indicates a tentative, impartial, and reflective approach to learning. High RO individuals rely heavily on careful observation in making judgments. They prefer learn-

Fig. 8.2. Sample items from *Learning Styles Inventory: Primary* (LSI:P), copyrighted. (Reproduced with permission.)

1. If there were no lights on in the classroom, only the light from the windows would it be:

    <u>1</u> easy for you to do your schoolwork?
    or
    <u>2</u> hard for you to do your schoolwork?

2. If you took a book to look at out of doors on a sunny day would the sunlight:

    <u>1</u> bother your eyes?
    or
    <u>2</u> not bother your eyes at all?

ing situations such as lectures that allow the role of impartial objective observers. These individuals tend to be introverts. A high score in active experimentation (AE) indicates an active "doing" orientation to learning that relies heavily on experimentation. High AE individuals learn best when they can engage in such things as projects, homework, or group discussions. They dislike passive learning situations such as lectures. These people tend to be extroverts.

The *Kolb Learning Style Inventory* describes the way one learns and how one deals with ideas and day-to-day situations in life. It is based on the works of John Dewey, Kurt Lewin, Jean Piaget, and J. P. Guilford. For more information regarding his learning style inventory, see the following:

Kolb, D. A. 1984. *Experiential Learning: Experience as the Source of Learning and Development.* Englewood Cliffs, N.J.: Prentice-Hall.

Smith, D. M., and D. A. Kolb. 1986. *The User's Guide for the Learning-Style Inventory: A Manual for Teachers and Trainers.* Boston: McBer and Company.

The cost for this instrument is $79.00 for 10 self-scoring booklets. It can also be administered online for $15.00 per person. For further information, call 1–800–729–8074 or e-mail Hay Resources Direct at haytrg@haygroup.com.

SILVER STRONG LEARNING PREFERENCE INVENTORY

Information from the *Silver Strong Learning Preference Inventory* helps individuals to make better decisions about learning and teaching. It consists of four areas: Sensing-Thinking

(Mastery), Sensing-Feeling (Interpersonal), Intuitive-Thinking (Understanding), and Intuitive-Feeling (Self-Expressive). People who score high on Mastery are good at working with and remembering facts and details, able to speak and write directly to the point, goal-oriented, focused on immediate tangible outcomes, concerned with utility and efficiency, and concerned with accuracy. Individuals who score high on Interpersonal are spontaneous, able to express personal feelings, able to learn through human interaction and personal experience, comfortable with activities regarding expression of feelings, able to persuade people through personal interaction, keen observers of human behavior, and interested in people. Those who score high on Understanding take time to plan and contemplate consequences of actions, are able to organize and synthesize information, can weigh the evidence and make judgments based on logic, and learn through books and other symbolic forms. People who score high on Self-Expressive are good at interpreting facts and can see the broader picture, are able to express ideas in new and unusual ways, can approach tasks in a variety of ways, are able to adapt to new situations and procedures quickly.

LEARNING TOOLS INVENTORY

The *Learning Tools Inventory*, developed by Philip Turner, is based partially upon the works of Allen (1975), Gagne (1975), Ausburn and Ausburn (1978), and Heiman and Slomianko (1985). The procedure is premised upon the belief that successful learners possess a variety of learning tools that enable them to acquire and process information successfully. These tools are often thought of as critical thinking skills or as metacognitive abilities.

The *Learning Tools Inventory* involves assessing learners' characteristics as to the degree of possession of each of eight learning tools as well as the tendency of the learner to employ the tool. These tools correspond roughly to the phases of learning posited by Gagne (1975). If a tool is not present to a sufficient degree, learning can be seriously impaired. The characteristics are as follows:

- *The ability and tendency to establish "set" prior to or immediately after entering a learning situation.* Establishing "set" is a process by which the learner creates a set of expectations for both content and delivery in the lesson. Learners with a high degree of this characteristic ready themselves for learning by becoming aware of what is to be learned in a particular instructional experience. They might employ the tool of imagining themselves successfully completing the task. Learners who possess this tool focus on instructional objectives and unit goals and direct their behaviors to meet these.

- *The tendency to structure information into a format that will aid learning.* Much instruction involves the presentation of poorly structured information. Heiman and Slomianko (1985, 17) view breaking down ideas and tasks into manageable tasks as one of the two skills central to learning. Learners high in this characteristic tend to provide an internal structure, using a variety of strategies such as creating outlines, flow charts, task checklists, and graphs. Learners who possess little or none of this characteristic tend to be more passive learners who, when they do attempt to organize information, do so in a haphazard manner that leads to their missing much of the information.

- *The ability to locate criterial information.* Learners high in this characteristic are able to concentrate on the important information in a visual or audio presentation and to filter out the "noise."

- *Tendency to generate questions regarding the material to be learned during the presentation.* Generating appropriate questions is the second skill viewed as central to learning by Heiman and Slomianko (1985, 17). A learner high in this characteristic routinely formulates questions regarding the important facts, concepts, and rules. The learner may engage in a covert dialogue with the author or speaker and may form hypotheses (Heiman and Slomianko 1985, 16).

- *Tendency to check self-perceptions regarding the material to be learned.* It should be evident that this tool can be utilized only when the previous characteristic is employed. This characteristic involves checking to see whether the answers to the self-generated questions are correct.

- *Ability to process information rapidly.* This involves reading and listening rates as well as processing pictorial information.

- *The tendency to want to learn.* This is the characteristic of motivation. Although motivation is certainly not a constant with any learner, students can be said to vary along a continuum as to interest in learning.

- *The tendency to summarize information after presentation.* Learners high in this characteristic tend to paraphrase the material as it is presented. They also will summarize the major concepts and generalizations that were to be learned.

There are instruments that are designed to measure a single one of these characteristics (for example, for the third characteristic see field dependence/independence under unidimensional procedures in this chapter). However, the *Learning Tools Inventory* is quicker and less expensive than employing such single-purpose instruments.

To analyze a particular learner, the teacher(s) or a combination of teacher(s) and instructional consultant rate each student on a 0 to 10 scale for each characteristic. A score of 0 indicates that the rater believes the learner possesses none of the characteristic—that is, does not possess the learning tool or does not employ it at the appropriate time. Conversely, a score of 10 indicates a perception that the learner possesses the learning tool to a high degree and uses it when called for by the learning situation. (See appendix F for a copy of the rating form.)

Each score has implications for the production, selection, and use of instructional materials as well as learner strategies and activities. These will be covered in detail in later chapters.

A strength of the *Learning Tools Inventory* procedure is that it is based on a widely accepted model of how humans learn, and the results are easily translated into design prescriptions. The appropriateness of this approach is reinforced by the incorporation of much of the terminology in works dealing with critical thinking skills and metacognition. Another strength is that it addresses critical learning skills that are not included in many of the other inventories.

The main weakness of the *Learning Tools Inventory* is that it involves a guesstimate on the part of the rater, with all the inherent pitfalls. There are, however, some generalizations that can help in rating:

- Most of these characteristics are strengthened developmentally. Learners usually obtain these tools as a result of maturation and experience. Therefore, the younger the child, the lower the expected score.

- Students who consistently fail to achieve often do not possess many of these tools. Therefore, a student who is doing especially poorly in class should be looked at closely.

The teacher can employ informal interview techniques to help reinforce original perceptions. Use of this procedure is highly recommended for young students and for low achievers. Because the procedure is limited primarily to cognitive characteristics, its use in conjunction with another type of learner analysis is advisable.

FREE LEARNING STYLE INVENTORIES

Several learning style inventories are available on the Internet. An example can be found at http://w3.tvi.cc.nm.us/~gbw/learnstyle.html [May 8, 2003].

TENTATIVE CONCLUSIONS AND RECOMMENDATIONS

Learner analysis is a construct that is constantly developing and changing. Although solid, research-backed conclusions are only now emerging, tentative observations and recommendations can be made:

- Relatively stable learner characteristics can be identified reliably.

- Many of these characteristics affect the way students learn.

- Instruction can be designed that will result in a greater probability of success for learners with a given characteristic.

On the basis of these three conclusions, the instructional designer should consider the following recommendations:

- Educators should attempt to individualize instruction on the basis of learner characteristics. Instruction should be directed to a learner's strengths.

- Learners should be encouraged to strengthen, whenever possible, learning styles or tools that are weak or nonexistent.

- If a teacher does not have the resources to individualize instruction completely, then instruction should be tailored to the smallest groups possible. This might entail dividing the class into small groups around certain characteristics or perhaps dividing the class into only two groups. If for some reason the class cannot be divided and all must be taught with the same materials and activities, then learner analysis results can be studied to determine whether a predominant class style exists.

- Learner analysis should be the focus of well-designed research projects by colleges and universities to deepen validity and heighten predictability of available procedures.

- School library media specialists should become familiar with various procedures, both to use in their instruction and to enable them to assist their teachers.

LEVELS OF INVOLVEMENT BY THE SCHOOL LIBRARY MEDIA SPECIALIST AT THE LEARNER ANALYSIS STEP

The learner analysis step of the instructional design process consists of selecting pertinent learner characteristics and diagnosing the strength of these characteristics in each learner.

The Initial Level

At the initial level of the learner analysis step of the instructional design process, the school library media specialist can assist the teacher by obtaining and maintaining learner analysis instruments and manuals. The school library media specialist can also maintain a collection of materials that will introduce and update the concept of learner analysis to teachers, administrators, and parents. Depending on the level of available resources, the school library media specialist should make available several of the instruments discussed in this chapter, as well as others that might be required by the circumstances in the particular school.

Learner analysis is a rapidly developing phenomenon. The library media specialist can do the faculty a great service by keeping up with the literature and constantly updating the professional collection's materials on this topic. The following are recommended materials.

Andrews, R. H. 1994. Three Perspectives of Learning Styles. *School Administrator* 51 (8): 19–22.

Association for Supervision and Curriculum Development. 1979. *Educational Leadership* 36 (4).

———. 1983. *Educational Leadership* 40 (5).

Atkinson, G,. and P. H. Murrell. 1988. Kolb's Experiential Learning Theory: A Meta-Model for Career Exploration. *Journal of Counseling and Development* 66: 374–77.

Brown, D. W. 2000. Libraries Can Be Right-Brained. *Book Report* 19: 19–21.

Carbo, M., R. Dunn, and K. Dunn. 1986. *Teaching Students to Read through Their Individual Learning Styles.* Englewood Cliffs, N.J.: Prentice-Hall.

Dunn, K. 1987. Dispelling Outmoded Beliefs about Student Learning. *Educational Leadership* 44: 55–61.

Dunn, R. 1981. A Learning Styles Primer. *Principal* 60 (5): 31–34.

———. 2001. Learning Style Differences of Nonconforming Middle-School Students. *NASSP Bulletin* 85: 68–74.

———, and S. A. Griggs. 1988. *Learning Styles: Quiet Revolution in American Secondary Schools.* Reston, Va.: National Association of Secondary School Principals.

Ebeling, D. G. 2001. Teaching to ALL Learning Styles. *Education Digest* 66: 41–46.

Garger, S. 1990. Is There a Link between Learning Style and Neurophysiology? *Educational Leadership* 48 (2): 63–65.

Garner, I. 2000. Problems and Inconsistencies with Kolb's Learning Styles. *Educational Psychology* 20: 341–49.

Haar, J., G. Hall, P. Schoepp, and D. H. Smith. 2002. How Teachers Teach to Students with Different Learning Styles. *Clearing House* 75: 142–45.

Hardy, I. R. 2000. Medal Winners. *School Library Media Activities Monthly* 16: 26–28.

Harpe, B., and A. Radloff. 2000. Informed Teachers and Learners: The Importance of Assessing the Characteristics Needed for Lifelong Learning. *Studies in Continuing Education* 22: 2.

Heffler, B. 2001. Individual Learning Style and the Learning Style Inventory. *Educational Studies* 27: 3–4.

Heiman, M., and J. Slomianko. 1985. *Critical Thinking Skills.* Washington, D.C.: National Education Association.

Hoerr, T. R. 2002. Engaging Learners in Your Classroom. *Early Childhood Today* 16: 40–46.

House, J. D., and E. J. Keely. 1996. Relationship between Learner Attitudes, Prior Achievement, and Performance in a General Education Course: A Multi-Institutional Study. *International Journal of Instructional Media* 23: 257–71.

Jenkins, J. M., C. A. Letteri, and P. Rosenlund. 1990. *Learning Style Profile Handbook: I. Developing Cognitive Skills.* Reston, Va.: National Association of Secondary School Principals.

Keefe, J. W. 1987. *Learning Style: Theory and Practice.* Reston, Va.: National Association of Secondary School Principals.

———. 1988. *Profiling and Utilizing Learning Style.* Reston, Va.: National Association of Secondary School Principals.

Klein, J. D., and J. M. Keller. 1990. Influence of Student Ability, Locus of Control, and Type of Instructional Control on Performance and Confidence. *Journal of Educational Research* 83: 3.

Koob, J. J., and J. Funk. 2002. Kolb's Learning Style Inventory: Issues of Reliability and Validity. *Research on Social Work Practice* 12: 293–308.

Ojure, L., and T. Sherman. 2001. Learning Styles. *Education Week* 21: 33.

Prescott, H. M. 2001. Helping Students Say How They Know What They Know. *Clearing House* 74: 327–32.

Smith, J. 2002. Learning Styles: Fashion Fad or Lever for Change? The Application of Learning Style Theory to Inclusive Curriculum Delivery. *Innovations in Education and Teaching International* 39: 63–70.

The Moderate Level

In order to move up to the moderate level at the learner analysis step of the instructional design process, the school library media specialist must become familiar with learning styles and specific learner analysis procedures. Because learner analysis is a relatively new area and one in which interest is rapidly increasing, there should be many opportunities for the kind of informal assistance characterized by the moderate level.

After deciding to move up to this level at this step and after preparation is completed, the school library media specialist must publicize the availability of assistance. This can be accomplished in one or more of the ways described in chapter 5. The following are two illustrations of moderate-level interactions that might occur at the learner analysis step.

SCENARIO 1

Lotsee Platmore, a seventh-grade social studies teacher, has seated herself beside Michelle Craig, the school library media specialist, at the opening of Elmwood City Junior High's drama club play. The conversation takes place during intermission.

Michelle: How is the unit on cities going? I know you were going to try a new approach this year. Groups or something?

Lotsee: Ughh. Cities! And I was enjoying the play.

Michelle: Sorry I brought it up. It's just that you were so excited in September. What happened?

Lotsee: Some of the students seemed to love it. They really blossomed and worked together fine. Others complained that they would rather do the work themselves, and still others said that they like to sit in a lecture and then discuss. What a group!

Michelle: Would you be willing to let some of the students work on individual projects, others in groups, and still others sit for a lecture and discussion?

Lotsee: Hmm . . . I think it could be managed. How would I split them up?

Michelle: Well, you could ask them what they want. Another possibility would be to diagnose their preferences.

Lotsee: Wow! Sounds technical. Do you have to stick electrodes in their heads?

Michelle: No, it's painless and actually very quick. I have a test that takes about fifteen minutes. Many students really enjoy taking the test and talking about the results.

Lotsee: And this test will tell me whether a student prefers to work in groups or not?

Michelle: Among other things. Why don't you stop by after school tomorrow, and we can talk about it?

SCENARIO 2

Bill Cabelerri has recently been asked to teach a section of ninth-grade science. This class is made up of very slow learners, and things have not been going well. Bill is dedicated and has tried to use quality audiovisual materials to help the students learn. However, the students consistently do poorly on tests that cover material included in the presentations. In this scenario, Bill is bringing a videotape back to the center and is looking for more materials. Ken Ramer, the school library media specialist, greets him.

Ken: Hey, Bill, how's it going?

Bill: Well, all is quiet on the classroom front. . . . They're not learning anything, but all is quiet.

Ken: Those materials (pointing to the videotape). Just didn't do the trick?

Bill: No, they did not. I know the information that I tested them on was in this videotape—and it sure is a beautiful videotape—but it didn't work. Those kids just seem to be missing something. They're not dumb, they just seem to have a lot of trouble learning. You know, the last few years I've been teaching the chemistry and physics advanced classes. Those kids spoiled me.

Ken: I think I might have something that could help you get a handle on this group's problems. It's called *Learning Tools Inventory.* It's a procedure in which the teacher rates each student on certain abilities. These abilities are crucial to effective learning,

Bill: Such as?

Ken: Okay, do your students generally have a clear idea as to what they are supposed to learn before a lesson begins?

Bill: (pauses) Well, I don't know . . . probably not. In fact, for most of them, I'm sure not.

Ken: Do most of your students have trouble getting the important information out of particular parts of the videotape?

Bill: Yes! Take this videotape for example. One of the things it is supposed to teach is an inclined plane. The videotape illustrates this with a boy pushing a motorcycle up a ramp into a van. Well, do you think they noticed the inclined plane? They were so excited by the Kawasaki 800 and the custom van that they missed the point entirely. . . . What did you call this procedure again?

Ken: *Learning Tools Inventory.* It's a simple procedure that provides some questions to ask about students. The answers to these questions can help you select and use materials better. Come in during your planning period sometime this week, and I can tell you a little more about the procedure.

The In-Depth Level

Many teachers will have heard of learning styles but will be unfamiliar with many of the concepts and with the instruments that can be used. The opportunities for in-depth-level activities are many.

IN-SERVICE

Learner analysis makes an ideal topic for in-services by the school library media specialist. The in-service can serve to introduce the construct of learner analysis in general or can concentrate on one or more specific procedures.

If specific procedures are presented, it is a good idea to have the teachers complete an analysis for themselves. Not only is this a good motivational technique, it can be very enlightening. As Barbe and Milone (1980) have suggested, teachers tend to develop teaching strategies that are congruent with their own preferences. Finding out their own learner characteristics, as well as procedures for determining their students' characteristics, are the first steps in teachers' broadening their range of strategies.

The article by Garger (1990) listed in The Initial Level section of this chapter is an excellent one to use as a discussion starter with a group of teachers. Teachers have struggled for so long with those students who just can't seem to sit still and who seem to need constant stimuli. Garger's article will help them to see the possibility that some students need special environments to help them function well.

INSTRUCTIONAL DESIGN TEAM PARTICIPATION

The learner analysis process does not have to be engaged in frequently. Because most learner characteristics are relatively stable, once a learner analysis is performed with a particular student, this information can be used in planning instruction for an extended period of time. This fact can motivate teachers to participate on a team to analyze their students in common, with leadership from the school library media specialist. The procedures that require subjective judgment on the part of the rater are made more reliable by more than one rater. The school library media specialist can serve as both educator and facilitator in this process.

THOUGHT PROVOKERS

1. Use the *Student Learning Styles—A Survey* procedure to analyze yourself. Then analyze at least one other person. Try to choose someone whose learning style you believe is different from yours.

2. Repeat your analysis using the *Learning Tools Inventory* procedure.

3. What is the most "important" category of learner characteristics? For example, if a learner was mismatched to the instruction for his or her physiological, affective, or cognitive characteristics, which mismatch would result in the greatest problem?

4. Respond to this statement: "Teaching students according to their learning characteristics is like giving them a crutch. If you don't force them to exercise their weak learning muscles, they will be crippled for life!"

(See appendix A for answers.)

REFERENCES

Allen, W. H. 1975. Intellectual Abilities and Instructional Message Design. *A V Communications Review* 23 (6): 139–70.

Ausburn, L. J., and F. B. Ausburn. 1978. Cognitive Styles: Some Information and Implications for Instructional Design. *Educational Communications and Technology Journal* 26: 337–54.

Barbe, W. B., and M. N. Milone, Jr. 1980. Modality. *Instructor* 39 (6): 45–47.

Crandall, V. C., W. Katkovsky, and V. J. Crandall. 1965. Children's Belief in Their Own Control of Reinforcements in Intellectual-Academic Achievement Situations. *Child Development* 36: 91–109.

Curry, L. 1987. *Integrating Concepts of Cognitive or Learning Styles: A Review with Attention to Psychometric Standards.* Ottawa, Ontario: Canadian College of Health Services Executives.

Doyle, W., and B. Rutherford. 1984. Classroom Research on Matching Learning and Teaching Styles. *Theory into Practice* 23 (1): 20–25.

Dunn, R. 1984. Learning Style: The State of the Science. *Theory into Practice* 23 (1): 10–19.

Dunn, R., and K. Dunn. 1978. *Teaching Students through Their Individual Learning Styles: A Practical Approach.* Reston, Va.: Reston.

Dunn, R., K. Dunn, and G. E. Price. 1981. *Learning Style Inventory Manual.* Lawrence, Kans.: Price Systems.

Dunn, R., K. Dunn, L. Primavera, R. Sinatra, and J. Virostko. 1987. A Timely Solution: Effect of Chronobiology on Achievement and Behavior. *Clearing House* 61: 5–8.

Dunn, R., J. S. Krimsky, J. B. Murray, and P. J. Quinn. 1985. Light Up Their Lives: A Review of Research on the Effects of Lighting on Children's Achievement and Behavior. *Reading Teacher* 38: 863–69.

Friedman, P., and R. Alley. 1984. Learning/Teaching Styles: Applying the Principles. *Theory into Practice* 23 (1): 77–81.

Gagne, R. M. 1975. *Essentials of Learning for Instruction.* Hinsdale, Ill.: Dryden Press.

Gagne, R. M., L. J. Briggs, and W. W. Wager. 1988. *Principles of Instructional Design.* New York: Holt, Rinehart and Winston.

Garger, S. 1990. Is There a Link between Learning Style and Neurophysiology? *Educational Leadership* 48 (October): 63–65.

Gregoric, A. F. 1982. Learning Style/Brain Research: Harbinger of an Emerging Psychology. In *Student Learning Styles and Brain Behavior,* ed. Thomas A. Koerner, 3–10. Reston, Va.: National Association of Secondary School Principals.

Heiman, M., and J. Slomianko. 1985. *Critical Thinking Skills.* Washington, D.C.: National Education Association.

Henson, K. T., and P. Borthwick. 1984. Matching Styles: A Historical Look. *Theory into Practice* 23: 3–9.

Hockey, R. 1979. Stress and the Cognitive Components of Skilled Performance. In *Human Stress and Cognition: An Information Processing Approach,* ed. V. Hamilton and D. M. Warburton, 141–77. New York: John Wiley.

Jenkins, J. M., C. A. Letteri, and P. Rosenlund. 1990. *Learning Style Profile Handbook: I. Developing Cognitive Skills.* Reston, Va.: National Association of Secondary School Principals.

Keefe, J. W. 1982. Assessing Student Learning Styles: An Overview. In *Student Learning Styles and Brain Behavior,* ed. Thomas A. Koerner, 43–53. Reston, Va.: National Association of Secondary School Principals.

Keefe, J. W., and J. S. Monk. 1990. *Learning Style Profile, Examiner's Manual.* Reston, Va.: National Association of Secondary School Principals.

Keefe, J. W., ed. 1988. *Profiling and Utilizing Learning Style.* (NASSP Learning Style Series.) Reston, Va.: National Association of Secondary School Principals.

Marshall, C. 1990. The Power of the Learning Styles Philosophy. *Educational Leadership* 48 (2): 62.

National Association of Secondary School Principals. 1982. *Student Learning Styles and Brain Behavior.* Reston, Va.: National Association of Secondary School Principals.

Price, G. E. Personal correspondence with the author, September 18, 1984.

Price, G. E., R. Dunn, and K. Dunn. 1976. *Learning Style Inventory: Research Report.* Lawrence, Kans.: Price Systems.

Project CITE. 1976. *Student Learning Styles—A Survey.* Unpublished learning-styles instrument. Wichita, Kans.: Murdock Teacher Center.

Spielberger, C. D., et al. 1980. *Test Anxiety Inventory.* Palo Alto, Calif.: Consulting Psychologists Press.

Turner, P. M. 1983. Anxiety and Cueing in a Concept Learning Task. *Educational Communications and Technology Journal* 31: 47–53.

———. 1985. Search Time and Test Anxiety in a Visual Location Task. *Contemporary Educational Psychology* 10: 292–301.

Witkin, H. A., et al. 1971. *Group Embedded Figures Test Manual.* Palo Alto, Calif.: Consulting Psychologists Press.

ADDITIONAL READINGS

Barbe, W. B., and R. Swassing. 1979. *Teaching Students through Modality Strengths: Concepts and Practices.* Columbus, Ohio: Zaner-Bloser.

Beglane, E. T. 2001. Principals Who Faced Obstacles to Learning Styles Instruction. *NASSP Bulletin* 85: 79–84.

Claxton, C. S., and P. H. Murrell. 1987. *Learning Styles: Implications for Improving Educational Practices.* ASHE-ERIC Higher Education Report No. 4. Washington, D.C.: Association for the Study of Higher Education.

Cohen, V. L. 2001. Learning Styles and Technology in a Ninth-Grade High School Population. *Journal of Research on Computing in Education* 33: 355–67.

Davidman, L. 1981. Learning Style: The Myth, the Panacea, the Wisdom. *Phi Delta Kappan* 62: 641–45.

Frymier, J. 1977. *Annehurst Curriculum Classification System.* West Lafayette, Ind.: Kappa Delta Pi.

Holland, R. P. 1982. Learner Characteristics and Learner Performance: Implications for Instructional Placement Decisions. *Journal of Special Education* 16: 1.

Hopper, B., and P. Hurry. 2000. Learning the MI Way: The Effects on Students' Learning of Using the Theory of Multiple Intelligences. *Pastoral Care in Education* 18: 26–32.

Manner, B. M. 2001. Learning Styles and Multiple Intelligences in Students: Getting the Most Out of Your Students' Learning. *Journal of College Science Teaching* 30: 390–93.

Oakland, T. 2000. Temperament-Based Learning Styles of Visually Impaired Students. *Journal of Visual Impairment and Blindness* 94: 26–33.

Rattanapian, V., and W. J. Gibbs. 1995. Computerized Drill and Practice: Design Options and Learner Characteristics. *International Journal of Instructional Media* 22: 59.

Root, J. R., and M. D. Gall. 1981. Interaction between Student Achievement, Locus of Control, and Two Methods of College Instruction. *Educational Communications and Technology Journal* 29: 139–46.

Sanchez, R. 2001. How to Start Somewhere When They All Learn Differently. *Exercise Exchange* 46: 3–5.

Schwen, T. M. 1972. Learner Analysis. *A V Communications Review* 22: 44–72.

Searson, R., and R. Dunn. 2001. The Learning-Style Teaching Model. *Science and Children* 38: 22–26.

Sieber, J. E., and H. E. O'Neil, Jr. 1977. *Anxiety, Learning, and Instruction.* New York: Halstead.

Smith, S. M., and P. C. Woody. 2000. Interactive Effect of Multimedia Instruction and Learning Styles. *Teaching of Psychology* 27: 220–24.

Stellwagen, J. B. 2001. A Challenge to the Learning Style Advocates. *Clearing House Press* 74: 265–68.

Witkin, H. A., C. A. Moore, and D. R. Goodenough. 1977. Field Dependent and Field Independent Cognitive Styles and Their Educational Implications. *Review of Educational Research* 47 (1): 1–64.

(See also purchases recommended in this chapter.)

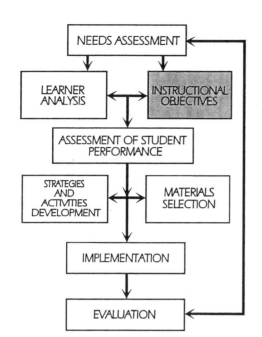

9

Instructional Objectives

This chapter provides information to help the reader

- understand the purpose and components of the instructional objectives step

- perceive advantages and disadvantages of the use of instructional objectives

- create goal-elaboration statements

- translate goal-elaboration statements into instructional objectives

- identify the category of learning represented by a given instructional objective

- identify the level of learning represented by a given instructional intellectual skill objective

- develop an instructional enterprise for a given primary instructional objective

- identify entrance skills and determine order of instruction

REVIEW OF STEP 1 IN THE INSTRUCTIONAL DESIGN PROCESS

In the first step of the instructional design process, needs assessment, the instructional content is determined. This content is most often expressed in terms of an instructional need or goal. Many needs assessment models call for goals to be written in precise and measurable terms, but most often they will fit Pipe's (1975, 62) definition of a goal as an "unmeasurable statement about instructional intent." Goal statements—such as the student will recognize geometric forms, the student will appreciate a litter-free classroom, and the student will be able to throw a softball well—might result from a small-scale needs assessment or from another method of deriving instructional content.

THE PURPOSE OF THE INSTRUCTIONAL OBJECTIVES STEP

The purpose of the instructional objectives step is to translate the instructional goal statement into an instructional objective. Given an instructional goal, an instructional objective answers the question, "What will a learner be able to do when the goal has been met?"

WRITING AN INSTRUCTIONAL OBJECTIVE

The Goal-Elaboration Statement

Many instructional goals are often written as a single sentence, but there may be some difficulty in creating a quality instructional objective without more detail. The instructional designer often needs to obtain more information before translating the goal into an objective. A useful technique is to create a goal-elaboration statement. This statement expands on the knowledge base that must be possessed in order for the goal to be met.

For the goal, "The student will recognize geometric forms," a possible goal-elaboration statement is: The student should understand the characteristics used to classify two-dimensional geometric figures including 1) the number of sides, 2) the length of these sides, and 3) the angles formed when these sides meet. The student should be familiar with the characteristics of squares, rhombuses, rectangles, and triangles.

There are many different ways to elaborate upon a particular goal statement. The teacher creates the elaboration based on the needs of the student and the overall instructional plan.

Parts of an Instructional Objective

Once the designer is comfortable with the goal, the next step is to translate it into an instructional objective. There is no one way to translate an instructional goal statement into an instructional objective. The readings listed in the Initial Level section of this chapter describe several ways. *A "correct" instructional objective will allow a reasonably competent person to determine, to an acceptable degree of certainty, whether the instructional goal has been reached.*

A useful method of writing instructional objectives, the ABCD method, was described by Armstrong, Denton, and Savage (1978). Their instructional objectives contain four parts:

A. a description of the audience (learner)

B. a description of the behavior that demonstrates that the goal has been reached

C. a description of the conditions under which the behavior will be performed

D. a description of the degree to which the stated behavior must occur for the instruction to be judged successful

Let us examine each of these parts in more detail.

AUDIENCE

Who is doing the learning? This question can be answered generally: "Second-grade students in Ms. Marreli's room." It can be answered more specifically: "The second-grade students in Ms. Marreli's room who are in the low-math group." It can be answered even more specifically: "The second-grade students in Ms. Marreli's room who are in the low-math group and who have exhibited a large amount of math anxiety during the year."

The possibilities for complexity of the audience statement are virtually unlimited. This can frustrate teachers who are beginning to use instructional objectives. The purpose of the more complex audience statements is to avoid confusion for whom the objective is designed and to provide important information relevant to steps 5 and 6 of the instructional design process. This benefit must be considered in terms of the cost in resources and in terms of patience for writing detailed audience statements. If a teacher is designing instruction for his or her own use, and if it is clear to the teacher for whom the objective is being written, then a simple audience statement such as "the learner" will suffice.

BEHAVIOR

This part of an instructional objective is by far the most important. Remember, an instructional objective is a statement that describes what the learner will be able to do when the goal has been met. The action verb(s) therefore must be chosen with great care. As we shall see later in this chapter, the verb(s) in the instructional objective provides a clue to the level of learning that will take place.

In order for the instructional objective to be useful, verbs must be chosen that will allow the teacher to be reasonably sure that the action described by the verb has taken place. Verbs such as *appreciate, know, become aware of,* and *understand* are useful in writing goal-elaboration statements but are not appropriate for instructional objectives. How will the teacher be reasonably sure that the student knows or understands? Statements of behavior such as *verbally state, write, throw,* and *select* can easily be judged by the teacher and are more effective as part of the instructional objective. The instructional designer should be able to design a test based upon the actions described in the behavior portion of the instructional objective.

CONDITIONS

Under what conditions will the behavior be performed? What information, tools, equipment, and so on, will be available to students when they attempt to perform the behavior described in the objective? What information, tools, and equipment will not be available to the student?

Examples of information include multiplication, periodical, logarithmic, and other types of tables as well as dictionaries, thesauri, and encyclopedias. Relevant tools and equipment might include calculators and computers, compasses and templates, or test tubes and telescopes. A condition for the instructional objective should not include any characteristic of the instruction itself. It is presumed that instruction always takes place.

The instructional designer could spend a great deal of time listing what will not be available to the student when the stated behavior is to be performed. A listing of the materials that will be used can also become ridiculous. ("The learner, given a paper, pencil, eraser, light, air, seat . . . ") Conditions do not have to be stated as part of every instructional objective. The instructional designer needs to keep in mind that certain information, tools, and equipment might be available in a real-life setting and should decide whether these are appropriate for the situation in which the objective will be tested. An awareness of the impact of these materials on the performance of the behavior described is what is most important.

DEGREE

To what degree must the learner perform the behavior in order for the goal to be reached? If the behavior is locating government Web sites, how many must the learner locate? If the learner must use APA Citation Style correctly, how many mistakes can be made by the learner?

There are several ways to describe the degree to which the behavior should be demonstrated, including

- *Time to completion* (Cone 1988). Example: Name seven Middle Eastern countries *within two minutes.*

- *Minimum number of correct actions.* Examples: List at least *four* U.S. presidents since 1960. List four currently used computer domains accurately.

- *Percent or proportion.* Examples: Write the "I" form of the past perfect tense of at least *50 percent* of the fifty irregular verbs provided. At least *three-fourths* of the students will locate Web sites appropriate for the topic of "gang violence in schools."

- *Limitation of departure from a fixed standard.* Examples: Must be correct to the nearest thousandth. Must land within five inches of the target.

- *Consecutiveness* (Cone 1988). Example: Tie shoes correctly for at least *three consecutive days.*

Writing the degree portion of the instructional objective is a process by which the teacher establishes a "self-contract." In effect, the teacher is saying, "If the student can perform the behavior to this degree, then I will judge the instruction a success." Conversely, if the learner does not meet the criteria, then the instruction was not successful, and some action—for example, reteaching—should take place.

The degree statement should clearly allow the teacher to see whether the contract has been fulfilled. Reliance solely on expert or instructor judgment often leads to less useful degree statements (Dick and Carey 1990). "The learner will be able to punctuate a given paragraph to the teacher's satisfaction" can be translated into "If the student can punctuate a given paragraph so that I am satisfied, I will be satisfied." This does not make sense. Neither does "Given the names of eight presidents, the learner will be able to write the dates of office of at least 40 percent of them." How do you write the dates of office for 3.2 presidents?

It should be noted at this point that some instructional designers do not include the degree statement as part of the instructional objective, but rather wait until the assessment of student performance step to decide upon criteria. This is a valid approach and provides for increased flexibility.

SAMPLE INSTRUCTIONAL OBJECTIVES

The following are three examples of instructional objectives.

- Given a sheet with line drawings of twenty geometric figures (five each of triangles, circles, squares, and rectangles) (conditions), the learner (audience) will put an X through (behavior) at least four of the triangles, and not through more than one of the other remaining figures (degree). (Note that the parts of the objective do not have to be in ABCD order.)

- Given a list of twenty singular nouns ending in *f* or *fe* (condition), the learner (audience) will correctly write the plural (behavior) of at least fifteen (degree).

- The students in the computer section of Mr. Wilson's EMR class (audience), each using a separate computer (condition), will type (behavior) one paragraph with no grammatical or spelling errors (degree).

THE USES (AND ABUSES) OF INSTRUCTIONAL OBJECTIVES

An instructional objective is a tool, and like any tool (wrench, hammer, or computer) it is inert. Instructional objectives have little or no meaning in and of themselves (Dick and Carey 1990). Unfortunately, the writing of objectives has become for many school systems sufficient evidence that innovation is being practiced. Teachers are required to turn in objectives for each week, and they are sometimes written after the instruction has been completed. Differing methods of writing objectives are foisted upon teachers, each as the one correct way. The writing of an objective in isolation from instruction has no more effect upon the instructional process than purchasing a computer and locking it in the closet.

The use of behavioral objectives has come under attack since its inception. With the increase in popularity of cognitive science, these attacks have intensified and become more focused. Barone (1987, 18) describes two "miseducative" features of objectives. First, he claims that objectives "close" educational content and prohibit spontaneous learning outside of the predetermined objectives. Second, objectives "particularize" educational content into discrete information blocks that are unrelated to other content.

Popham (1987), responding in defense of the use of objectives, acknowledges that the focus on increasingly smaller segments of post-instruction behavior has proved frustrating to the teacher and a barrier to spontaneity. He cautions that less is more.

There is no doubt that a compromise area exists between the rabid behavioralists who promote the total mechanization of teaching and the radical humanists who would let the instructional experience "happen" with no planning whatsoever. Although there may be perfect teachers who can step into the classroom with no planning and guide the students through an excellent learning experience, most teachers, and therefore their students, would benefit from planning instruction. The instructional design process, including the creation of objectives, helps the teacher create a map of the instructional journey. As will be seen later in this chapter, Barone's concerns are largely answered by considering instructional objectives within the context of mental models.

Let's look at an example of the planning process. Suppose a teacher has selected the following statement as an instructional goal for a lesson: "The student will know about the recent presidents of the United States." How difficult would it be to select instructional materials and activities and to design an assessment based upon this goal statement? Would you use a videotape about John Kennedy? Would each student write a book report on a biography of a president? In reality, this goal statement opens up a Pandora's box of possibilities. Selection of materials and activities and the design of assessment become a matter of chance. The procedure becomes a little like someone preparing to take a trip who throws supplies into the car at random, looks into the car, and then decides the destination of the trip on the basis of what's in the car.

The creation of a goal-elaboration statement assists the teacher to describe more clearly what is desired. Here are two of the many possible goal-elaboration statements:

- The learner should be able to recall most of the presidents who served in the last half of the twentieth century and know their term of office.

- The student should understand the relationship between the presidency and the legislative branch of the federal government, with particular emphasis on the impact of the president's party being the minority party in Congress. The student should understand how the use of the veto can offset the effect of the majority party.

It is obvious that the teacher who creates the first elaboration statement has a significantly different instructional intent than does the teacher who creates the second. The next step in planning for instruction would be to determine what students would have to be able to do in order to demonstrate that the goal had been met. That next step is writing instructional objectives.

There are numerous ways in which the students can demonstrate that the goal has been reached, though the arena is not as large as it would have been if the objectives had been derived from the original goal statement rather than the goal-elaboration statement. Possible instructional objectives for the preceding goal-elaboration statements follow:

- The learner will list at least six of the presidents since Coolidge and correctly list the dates of office for each.

- The learner will write an essay comparing the use of the veto by Lyndon Johnson, Richard Nixon, and Bill Clinton. The essay should describe a significant veto action by each president and the result of that action. The essay should contain an explanation of the impact that the president's party membership, in relation to the dominant party in Congress, had on the process and outcome.

The teacher can begin instruction based on the goal alone, based on a goal-elaboration statement, or based on the instructional objective. Many curriculum guides contain cryptic goal statements such as "The student will know about the recent presidents of the United States." Instruction is often based on such statements and often results in confusion and frustration. The process of elaborating goal statements and creating instructional objectives takes time and effort. Why should the effort be made? This expenditure of resources is worth it because the selection of instructional materials, strategies, and activities will be easier, with much more probability of success, if a goal-elaboration statement and instructional objectives are created.

It should be noted that instructional objectives play a critical part in distance education as well. A key consideration for the success of a distance learning environment is whether or not, and to what degree, instructional objectives can be met using different delivery technologies. Using today's advanced distance learning technologies it is possible to achieve instructional objectives without the presence of the instructor or without all learners being in one physical area. It is important to evaluate all instructional objectives associated with a course or learning module before considering whether, and to what degree, distance learning technologies are most effectively (for cost and instructional integrity) used to achieve those objectives (Belanger 2000).

CATEGORIES OF LEARNING

As stated previously, the most important use of a set of instructional objectives is as a guide to the selection of instructional materials, strategies, activities, and the design of assessment of student performance. This use can be greatly facilitated by creating categories of learning under which instructional objectives can be grouped and which require certain types of materials and activities.

Gagne (1975, 6) maintained that learning is a process that can be inferred to have occurred "when a change or modification in behavior occurs, which persists over relatively long periods during the life of the individual." Gagne (1972) grouped the outcomes of learning into five categories. For the sake of simplicity, these will be condensed into the following three categories:

1. *Intellectual skills.* This category involves types of learning in which the learner is required to "know" and to think or reason. Although not necessarily the most important learning outcome category, this has been the focus of the greatest amount of resource expenditure in education.

2. *Affective or attitudinal learning.* Many of the goals of instruction involve a change in attitude on the part of the student. This may be as complex as valuing democracy as a form of government or as simple as wanting to pay attention to an instructional message. The teaching of values, although a source of controversy, is extremely important in the educational process.

3. *Motor skills.* Motor skills are an important part of a person's behavioral repertoire. Not only are they important for a satisfactory physical existence, they are required for the performance of many jobs and are prerequisite to basic forms of communication such as writing and typing.

With regard to Web-based learning, the three categories remain intact. For example, an objective might describe the behavior of voluntarily visiting a Web site that provides ways in which individuals can address local water pollution. One example of a lower level psychomotor skill that can be improved in distance learning is typing. Higher-level motor skills include using multimedia technologies that develop motor skills in hazardous environments. (For example, aircraft simulators allow students to make and learn from errors in a simulator, where in real life the mistake might cost them their life.) Each of these categories of learning will now be covered in more depth.

Intellectual Skills

In any course, there are likely to be hundreds of possible instructional objectives. Given the rapidly expanding base of human knowledge, the number of possible objectives is almost limitless.

It has been long recognized that learning, whether it is described in a formal manner or not, varies as to complexity. The level of complexity will, of course, have an impact on how this learning is to be achieved. There have been several attempts to group intellectual skills into categories by complexity so that these categories can be related to instructional decisions. The premise upon which these attempts rest is that categories of learning outcomes cut across subject boundaries. For example, the activity of conjugating regular Spanish verbs in the present tense and borrowing in subtraction represent two different subjects, but they both can be the result of the same kind of mental process.

Probably the most widely used of these taxonomies is that of Bloom (1956). Although this taxonomy is among the easiest to use initially and can be very useful, the connection between the taxonomy category and material and activity selection is not as readily apparent as with some other taxonomies. This is especially true for the higher levels.

Gagne, Briggs, and Wager (1988) posited a continuum of learning outcomes that, although seemingly more complex at first sight, has the advantage of being directly tied to the selection of materials, strategies, and activities. This system considers not only the content to be learned but also the thinking process that must take place during learning.

Merrill, Li, and Jones (1990b) used many of the concepts from cognitive science to create a system of knowledge representation that places an even higher emphasis on the internal processes that take place during learning. According to the authors, an intelligent-adviser system can be created and used on a computer to provide real-time connections between the content, the learner, and instructional strategies.

LEVELS OF INTELLECTUAL SKILL LEARNING

Humans learn from the moment they are born and continue until they die. The purpose of instruction is to facilitate this learning. Instructional designers have come to realize that humans are not passive learners who mirror the instruction exactly. Rather, learners "construct" what they learn from an almost infinite set of stimuli and make connections between current and previous learning.

The best way for students to construct what they learn is through abstractions, and the most powerful tool by which these abstractions are used is language. In the play, *The Miracle Worker*, Anne Sullivan says, "She has to learn that everything has its name! That words can be her *eyes, . . .* what is she without words? With them she can think, have ideas, be reached, there's not a thought or fact in the world that can't be hers" (Gibson, 1957, 79).

It is true that language is not necessary in learning to carry out high-level tasks. Through extensive experience but with a very limited vocabulary, a primitive farmer could learn to decide when is the best time to plant and to predict rain. The same farmer could learn to identify poisonous plants and to decide the best place to look for underground water.

Language, and the ability to create abstractions and models, does speed up the rate of learning. Language is also the catalyst in the instructional process. A student can learn by observing in an apprenticeship role, but the process of learning is facilitated markedly through the use of symbols. Leamonson (1992, 8), in a response to a proposal to emphasize oral culture, warned that movement in the direction of a secondary orality was regressive: "This is regressive because only literate cultures can deal with metaphor, analogy, and abstraction."

The model in figure 9.1 shows the levels of intellectual skill learning. This model represents, from the bottom up, the process that a learner goes through in acquiring increasingly more complex intellectual skills. Although learning at all levels might occur at practically any age, progress up the levels is usually developmental. The bulk of learning in a very young child takes place at the lowest levels, and the reverse is true for normal adults.

The model combines aspects of several models of learning, most particularly that of Robert Gagne. When we consider this or any other model, we should keep in mind that instructional science is still relatively new and is far from perfect. We can only estimate the process through which humans learn and the best way that we can help this process. Indeed, there are those who propose that we scale back the process of diagnosing and planning in favor of cognitive apprenticeships (Brown, Collins, and Dugdid 1989). Despite the limits of models of intellectual skills, it is our premise that we must teach children and young adults to think and reason at a high level, and that we must continue to investigate the foundation of these higher-order skills.

ASSOCIATIVE LEARNING

Imagine a child, who is just learning to speak, standing with an adult in the front yard of their home when a bright red dump truck passes by. The adult points to the truck and says, "Truck!" This occurs several times until, one time, the child sees the same red dump truck, points, and says, "Truck!" This child has *associated* the *particular* bright red dump truck with the sound *truck.* This is a very elementary type of learning in which the learner associates or "chains" two or more words or images. It is important to remember that the learner need not *understand* the meaning of the words. Listening to a child say the pledge of allegiance or sing the national anthem ("Jose can you see?") often provides an opportunity to view this type of learning. Learning to recite an unfamiliar poem in an unfamiliar language is another example of associative learning.

Fig. 9.1. Levels of intellectual skill learning

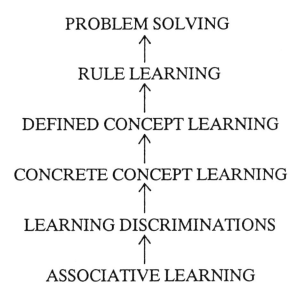

PROBLEM SOLVING
↑
RULE LEARNING
↑
DEFINED CONCEPT LEARNING
↑
CONCRETE CONCEPT LEARNING
↑
LEARNING DISCRIMINATIONS
↑
ASSOCIATIVE LEARNING

Sample instructional objectives:

- When shown a *particular* picture of a square, the learner will say "square."

Notice the emphasis on *particular*. In this objective, the student is expected to associate one certain figure with the response "square." If the figure is 2 by 2 inches and blue, then that is the only figure that the student should be expected to respond to. At this very elementary level of learning, the learner is not expected to understand "squareness."

- When prompted with the question, "What is the area of a triangle?" the learner will respond, "One-half the altitude times the base."

This objective does not call for the student to be able to know what a triangle, altitude, or base is. The learner does not have to know how to find the area of a triangle. The learner must simply verbally respond to a verbal stimulus in a certain way.

This type of learning is often known as "learning facts." It is elementary, a prerequisite for all the other levels.

LEARNING DISCRIMINATIONS

Consider our child and the bright red dump truck again. If the truck is followed by a bright red minivan, the child does not say "truck" for the minivan. Why? The child can *discriminate* between the two objects. This discrimination does not require that the child understand the essence of trucks or minivans but rather that the child knows that the minivan is not the same object as the truck.

Gagne, Briggs, and Wager (1988, 57) define a discrimination as the "capability of making different responses to stimuli that differ from each other along one or more physical dimensions." At this elementary level of learning, the learner is able to react differently to a variety of stimuli without necessarily understanding those stimuli. If a student is shown a slide of five healthy cells and one cancerous one, the student might be able to point out the cell that is different. The student might not know which cells are healthy or even that what he or she is seeing are cells. The student simply would be able to recognize that one was different from the others.

Sample instructional objectives:

- Shown the following set of shapes (see fig. 9.2), the learner will point to the one that is different from the others.

The learner does not have to know what a square or a parallelogram is to meet this instructional objective.

- Given three examples of dictionaries and three of encyclopedias, the learner will make two piles, each pile containing all the books of each type.

Fig. 9.2. Figures for discrimination task

Again, the learner does not have to know what a dictionary is to meet this objective. The learner would just have to be able to recognize the physical similarities and differences so that he or she can group dictionaries with dictionaries and encyclopedias with encyclopedias

CONCRETE CONCEPT LEARNING

Now imagine that our child has had a wide variety of trucks pointed out, each accompanied by the sound "truck." The child has learned to associate each specific instance with the sound. Then one day, the child sees a new example of a truck and identifies it as a truck. If the child can do this with regularity, and with a wide variety of trucks, we can say that the concrete concept "truck" has been learned.

In acquiring a concrete concept, the learner relates direct experiences to words. Andre (1986, 187), in discussing concrete concepts, uses a metaphor of making black-and-white silhouettes of various shapes of birds. If all of these silhouettes were made the same size and then put together, the shadow that they would throw might represent the concrete concept "bird." Andre uses the term *prototype* for this very basic-level concept.

Another way of thinking of concrete concepts is as symbols. When a concept is mentioned, what picture comes to mind? If the concrete concept is "square," perhaps one thinks of the face of a bright red cube that was in one's room as a child.

Note that learning a concrete concept requires that learning at the lower levels has taken place. The learner must have *associated* any number of examples of the concept with the name and must have *discriminated* examples from non-examples. Learners can be said to have learned a concrete concept when they can *select examples of the concept set from non-examples, having previously seen neither.*

Sample instructional objectives:

- Given five photographs of oak leaves and five photographs of other kinds of leaves, when requested to pick out the oak leaves, the learner will do so. (All ten examples are novel to the learner.)

- Upon hearing ten words in Spanish, each containing either a single or double *r*, the student will indicate whether the *r* is single or double. (The words will be novel and will be pronounced by various persons.)

- Given ten photographs of protists such as flagellates and sporozoans, the learner will point out the nucleus in each. (All ten examples are novel to the learner.)

DEFINED CONCEPT LEARNING

Andre (1986, 188) points out that the use of the prototype to determine members and non-members of a concept class works well for clear-cut examples and non-examples. However, for ambiguous cases, the prototype may not be sufficient. (Is a saddle a chair?) As learners become exposed to many and varied examples and non-examples, they will tend to build mental models of concepts. Such a model is often called a schema (plural: schemata) and might contain particularly important examples and non-examples, definitions of the concepts, and procedures for classifying the concepts.

A definition as part of a schema is critical for concepts that do not have an experiential basis but rather are based on semantics. For example, a brother can be pointed out, but the defined concept "brother" must be learned through the formulation of a definition. One might possess a multitude of concrete images of brothers. Perhaps one has a prototype brother in mind—for example, Boys Town's famous "He ain't heavy, he's my brother" picture. There is still a need to possess this concept at a higher level through more abstraction.

Fig. 9.3. Schema for the defined concept "transportation"

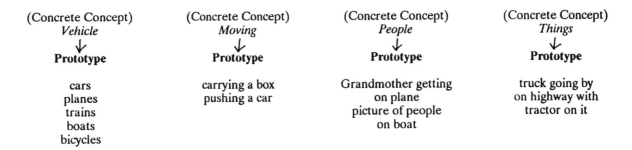

SCHEMA FOR THE DEFINED CONCEPT "TRANSPORTATION"

Transportation are the vehicles used for moving people and things.

(Concrete Concept) *Vehicle* ↓ **Prototype**	(Concrete Concept) *Moving* ↓ **Prototype**	(Concrete Concept) *People* ↓ **Prototype**	(Concrete Concept) *Things* ↓ **Prototype**
cars planes trains boats bicycles	carrying a box pushing a car	Grandmother getting on plane picture of people on boat	truck going by on highway with tractor on it

Our child, now somewhat older, is introduced to the concept "transportation." On a concrete level, specific modes of transportation can be identified as being examples of transportation, but the concept is not truly mastered until the child can state the definition, separate examples from non-examples, and possess each of the concepts within the definition. In the example in figure 9.3, the concepts in the definition are possessed at the concrete concept level, and the possession of these concepts, along with the definition, indicates the possession of the defined concept "transportation."

The *minimum* criteria for learning a defined concept, therefore, are as follows:

1. *Selecting examples of the concept set from non-examples,* having previously seen neither. Example: A student is given pictures and descriptions of a mammal, a fish, a bird, and two reptiles, none of which have been seen before. The student selects the mammal as an example of the concept "mammal."

2. *Stating the definition of the concept.* Example: A mammal has hair and a temperature-regulation system, gives birth to live young, and nurses its young.

3. *Possessing the relevant concepts in the definition.* For example, to possess the defined concept "aunt," the learner must

   a. select examples of an aunt from non-examples,

   b. be able to state the definition of an aunt, and

   c. possess the concepts "sister" and "mother."

Note that the concepts "sister" and "mother" can be possessed at the concrete level or as defined concepts. If they are possessed at the defined level, then the schema would include definitions for the concepts "sister" and "mother."

Sample instructional objectives:

• The learner will state the definition of a moon and will select from a list of descriptions of objects in space those that are moons.

• Given descriptions of ten common household products, not previously covered in class, the learner will identify each as an acid, base, or salt.

Notice in the second example that the learner is not required to state the definition of the concepts. Rather, it is presumed that knowledge of the definition is required to carry out the objective. It is also important to realize that the student must possess each of the concepts in the definition, either at the concrete or the defined level.

One goal of instruction is to assist the learner in enhancing the elaborateness and richness of the schema for a particular concept. Tessmer, Wilson, and Driscoll (1990) point out that concepts should be regarded as tools, and not simply as something to be memorized. They provide several possibilities through which concept attainment can be determined. By using these methods, we can determine the richness and depth of the learner's schema for a concept. These methods include:

- *Using the concept in conversation, writing, and argumentation* (Brown, Collins, and Dugdid 1989). Example: The student will write a one-page paper describing the life cycle of a frog and will use the term *adaptation* correctly.

- *Simulating or role-playing the concept* (Tessmer, Jonassen, and Caverly 1989). Example: The learner will write original biographies and job descriptions of the leaders in fictional countries that are dictatorships, democracies, and oligarchies.

- *Making inferences about membership of the concept in a larger class* (Anderson and Ortony 1975). Example: The learner will answer, and justify the answers, for the following questions using Internet sources: Can a friend be an enemy? Can a promise be a threat? Can a weed be a flower?

- *Making inferences about properties or functions of the concept that are not directly given as defining attributes.* Example: The learner will answer, and justify the answer to, the following question: Can a baseball float?

- *Using the concept in an analogy.* Example: The learner will complete the following analogy: Photosynthesis is to phototropism as food is to _____ (answer: movement).

RULE LEARNING

If our child from the previous examples is now an adolescent and is taught how to calculate the energy output from the same volume of different fuels (methanol, gasoline, and liquefied petroleum gas), he or she would be learning a rule. A rule is a statement that describes the relationship between concepts. Rules enable us to generalize about our environment and to make predictions.

Being able to state the rule (associative learning) is usually part of the demonstration that the rule has been mastered, but stating the rule is certainly not sufficient. Rules are learned when the mental models, or schemata, of the relevant concepts are connected. Therefore, the rule itself serves as an activating mechanism for the connection to be made between the schemata. It should be obvious, then, that the more thoroughly the component concepts have been mastered (the richer their schemata) the more powerful the rule that connects these concepts will be.

Consider the rule $F = M \times A$. If a student was asked to find F, given $M = 10$ kilograms and $A = 1$ meter/sec^2, the student could answer, "The force is 10 k/m/s^2" and could do so with only a surface understanding of the concepts force, mass, and acceleration (with poorly developed schemata for these concepts). However, a student with schemata for force, mass, and acceleration (see fig. 9.4) could form a mental model of the rule and thus have a firm understanding of the rule.

Notice that in the schema in figure 9.4, the concept's force and mass are possessed at the concrete level. Because acceleration is possessed at the defined concept level, each concept in the definition must be addressed to ensure that they are possessed by the learner.

Fig. 9.4. Schema for a rule

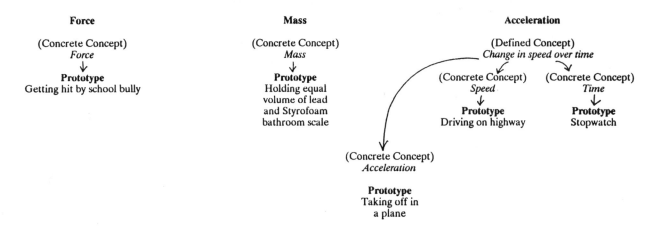

SCHEMA FOR THE RULE

The net force of an object is determined by the product of its mass times its acceleration

Force

(Concrete Concept)
Force
↓
Prototype
Getting hit by school bully

Mass

(Concrete Concept)
Mass
↓
Prototype
Holding equal
volume of lead
and Styrofoam
bathroom scale

Acceleration

(Defined Concept)
Change in speed over time

(Concrete Concept)   (Concrete Concept)
Speed   *Time*
↓   ↓
Prototype   **Prototype**
Driving on highway   Stopwatch

(Concrete Concept)
Acceleration
↓
Prototype
Taking off in
a plane

Sample instructional objectives:

- Given the height of a building, the learner will be able to calculate the speed at which an object will hit the ground when dropped from the top.

The learner, it is presumed, has been given the rule "The velocity of a freely falling object will be equal to the time it has been falling in seconds times 32 feet per second squared (32 ft/sec^2)" at a previous time. The learner must recall the rule and apply it. The goal of this rule acquisition is to enable the learner to relate the schemata for the concepts used in the rule.

- Given a computer "map location" Web site (e.g., MapQuest), the learner will answer questions regarding direction, distance, and size. Examples: Find the Black River. How many bridges cross it? How many towns over 5,000 population are east of the north/south railroad?

Again, this objective could be taught as a very elaborate chain of "facts" learned at the associative level. Rule learning for this objective would assume that the learner possessed well-developed concept schemata for "river," "town," "city," "bridge," "population," and many other concrete and defined concepts. The goal for this learning enterprise is to establish rules that relate these concepts to symbols on a computer location map.

- Given a tablecloth and all place-setting materials, the learner will set the table correctly.

At first glance, this seems like a very rudimentary rule. But if the forks, knives, spoons, plates, and so on that are used are ones the learner has not seen before, then the learner is relating the concrete concepts for these items according to a rule. This type of rule is a procedure, or what Gagne and Merrill (1990, 27) call a "manifesting enterprise." In learning this rule, the student connects the concepts in the applicable manner to form a "master" schema for this type of behavior. This schema could then be connected to others involving rules for determining selection of dishware and menu, seating of guests, introductions, and so on.

Note that just as a definition can consist of concrete concepts, a rule may be a combination of concrete concepts.

PROBLEM SOLVING

In this type of learning, learners are not provided with the rule that activates the mechanism to connect the concept schemata. Rather, learners arrive at this connection on their own. Of course, strategic teaching may provide a variety of levels of guidance to position the learner to make this connection.

There continues to be a constant call for increasing the learner's involvement in the higher level, or critical, thinking that is required to meet problem-solving-level objectives. Unfortunately, what is actually tested in both elementary and secondary schools can often be achieved by low-level learning. Perhaps if more teachers were aware of the levels of learning, more would strive to include the higher levels.

Sample instructional objectives:

- Based on the chemical requirements for photosynthesis and respiration, the student will explain why the leaves of many plants fold up at night.

Students should relate the concepts within the chemical processes to the appropriate portions of their schema for "night."

- The learner will write an essay relating John Kennedy's personal prejudices and his policies as president.

In order for this objective to be at the problem-solving level, learners must not be repeating a list of statements provided at an earlier date. Learners must possess elaborate concept schemata for personal prejudices and Kennedy's presidential policies, as well as for many other concepts. They must then "connect" these on their own to arrive at their conclusions.

- Given a list of single nouns ending in y and the correct plural of each, the learner will arrive at the rules for forming the plural when the y is preceded by a vowel and by a consonant.

A powerful characteristic of the levels of intellectual skill learning is that they provide a model for both the developmental stages of learning and for short-term learning. It should be clear that in order for a high-level objective to be reached, the instructional designer must be certain that the appropriate foundation consisting of the lower levels is in place. Each level is a prerequisite for all of the higher ones. In order for learners to master a defined concept, they might have to master any number of concrete concepts, discriminations, and associative learning tasks. The defined concept, once mastered, might in turn be used in conjunction with other concepts as the basis for rule learning and problem solving. Learning can be seen as a natural progression of complexity and sophistication.

COGNITIVE STRATEGIES AND METACOGNITION

Suppose a student is faced with the task of being able to recall the names of ten states and the chief crop of each state. Many learners would employ some type of cognitive strategy that would help them in this task. For example, one student might make drawings containing the state name on top of the crop. Another student might make up a silly dialogue, such as

Person A: "What state has the potato as its main crop?

Person B: "I don't know."

Person A: "You're right. Idaho!"

These actions are examples of cognitive strategies or of activating "learning" tools without being directed to do so. Gagne and Medsker (1996) describe several varieties of cognitive strategies. These are:

Attending. In a very complex environment, successful learners might develop methods to make sure that they are paying attention to the correct stimuli. This strategy might be particularly important if the instruction is over the Web and the learner is not in a classroom but in an environment with competing stimuli.

Encoding. These are strategies by which the learner rehearses, elaborates upon information, and organizes information. Such activities include note taking, mental practice, outlining, paraphrasing, and summarizing.

Retrieval. These include mnemonic devices such as the examples given above on state names and crops.

Employing a cognitive strategy may be part of a larger process called metacognition. A student who possesses a number of cognitive strategies, knows that he or she possesses these, and uses them selectively in the learning process, is involved in metacognition. Metacognitively controlled implementation of cognitive strategies can have a significant impact on reaching instructional objectives at all levels. In fact, examples of instructional objectives at the concrete and defined concept levels given earlier employ cognitive strategies of elaboration and metaphor as part of the instructional objective. Metacognition and cognitive strategies will be addressed in more detail in chapter 11, "Strategies and Activities Development."

INSTRUCTIONAL ENTERPRISES

Instructional design has always had a firm foundation in behavioral psychology. The instructional designer performed instructional analyses that divided the content into smaller and smaller entities. This division allowed the instructional designer to clarify the sought-after behavior more precisely and therefore was an advantage. Unfortunately, this process often resulted in a loss of a sense of the integrated whole being pursued in the instructional process (Merrill, Li, and Jones 1990a). Through an excess concentration on the trees, instructional designers were losing a sense of the forest. To extend the metaphor, instructional designers were sometimes concentrating on the individual cells of the leaves and losing touch with the relationship of the cell to the rest of the forest.

Cognitive psychology recently has had an influence on instructional design, pushing the designer to look for connections while analyzing instructional content. This second generation of instructional design emphasizes that connections and elaborations are necessary to build the mental models required for higher-level learning (Merrill, Li, and Jones 1990b). There are several strong theoretical foundations to guide instructional design for the Web-based learning environment. For example, Spiro, Feltovich, Jacobson and Coulson (1991) argue that there are special requirements for attaining advanced learning goals given the barriers that often result from how knowledge is organized. They describe the value of a crisscross landscape, multiple dimensions of knowledge representation, and multiple interconnections across knowledge components—all elements of learning that are readily supported by hypertext domains and communication facilities of the Web. Jonassen and Reeves (1996) use the term "cognitive tools" to describe computer-based learning applications that assist learners in representing their own knowledge of the external world. Cognitive tools when used appropriately can engage learners in higher-order thinking and learning, providing opportunities for the acquired knowledge to be generalized to new and alternative learning situations.

This push for connections can be seen in the writings of Robert Gagne, upon whose work the most widely applied instructional design models have been based. Gagne and Merrill (1990) observe that the process of working backward from goals to instructional events has been, and still is, a very useful technique. They point out that "when the comprehensiveness of topics reaches a level such as often occurs in practice, instructional design is forced to deal with multiple objectives and *the relationship among these objectives*" (emphasis added, p. 24).

We will employ a construct called an instructional enterprise to describe the network of instructional objectives that represents the learning of anything beyond the simplest of content. This construct is based upon that of an "enterprise scenario" put forth by Gagne and Merrill (1990).

A useful metaphor for an instructional enterprise is that it should represent a map of the mind of someone who has met the specified instructional goal. This map contains all of the schemata necessary, and the links between these schemata. To illustrate an instructional enterprise, let us take a typical instructional goal and develop an enterprise for achieving it. Our goal statement is: The student will be familiar with three common forms of government.

Because this goal is written in a cryptic manner, we would need to develop a goal-elaboration statement. One such elaboration might be: The learner should understand that the factor that most significantly determines the type of government that exists is where the authority or power resides; that the formal government structure might not be the "real" government. Therefore, the learner must understand power in depth. The learner must also be familiar with the most typical organizational patterns in which power can be vested (dictatorship, oligarchy, and democracy).

The instructional designer translates this goal elaboration into a "primary" instructional objective, which represents the performance that demonstrates attainment of the goal. A possible primary instructional objective is: Given nine descriptions of governments, novel to the learner, the learner will identify each as a dictatorship, oligarchy, or democracy. Sample description: In this country, ten families own 80 percent of the land and 75 percent of the manufacturing capability. The president is not a member of any of the families. The supreme commander of the armed forces is the head of the richest family.

This primary instructional objective represents the defined concept-level of learning. In fact, this objective brings together three defined concepts (dictatorship, oligarchy, and democracy). Each of these concepts is a schema cluster, or a grouping of schemata that form the model of that concept in the learner's mind. Notice in figure 9.5 that each of these schema clusters contains a definition of the concept, learned at the associative level. Each cluster also contains a concrete concept of the type of government that contains the prototypes of the concept stored in the learner's memory.

Each of these concepts is linked to a schema cluster for the defined concept "government," which is linked to a schema cluster for the defined concept "power." There is a further link to other defined concepts, including "law enforcement," "military," and "economics."

The information on the left side of the instructional enterprise model indicates that each of the schema clusters for the type of government is linked to a variety of schema clusters for defined and concrete concepts such as "one," "people," "share," and "family."

CREATING THE INSTRUCTIONAL ENTERPRISE

The first step, of course, is to create a goal-elaboration statement and a resultant primary instructional objective. The instructional designer then creates a map containing the schema clusters for each concept and their connections, which must be present to realize this objective. Each schema cluster will be headed by an enabling objective that is a description of the performance required to demonstrate possession of the schema cluster.

Initially, the process of determining schema clusters and their relationships can be confusing. Imagining that one is the learner and being sensitive to the thought processes that occur is helpful to many instructional designers. Talking the learning process through with someone else can also be useful. Most people find that creating a visual model of the instructional enterprise is necessary. Using index cards for each instructional objective provides flexibility. There are many models for representing learning in a spatial mode (Holley and Dansereau 1984).

Fig. 9.5. Instructional enterprise goal: Understand the three main types of governments

Goal Elaboration Statement: The learner should understand that the main determining factor of the type of government is where the power resides. Therefore, the student should understand power in depth. The student should also be familiar with the most typical organizational patterns in which power can be vested.

Primary Instructional Objective: Given nine descriptions novel to the learner, of a government, the learner will identify each as a dictatorship, oligarchy, or democracy. (Sample description: In this country, ten families own 80% of the land and 75% of the manufacturing. The president is not a family member of one of these families. The commander of the armed forces is the head of the most wealthy of the families.) (Rule Learning)

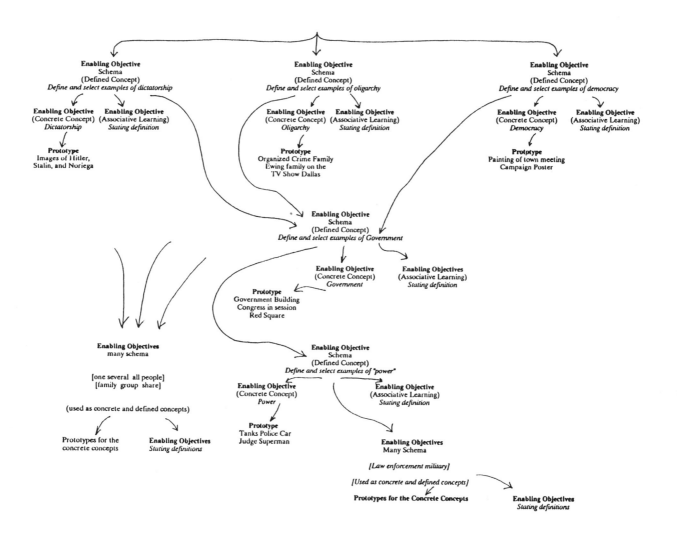

There are two characteristics of an instructional enterprise that the instructional designer should be aware of:

- The level of learning of the primary instructional objective is generally the highest level of any instructional objective in the enterprise. The network of schemata that represents an instructional enterprise generally takes the form of an inverted V. The model of the enterprise generally branches downward to contain smaller networks of instructional objectives that support the schemata above. These enabling objectives can be at the same level as the primary objective, but not higher.

- The instructional designer must limit the number of enabling-objective schema clusters in the enterprise. Taken to its ultimate conclusion, the design of every instructional enterprise would result in a virtually infinite number of enabling-objective schema clusters. A study of figure 9.5 can yield many possible schema clusters that were not included. The concept of an instructional enterprise as a map is useful here. The mapmaker must decide which items are included in the map and chooses only those that are deemed necessary for the map user to reach the objective. The designer of the instructional enterprise must also carefully choose the schemata that are represented.

Let's take a minute to review: The instructional enterprise is the collection of all the schema clusters required to master the primary instructional objective. A schema cluster is the map for each concept. Note that the schema cluster for a defined concept could consist of a number of smaller schema clusters, as in our example for "aunt."

A prototype is the synthesis of experience regarding the concrete concept. It may be in the form of an image and is usually nonverbal. All schemata should terminate with concrete concepts and prototypes, though these might be assumed to be possessed before instruction. The place of concrete concepts and prototypes as the foundation of learning is the rationale for providing young children with an experiential base.

ENTRANCE SKILLS AND ORDER OF INSTRUCTION

Once the instructional designer has created the instructional enterprise, the next step is to determine which enabling objectives must be taught and which can be assumed to be already possessed by the learner. The latter are termed entrance skills and are included and retained in the instructional enterprise to remind the instructional designer that these skills are essential to mastering the remaining objectives. For example, in the instructional enterprise in figure 9.5, many of the concepts on the left side (one, all, group, etc.) would probably be considered entrance skills. For concrete concepts, the instructional designer must make the decision as to whether an adequate prototype exists. If the instruction is aimed at predicting various types of precipitation, does the student have an experiential base for the concrete concept "snow?" The presence or absence of this base will determine whether the concept is designated an entrance skill.

The instructional designer, of course, does not designate entrance skills in isolation. They are designated upon careful consideration of the learner. For a particularly crucial entrance skill, an assessment activity might be used to determine possession of the skill.

The final step is to determine in which order the instructional objectives are to be taught. Often, the instructional sequence proceeds from the base of the enterprise upward, covering the foundational enabling objectives first. Another tack would be to introduce the associative-level definition objectives first, followed by a discussion of the prototypes of the concepts that each student possesses. In one of the earlier examples, students might learn the definition of the three types of governments and then describe and discuss the images that each of these concepts evokes.

Affective or Attitudinal Learning

Attitudes can be viewed as either means or ends (Anderson and Anderson 1982). Each learner will possess an attitude toward what is to be learned, and toward the process by which it is to be learned. For example, some students might be very interested in learning how snakes lose their skins; others might not. Some students might be motivated in a positive manner if they can work with peers; other students might find this a negative influence.

Educators might want to instill an attitude. In this case, the attitude is considered as an instructional objective, and instruction must be designed to achieve this objective.

Writing instructional objectives for affective instructional goals presents a tremendous challenge. Attitudinal goals seem to be more what Mager (1972) called "fuzzy" than any other type, for human emotions are very difficult to define. In writing any attitude goal in precise and observable terms, there is the danger that the essence of the attitude will be lost. Nevertheless, the instructional design procedure calls for the delineation of instructional objectives that can be judged as met or not met by some agreed-upon criteria.

In real-life settings, learners often learn through interactions with those who are more experienced. The design of situated learning environments benefits from the development of instructional activities involving the observation of, and participation in, what are ostensibly real-life episodes (Collins 1988; Collins, Brown, and Newman 1989; Lave and Wenger 1991; Resnick 1987).

Based upon the procedure put forth by Mager (1972), the following steps represent a relatively simple method for creating affective instructional objectives.

1. The attitude goal is formulated. Instructional goals are usually in unmeasurable form, and attitude goals are no exception. Example: The student will develop a value for a litter-free environment.

2. The instructional designer brainstorms observable actions that a student who possesses the value would or would not perform. Example:

Would do

pick up litter of others

dispose of own litter properly

join an anti-litter club

choose a topic dealing with the dangers of litter

volunteer for after-school cleanup team

donate money for trash baskets for schoolyard

clean up room at home

Would not do

throw litter in inappropriate places

tip over wastebaskets

make fun of students who dispose of litter properly

3. The instructional designer writes an instructional objective based upon the actions derived in step 2. This objective can contain one or more actions from the would-do and would-not-do categories. These actions would be selected as a result of considering many factors, including ease of implementation and degree of representation of the value indicated. Example: On three successive Thursdays, after eating their ice cream snacks, at least 90 percent of the students will properly dispose of their sticks and wrappers.

At this point, it should be noted that the instructional objective will not be truly representative of the original goal if the instruction is directed specifically at the objective. In this case, if all of the instruction was directed at disposing of ice cream sticks and wrappers, obtaining the behavior described in the instructional goal would *not* indicate that the original goal had been achieved. Rather, the instruction should be more generally directed at the value of a litter-free environment.

Motor Skills

Motor skills are best approached by analyzing the behavior implied in the goal and breaking this behavior down into two categories: *component-part skills* and *executive subroutine* (Gagne, Briggs, and Wager 1988). The component-part skills are the individual actions that must occur in order for the behavior to occur.

For the motor skills instructional objective "The learner will come about in a sloop-rigged sailing craft so that momentum is maintained," the following component-part skills are involved:

releasing main sheet from leeward side cleat

swinging tiller hard to leeward

ducking boom

shifting weight to opposite side of boat

dealing mainsheet to new leeward side

Each of the component-part skills might also have component-part skills and subroutines. The executive subroutine is the knowledge of the order in which the component-part skills are executed. The ability to perform the component-part skills without knowing their proper order is not sufficient. (Anyone who has been struck in the head by a boom knows this.)

For motor skills instructional objectives, the component-part skills and executive subroutine become hierarchically arranged enabling objectives. Notice that enabling objectives for motor skills instructional objectives always include at least one intellectual skill/verbal information type of objective.

INSTRUCTIONAL OBJECTIVES AND INFORMATION SKILLS

Chapter 7 contained examples of determining the content of the information skills to be taught with a particular unit. The output of the needs assessment procedure to determine the subject content served as the input for a similar process to determine the appropriate information skills. The more complex the content, the higher the level of information skills that would generally be required.

Now that we have covered the instructional objectives step, it should be evident that goals translated into performance objectives are a more powerful tool for selecting information skills than the goals themselves. The level of learning targeted by each objective, and the relationship of the objective to other objectives, should provide considerable guidance to the school library media specialist in selecting information skills.

LEVELS OF INVOLVEMENT BY THE SCHOOL LIBRARY MEDIA SPECIALIST AT THE INSTRUCTIONAL OBJECTIVES STEP

The instructional objectives step involves creating goal-elaboration statements, translating these into primary instructional objectives, identifying enabling objectives and entrance skills, classifying objectives as to category of learning, and arranging the objectives into a teaching hierarchy.

The Initial Level

The school library media specialist can assist teachers in the instructional objectives step at the initial level by gathering and making available collections of instructional objectives. These collections can come from local and commercial sources. The school library media specialist can also make professional materials available that will help teachers improve their ability to perform this step. The following are recommended titles:

Dick, W., and L. Carey. 2000. *The Systematic Design of Instruction.* 5th ed. Boston: Addison-Wesley.

Gagne, R. M., L. J. Briggs, and W. W. Wager. 1992. *Principles of Instructional Design.* 4th ed. New York: HBJ College and School Division.

Horton, W. K. 2000. *Designing Web-Based Training: How to Teach Anyone Anything Anywhere Anytime.* Hoboken, N.J.: John Wiley and Sons.

Mager, R. F. 1997. *Goal Analysis: How to Clarify Your Goals So You Can Actually Achieve Them.* 3rd ed. Atlanta, Ga.: The Center for Effective Performance.

———. 1997. *Preparing Instructional Objectives: A Critical Tool in the Development of Effective Instruction.* 3rd ed. Atlanta, Ga.: The Center for Effective Performance.

Roblyer, M. D. 1999. *Integrating Educational Technology into Teaching.* 2nd ed. Upper Saddle River, N.J.: Prentice-Hall.

The Moderate Level

Instructional development consultation by the school library media specialist at the moderate level consists of informal assistance, often provided spontaneously as the result of a request by the teacher. At the instructional objectives step, there are many possibilities for such assistance. Writing instructional objectives is probably the aspect of instructional technology that has made the greatest inroads into actual educational practice.

Unfortunately, this movement has too often been the result of coercion by higher-ups who have viewed instructional objectives as an end rather than as a means. As a result, teachers often regard instructional objectives with distrust and even hostility. (One teacher I worked with called them "behavioral objections.") The school library media specialist can help counter this attitude by demonstrating that instructional objectives are but one step in the process of designing instruction, and that, in isolation, they are of limited use. The school library media specialist can also illustrate the usefulness of instructional objectives by using them in planning information skills lessons and programming.

One of the advantages of the emphasis on instructional objectives for a school library media specialist planning to target the moderate level is that there are usually several teachers looking for assistance. Such assistance may include helping a teacher write an initial instructional objective from a goal. Writing instructional objectives is very difficult for some teachers. Explaining the ABCD format often helps. Remember to concentrate on the action portion of the objective and try to keep the objectives as simple as possible.

A SCENARIO

The teacher, Marlene Wilder, has been at the school for nineteen years. The principal, following a directive from the central office, has instructed all teachers to submit instructional objectives in writing each Friday afternoon for the following week's instruction. Marlene has repeatedly had her objectives criticized as "improper." This conversation takes place on Thursday, right after school, in the library media center. Marcia Billings is the school library media specialist.

Marlene: Hello, Marcia. Mind if I stop in here for a few minutes to rest?

Marcia: Hello, Marlene. No, make yourself at home. Cheer up. Remember, tomorrow is Friday.

Marlene: I'm afraid I don't like Fridays anymore. Not since we had to start turning in those instructional objectives— yechh!

Marcia: You and objectives don't get along? What seems to be the problem?

Marlene: I have tried! But whatever I do, you-know-who isn't satisfied.

Marcia: Do you happen to have any with you? Maybe I could take a look.

Marlene: I was hoping you'd say that. Here, this is what I'm going to turn in tomorrow. Now, what is wrong with "To teach the students about Haiku poetry"?

Marcia: Nothing is wrong with teaching the students about Haiku poetry. That sounds like a great goal for a week's lessons. I think the problem is that instructional objectives need to be written in terms of what the student will do.

Marlene: That's easy! The student will learn about Haiku poetry.

Marcia: Well, it's on the right track, but those instructional objectives want more. They need to be written in terms of student actions that can be observed. In other words, after your students have learned about Haiku poems, what will they be able to do?

Marlene: Hmm. . . . Pass a test?

Marcia: I hope so. But what would they need to do to pass the test?

Marlene: That's difficult. I usually don't make up the test until after the lesson is over. I suppose they should be able to tell me a little of the history of Haiku poetry, like where it comes from and what it was used for. They should know the rules for writing a Haiku poem, and they should be able to write one, given a picture to describe. How about that?

Marcia: Terrific. I would write those down and turn them in tomorrow. They might come back with some negative comments, but they are pretty good. Come and see me next week before Thursday afternoon, and we can work some more.

Marlene: I will, and thank you. I hated not to look forward to Friday.

Notice that the school library media specialist did not insist that the teacher write a full-blown instructional objective but rather concentrated on the action portion. Teachers will often balk at going from not knowing how to write objectives at all to producing a very technical rendition. Also, school library media specialists often do not have the time at any one sitting to cover the entire topic.

The school library media specialist may also assist by helping a teacher classify an instructional objective as to type and level of learning or by helping a teacher select instructional objectives with higher levels of learning.

A SCENARIO

The teacher, Betty Carlisle, is one of the best at Bridgewood High School. She is a regular client of Bill Walby, the school library media specialist.

Betty: Bill, I'm hoping you can help me with a problem. You know we've started writing instructional objectives for our lessons. I thought it was a good idea because it really seemed to help me structure my lessons. The kids seem to like it, too. I give them a copy of the objectives for the week, and we go over them and discuss them.

Bill: That's a great idea! Particularly the discussion part. But you don't seem so convinced now.

Betty: Well, I can't seem to vary my student actions. You know, "write, list, state." There must be more to life than that.

Bill:	There should be. Tell me one of your instructional objectives.
Betty:	Okay. We're studying the circulation system now. "The learner will list the four subchambers of the heart."
Bill:	That sounds like associative level. How about, "The learner will write a statement describing the benefits of the heart being located where it is. In this statement, the learner will include a description of the parts of the circulatory system, the functions of the circulatory system, and the route the blood takes." Now that's off the top of my head. It does include your objective, but it also makes them do a little problem solving.
Betty:	I'm impressed. However, I still don't see how you did it.
Bill:	I'd like you to read some material I have on levels of learning. Once you begin thinking of objectives as being at certain levels, writing higher-level objectives is not so hard.

Finally, the school library media specialist may assist by helping a teacher establish an instructional enterprise, connecting enabling objectives to the primary objective, or by helping a teacher establish the order of instruction from an instructional enterprise.

The In-Depth Level

IN-SERVICES

Creating instructional objectives, identifying levels of learning, and designing instructional enterprises are good topics for in-services. Instructional technology has evolved considerably in the past twenty years, and many teachers have not kept up. Teachers often need help, and the principal is often very grateful to anyone who will provide it. Be very careful, however, to determine the needs of the teachers in this area. An in-service should not cover too much and should contain a large number of examples. Try to show the teachers how efforts at the instructional objectives step will help make their teaching easier by aiding in the selection of materials and the planning of activities.

INSTRUCTIONAL DESIGN TEAM PARTICIPATION

At the highest level of instructional consultation, the school library media specialist can work with a teacher or group of teachers in the selection of a goal or goals, in the translation of goals into instructional objectives, in the identification of types and levels of learning, in the design of an instructional enterprise, and in the formulation of a teaching sequence. Example:

1. As part of a unit on weather, the instructional goal is "Teach about precipitation."

2. The school library media specialist and the teachers use the goal as the basis for creating a goal-elaboration statement. They take into account the instructional needs and abilities

Fig. 9.6. Instructional enterprise goal: Understand precipitation

Goal Elaboration Statement: The learner should understand that the type of precipitation that occurs is related in a predictable manner to the temperature and positions of air masses.

Primary Instruction Objective: Students in 7th grade general science will be able, given weather conditions describing characteristics and positions of air masses, to predict and explain the type of precipitation which will occur. (Rule Learning)*

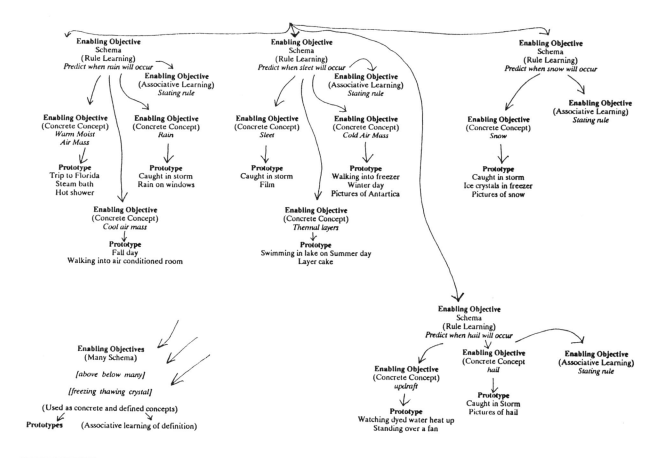

---

* Although the primary objective is at the rule learning level, the team in this case decided that the students needed to have experience-based instruction. Therefore, many of the concepts are at the concrete instead of the defined level.

of their students, and the time and resources available, and decide to cover four types of precipitation: rain, sleet, snow, and hail (see fig. 9.6).

3. Based on the goal-elaboration statement, the instructional team creates the primary instructional objective: Students in seventh-grade general science will be able, given weather conditions describing characteristics and positions of air masses, to predict and explain the type of precipitation that will occur (rule learning).

4. Four enabling objectives are created at the rule-learning level, one for each type of precipitation. The team also identifies several concepts that must be possessed in order to reach the primary instructional objective but that the students are assumed to possess already.

5. The instructional team decides that for these students the instruction needs to be based more on concrete experience than on abstractions, and the rule for predicting the type of precipitation should be based on concrete rather than on defined concepts. For example, the concept "thermal layer" should be approached through a sensory experience such as recalling swimming in a lake during a hot summer day and feeling the cold layer of water under a thin, warm layer.

6. Enabling objectives at the concrete concept level are created and prototypes are suggested for each. The team realizes that many students will have different prototypes for each concept, and some may possess no prototypes at all. In the latter case, the instruction will have to provide the experience to enable the student to form the appropriate prototype. (See fig. 9.6 for the complete instructional enterprise.)

7. In creating an order of instruction, the instructional team decides to approach each type of precipitation individually, beginning with the one that is most familiar (rain). In each case, those students who lack appropriate prototypes will be provided with experience and guidance to form them.

THOUGHT PROVOKERS

1. Which type of learning (intellectual skills, affective/attitudinal, or motor skills) would each of the following goals entail when translated into instructional objectives?

   a. The student will know how to add mixed numbers.

   b. The student will be able to toss a horseshoe correctly.

   c. The student will know how to add suffixes to words ending in *y*.

   d. The student will know about the art of the Renaissance.

   e. The student will value science.

2. Translate each of the previous goals into an instructional objective. (For the intellectual skills category of objectives, don't forget to create a goal-elaboration statement before creating the primary instructional objective.)

3. Which level of intellectual skills is represented by each of the following objectives?

   a. Given a paragraph in which none of the words is capitalized, the student will underline at least ten of the twelve proper nouns and no more than one word that is not a proper noun.

   b. The learner will be able to state the capital cities of at least forty states of the United States when presented with a list of all fifty states.

   c. Given a pendulum and a stopwatch, the learner will derive the law for the period of a pendulum.

   d. Given a computer display of fifteen animals, the learner will select at least four of the five mammals and not more than one of the non-mammals.

   e. When shown a picture of eight trucks, the learner will put an X over the one with the different number of wheels.

    f.   Given fifteen problems involving four-digit dividends and two-digit divisors, the learner will find the correct quotient in at least twelve of the problems.

    g.   Given twenty regular Spanish verbs, the learner will conjugate each correctly in the present tense.

    h.   Given fifteen declarative sentences, the learner will be able to identify correctly at least thirteen as to whether the statement is fact or opinion.

    i.   The learner will state the definition of air transportation and give at least one example not covered in class.

    j.   The learner will name the planets of the solar system in order, starting with the planet closest to the sun.

4.   Develop a goal-elaboration statement, a primary instructional objective, and an instructional enterprise with enabling objectives for the following instructional goal: The student will know how to add fractions with like denominators. Identify each objective as to level of learning.

5.   Identify which enabling objectives in exercise 4 can be considered entrance skills and justify this designation. Establish and justify an order of instruction.

(See appendix A for answers.)

REFERENCES

Anderson, L. W., and J. C. Anderson. 1982. Affective Assessment Is Necessary and Possible. *Educational Leadership* 39 (4): 524–25.

Anderson, R. C., and A. Ortony. 1975. On Putting Apples into Bottles: A Problem of Polysemy. *Cognitive Psychology* 7 (6): 176–80.

Andre, T. 1986. Problem Solving and Education. In *Cognitive Classroom Learning: Understanding, Thinking, and Problem Solving*, ed. T. Andre and G. D. Phye, 169–99. New York: Academic Press.

Armstrong, D. G., J. J. Denton, and T. V. Savage, Jr. 1978. *Instructional Skills Handbook*. Englewood Cliffs, N.J.: Educational Technology Publications.

Barone, T. E. 1987. Aesthetic or Anaesthetic? The Educational Experience and Behavioral Objectives. *Momentum* 18 (May): 17–19.

Belanger, F. 2000. *Evaluation and Implementation of Distance Learning*. Hershey, Pa.: Idea Group Publishing.

Bloom, B. S., ed. 1956. *Taxonomy of Educational Objectives. Handbook I: Cognitive Domain*. New York: David McKay.

Brown, J. S., A. Collins, and P. Dugdid. 1989. Situated Cognition and the Culture of Learning. *Educational Researcher* 16 (January–February): 32–42.

Collins, A. 1988. *Cognitive Apprenticeship and Instructional Technology* (Technical Report 6899). BBN Labs, Cambridge, MA.

Collins, A., J. S. Brown, and S. E. Newman. 1989. Cognitive Apprenticeship: Teaching the Crafts of Reading, Writing, and Mathematics. In *Knowing, Learning and Instruction: Essays in Honour of Robert Glaser*, ed. L. B. Resnick, 453–94. Hillsdale, N.J.: Learning Education Association.

Cone, J. D. 1988. Elaboration of the Criterion Portion of Three-Part Behavioral Objectives. *Educational Technology* 28 (June): 37–39.

Dick, W., and L. Carey. 1990. *The Systematic Design of Instruction.* Glenview, Ill.: Scott, Foresman.

Ertmer, P. A., and T. J. Newby. 1993. Behaviorism, Cognitivism Constructivism: Comparing Critical Features from the Instructional Design Perspective. *Performance Improvement Quarterly* 6: 50–72.

Gagne, R. M. 1972. Domains of Learning. *Interchange* 3: 1–8.

———. 1975. *Essentials of Learning for Instruction.* New York: Holt, Rinehart, and Winston.

———. 1977. Analysis of Objectives. In *Instructional Design: Principles and Applications,* ed. L. J. Briggs, 115–45. Englewood Cliffs, N.J.: Educational Technology Publications.

Gagne, R. M., and M. D. Merrill. 1990. Integrative Goals for Instructional Design. *Educational Technology Research and Development* 38 (1): 23–30.

Gagne, R. M., and Medsker, K. 1996. *The Conditions of Learning.* Ft. Worth, Tex.: Harcourt Brace.

Gagne, R. M., L. J. Briggs, and W. W. Wager. 1988. *Principles of Instructional Design.* New York: Holt, Rinehart, and Winston.

Gibson, W. 1957. *The Miracle Worker.* Toronto, Ontario: Samuel French.

Holley, C. D., and D. F. Dansereau. 1984. Networking: The Technique and the Empirical Evidence. In *Spatial Learning Strategies Techniques, Applications, and Related Issues,* ed. C. D. Holley and D. F. Dansereau, 81–108. New York: Academic Press.

Jonassen, D., and T. Reeves. 1996. Learning with Technology: Using Computers as Cognitive Tools. In *Handbook of Research for Educational Communications and Technology,* ed. D. Jonassen. New York: Macmillan.

Lave, J., and E. Wenger. 1991. *Situated Learning: Legitimate Peripheral Participation.* New York: Cambridge University Press.

Leamonson, R. 1992. Letters to the Editor. *Atlantic Monthly* 270 (2): 8.

Mager, R. F. 1972. *Goal Analysis.* Belmont, Calif.: Fearon.

Merrill, M. D., Z. Li, and M. K. Jones. 1990a. Limitations of First Generation Instructional Design. *Educational Technology* 30 (January): 7–11.

———. 1990b. Second Generation Instructional Design (ID). *Educational Technology* 30 (February): 7–14.

Pipe, P. 1975. *Objectives—Tool for Change.* Belmont, Calif.: Fearon.

Popham, W. J. 1987. Instructional Objectives Benefit Teaching and Testing. *Momentum* 2 (May): 15–16.

Resnick, J. 1987. Learning in School and Out. *Educational Research* 16: 13–20.

Spiro, R. J., P. J. Feltovich, M. J. Jacobson, and R. L. Coulson. 1991. Knowledge Representation, Content Specification and the Development of Skill in Situation Specific Knowledge Assembly. Some Constructivist Issues as They Relate to Cognitive Flexibility Theory and Hypertext. *Educational Technology* 31: 22–25.

Stuart, J. A. 1984. The Thinking Process: A Proposed Instructional Objectives Classification Scheme. *Educational Technology* 24: 21–26.Tessmer, M., B. Wilson, and M. Driscoll. 1990. A New Model of Concept Teaching and Learning. *Educational Technology Research and Development* 38: 45–53.

Tesser, M., B. Wilson, and M. Driscoll. 1990. A New Model of Concept Teaching and Learning. *Educational Technology Research and Development* 38: 45–53.

Tessmer, M. A., D. P. Jonassen, and D. C. Caverly. 1989. Learning Strategies: A New Instructional Technology. In *World Yearbook of Education for 1988: Education for the New Technologies,* ed. D. Harris, 29–47. London: Kogan Page.

ADDITIONAL READINGS

Atkins, D. H., K. T. Kelly, and G. S. Morrison. 2001. Development of the Child Evaluation Measure: An Assessment of Children's Learning across Disciplines and in Multiple Contexts. *Educational and Psychological Measurement* 61: 505–11.

Baker, S., R. Gersten, and D. Scanlon. 2002. Procedural Facilitators and Cognitive Strategies: Tools for Unraveling the Mysteries of Comprehension and the Writing Process, and for Providing Meaningful Access to the General Curriculum. *Learning Disabilities Research and Practice* 17: 65–77.

Carpenter, D. D. 2001. Teaching Lessons Learned. *Journal of Professional Issues in Engineering Education and Practice* 127: 141–43.

Dwyer, F. M., and D. M. Moore. 2001. The Effect of Gender, Field Dependence and Color-Coding on Student Achievement of Different Educational Objectives. *International Journal of Instructional Media* 28: 309–408.

Frudden, S. J., and S. B. Jones. 1985. Eight Elements of Effective Preinstructional Planning. *Education* 106: 218–22.

Gagne, R. M., and K. L. Medsker. 1996. *The Conditions of Learning: Training Applications.* Ft. Worth, Tex.: Harcourt Brace College Publishers.

Keil, F. C. 1989. *Concepts, Kinds, and Cognitive Development.* Cambridge, Mass.: MIT Press.

Markman, E. 1989. *Categorization and Naming in Children.* Cambridge, Mass.: MIT Press.

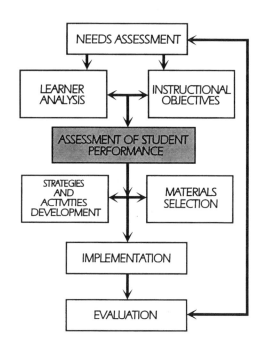

10

Assessment of Student Performance

This chapter provides information to help the reader

- understand the integration of assessment and instruction

- recognize the characteristics of authentic assessment

- understand the advantages of authentic assessment

- create the classroom conditions for authentic assessment

- know the types of authentic assessment

- write authentic tests

- plan portfolios as a means of authentic assessment

- plan performances as a means of authentic assessment

- understand assessment through teacher-student personal contact

- incorporate teacher and student reflection into the assessment plan

The fourth step in the instructional design process is planning the assessment of student performance. Traditionally, this assessment has been conducted through locally produced or nationally standardized testing. Because testing often does not provide a complete picture of students' achievements (revealing only a limited view of students' knowledge at a particular point in time), educators are augmenting or replacing traditional testing with assessment that is ongoing, open-ended, and in a real-life context. This type of assessment is often referred to as authentic assessment.

Despite the shift in the methods of assessment, the characteristics of good assessment have not changed: Assessment must measure how well students have mastered the objectives; assessment must be reliable (accurately reflecting students' abilities and not a particular evaluator's idiosyncrasies); assessment must allow students to demonstrate what they know rather than what they do not know; assessment must provide feedback to teachers on the effectiveness of instructional techniques, materials, and activities.

This chapter was contributed by Barbara K. Stripling.

THE PURPOSE OF THE STUDENT ASSESSMENT STEP

Assessment must be considered at this stage of the instructional design process because assessment is integral to any instructional unit. Assessment plans will influence the choice of activities, materials, and instructional strategies. Teachers can plan to assess student progress and teaching effectiveness either formally or informally at any point during the unit.

Four questions can guide the development of an assessment plan: 1) What do we want students to know and be able to do? 2) What will count as acceptable performance? 3) How can we ensure expert judgments? and 4) How can we provide feedback? (Diez and Moon 1992). Teachers must answer these questions during the student assessment step of the instructional design process.

If an English teacher, for example, wants students to connect themes in the literature they are studying with specific values held by the society at the time, the teacher must make a series of decisions. First, the teacher must decide how students can best demonstrate their understandings—through an essay, a talk-show script, a travel-back-in-time brochure, or some other product. Second, the teacher must select or create models to show students the standard of performance expected. Third, the teacher must design evaluation rubrics with specific descriptions of behavior for each level of performance in order to ensure reliable judgments from evaluators, which could include fellow students, teachers, or community members. Finally, the teacher must decide how and when to give feedback and whether to include peer comments, opportunities for revision, conferencing, and student self-evaluation.

CHARACTERISTICS OF AUTHENTIC ASSESSMENT

Authentic assessment can encompass various techniques including testing, questionnaires, interviews, ratings, observations, performance samples, and work products (Chittenden 1991). Authentic assessment often involves a performance of some kind, but it is not authentic unless "the student completes or demonstrates the desired behavior . . . in a real-life context" (Meyer 1992). Authentic assessment can be conducted at any point in a unit and for any level of instructional objectives. In other words, if a teacher wants to assess student performance on low-level objectives in the middle of a unit about the Middle Ages, the teacher might ask each student in a testing situation to select and explain the facts about life in the Middle Ages that would be most important to portray in a television miniseries, with rationales for the decisions. The teacher's high-level objectives for the final project of the unit might be assessed by asking students to create an actual script for an episode in the miniseries. The script should make the Middle Ages come alive.

To be a reliable picture of a student's understandings, authentic assessment must be ongoing, measuring student performance throughout the process of learning. Some research has shown that from eight to twenty samples are required to produce a reliable assessment of an individual's problem-solving ability in a given content area (Herman 1992).

Authentic assessment is a learning experience in itself. Unlike generic multiple-choice tests that categorize and limit the options, authentic assessments must be open-ended to allow many different approaches and products. Students are expected to synthesize, using their learning to create new ideas during the assessment process.

Peters (1991) has said that authentic assessment must be based on authentic content, and he has suggested five guidelines for selecting authentic content:

1. Material should be based on important concepts. Teachers should decide the essential themes and ideas to be learned; assessment should be directly related to these ideas.

2. Material should be consistent with state, school district, and school curriculum guidelines. This consistency will enable students to make connections with what they have previously learned and with what they are being taught in other subject areas.

3. Material should have real-life experience as its basis. Students should expect to encounter problems and concepts that have application to the world outside the school environment.

4. Material should take into account the developmental progression of students and build on prior knowledge. Teachers must determine when needed background is missing and then must include that information in the course content.

5. Material should demand a high level of thinking from the students.

An essential component to authentic assessment is reflection, by both the teacher and the students. Students must be asked to appraise their own learning and to reflect on their strengths and weaknesses. In some authentic-assessment formats (portfolios, for example), students start the process of assessment by setting goals for their own learning. They end the process with metacognition as they evaluate their own progress, their level of thinking, and their uses of processes and strategies to accomplish the goals they have set. Teachers must reflect on the appropriateness of the assessment for the content being taught and on the effectiveness of activities and instructional strategies.

CONDITIONS FOR AUTHENTIC ASSESSMENT

The learning environment in the classroom must allow the characteristics of authentic assessment to flourish by nurturing the students' complex thinking and reflection, by establishing assessment as a learning experience in itself, and by valuing students' progress as well as final achievements (Zessoules and Gardner 1991). Newmann has identified four additional classroom conditions that are essential for authentic assessment to take place: collaboration, access to tools and resources, discretion and ownership, and flexible use of time (Newmann 1991).

In a collaborative classroom, students help one another accomplish the learning objectives. Students recognize that they are expected to perform to a standard of achievement; they will not be weighed one against another during evaluation. Projects often entail group work, although each individual is held accountable for mastering all the learning objectives. The teacher in a collaborative classroom regards students as partners in the learning process and invites participation by other teachers and community members.

A second condition for authentic assessment is that students must be free to use whatever tools and resources they need. Because the assessment involves creative thinking beyond rote learning, teachers must allow students to use many information sources for details and specifics, just as the students would have those sources available in real-life, problem-solving situations. Students can consult a handbook of mathematical theorems, a chart of chemical properties, the textbook, a variety of Web sites, class notes, library sources, even experts in the field. The teacher is measuring the students' understanding and ability to manipulate information in creating new ideas, not the students' memorization of specific facts.

The classroom that fosters authentic assessment involves students in the learning and in the assessment process. Students help decide what is important and how their achievements should be measured. For example, a key characteristic of portfolios is that the students select the components and justify their choices in a reflective introduction to each piece. In performance assessments, once the teacher has structured an authentic situation, students have great leeway in determining the framework and content of their own performance.

Finally, the authentic classroom allows flexible use of time. Every student is expected to perform to a standard; some students may take longer to reach it than others. One student may take seven weeks to complete a project and another only three, but both are allowed the time necessary to achieve the standard. Projects are not arbitrarily ended because a grading period is over or because the teacher initially predicted completion in a shorter amount of time.

An ongoing, daily commitment to authentic assessment in the classroom changes the very nature of the curriculum. Consider, for example, a low-level math classroom in the junior high or high school in which students are struggling with calculations that they should have learned in elementary school. A typical instructional plan for teaching measurement to these students might involve large-group instruction, individual practice by working all the measurement problems in the book, and then a multiple-choice test. A plan based on authentic assessment might include instruction in measurement; individual or group practice by measuring items in the classroom and figuring out logical proportions for furniture and room dimensions; and group performance by designing, measuring pieces for, and constructing a dollhouse for an elementary classroom. Although the assessment of learning is much more difficult when students construct a dollhouse than when they take a test, the learning is probably more interesting, involving, and effective for the students.

TYPES OF AUTHENTIC ASSESSMENT

Four main categories of authentic assessment can be identified: tests, portfolios, performances, and personal contact with the student.

Tests

Grant Wiggins (1989, 1992) has suggested that for tests to be authentic assessment, they must be designed using eight criteria:

1. The test must measure essential content, something that is meaningful for the student to learn. It should concentrate on areas that are usually ignored, such as problem solving, thinking, and writing, and should stress depth rather than breadth. The test should not be an interruption in the learning process but should stimulate the thoughtful use of knowledge.

2. The test should include enough items that it is a valid measure of what it purports to measure. Students must be allowed to show their strengths. Only then can generalizations be drawn about a student's learning.

3. Scoring should be based on essential elements to understanding, not on what is easiest to measure. The scores should be multifaceted, not a single grade. Self-assessment is an important component.

4. Standards should be established that are reasonable for the real world, not arbitrarily easy for the school. Tests should never be graded on the curve.

5. The problems on the test should have detailed, enticing, realistic contexts so that students enjoy thinking about and working on them. Students with different learning styles should be allowed to approach the problems in their own ways.

6. The tasks on the test should be validated by giving them to a small group of students or teachers before the administration of the test. Items that are confusing or that do not seem to measure the objectives should be eliminated or revised.

7. The scoring should be feasible and reliable. Scoring rubrics can be constructed to increase reliability.

8. The results of the assessment should be used by students, teachers, and administrators to facilitate future learning and improve the learning environment.

Murray (1990) has suggested some variations to the prevalent one-student-per-test-at-the-end-of-the-chapter testing. Students might get second chances or access to additional information. The teacher might give an exam in class but then allow students to have a second copy of the exam to work on at home with their textbooks, computers, and so forth. The students would then discover answers to the questions that troubled them on the earlier exam. Other teachers might use take-home exams. In one variation, students receive the questions before the test. They can take the questions home and prepare, then write the exam in class without referring to their notes.

Other suggestions by Murray include various group-testing situations. In one, students work together to figure out answers to thought-provoking questions. Students compose a group answer, but in Supreme Court fashion, individuals can file dissenting opinions. In another situation, students work in groups to discuss multiple-choice test questions and teach each other. Students fill out their own answer sheets based on their group work.

Murray also suggests that students can work in pairs to take tests. Students answer some of the test questions on their own but combine into randomly selected pairs to answer an equal number of questions (although each student still maintains an individual answer sheet). A suggested variation is an essay test on which students work in pairs to write one essay answer to each question.

In summary, authentic tests must follow the guidelines identified for authentic assessment. Tests must measure important content, not incidentals. Tests must require thinking; simple repetition of memorized facts is boring and useless to the students and the teacher. Tests must require students to apply their understandings to real-life situations. Until students can work with the information they have acquired, they have gained no understanding of the material. Although authentic tests may be relatively easy to grade (compared to portfolios and performances), they can be extremely difficult to construct.

Portfolios

A portfolio is a selected collection of a student's work. The students have control over their portfolios—they set the initial goals for their portfolios; they select the works to be included, based on criteria they have established; they often write introductions in which they assess their own learning and their understanding of the subject concepts; and they write reflective pieces about each work included (Paulson, Paulson, and Meyer 1991). A portfolio reveals a student's understandings, abilities, progress, and mental processes. Students can compile portfolios for their entire school program or for individual classes.

Portfolios are student-directed; therefore, students learn to assume responsibility for their own learning. Teachers who have tried portfolio assessment have discovered that students compile their best work with pride, holding themselves accountable for higher standards than if they were simply turning in teacher-directed assignments for a grade. Students willingly revise pieces for their final portfolios based on revision comments from teachers and peers. Students are also effective evaluators of their own progress when they write reflective essays about their portfolio work. Students have commented that they learn almost as much from their reflections as they do from the original work.

Portfolios can vary a great deal in their content and form. Vavrus (1990) has suggested some questions for teachers and students to answer as they compile their portfolios.

- *What will the portfolio look like?* The portfolio can be arranged in several ways—chronologically, topically, by format, by rate of success (worst to best). It can be in a folder, a box, or any other container. The only requirement is that it should be planned to match the goals for the portfolio.

- *What should go into a portfolio?* The portfolio should include work that demonstrates mastery of the goals set by the student and teacher. It can include finished work only or all drafts and revisions as well as the finished work. Students must include pieces of self-reflection. Some portfolios contain only written work, but in a variety of formats including essays, tests, learning logs, journals, creative pieces, and samples of homework. Other portfolios contain videotapes of student performances, artwork, audiotapes, videodisks, HyperCard stacks, and whatever else the students feel demonstrates their proficiency.

- *When and how do students select the work to be included in the portfolio?* The teacher and students should set up a timeline at the beginning of the year for final portfolio completion. Individual pieces are added as the students select and revise them during the year. The final work on the portfolios should be finished in time for the students to present them to the teacher, an evaluation panel (if used), their peers, or their parents.

  Students select the works based on their own and the teacher's goals. If the teacher's main goal is to see growth in understanding of themes of history, the students should select work on the themes of history from various points during the year. If a student's goal is to develop creativity, the portfolio should also include the student's creative pieces from throughout the year.

- *How will the portfolios be evaluated?* The teacher sets standards of performance that would be acceptable outside of the school. Work in the portfolios is judged against those standards, probably through the use of a rubric that contains descriptive phrases rather than evaluative comments. For example, for a history unit on change, an excellent student essay might be described as "Demonstrates solid knowledge of the social, economic, and political disruption caused by change. Has developed a personal understanding of the effects of change on people's lives. Expresses concepts and feelings in understandable language and with conviction." A mediocre piece might be described as "Demonstrates knowledge of the surface effects of change on society (changing fads and fashions) but does not connect those effects with changes in the social, economic, and political structures. Appreciates change only as it happens to other people at other times; has made little personal connection to the concept of change. Expresses concepts and feelings understandably but with little personal conviction." The rubric might also include the following description for a poor piece: "Displays little understanding of the concept of change and the effects of change on society. Offers no personal insight into change; has formed no personal connection to the unit. Expresses ideas in a manner that cannot be easily understood by others."

  With such a rubric, evaluations can be conducted reliably by the classroom teacher, other teachers, students, and community members. Many teachers have discovered that by opening up the evaluation process, they help the students see that their work is preparing them for the world outside the classroom. That understanding adds value to their classroom work.

  Portfolios should be evaluated according to external standards, but that evaluation can be tempered with an assessment of student growth. More than any other method of assessment, portfolios offer teachers the opportunity to see student growth in ideas, skills, and attitudes. When students document how much they have learned, they can be rewarded through the assessment process.

- *What should be done with portfolios after the year has ended?* Once portfolios become more widely accepted in our schools, teachers will have the opportunity to review students' portfolios from previous years, which will help them gain a clear picture of the students' learning. With this insight, teachers can structure a curriculum that builds on the skills that most students have already developed and emphasizes those areas where students have faltering skills. A higher degree of individualization is also possible when teachers have access to students' previous portfolios. Students who can write a cogent, well-organized essay at the end of one year can be directed to write more sophisticated essays the next year.

Performances

Some learning is best demonstrated in performances. Certainly drama, music, speech, physical education, and athletics require performances in order for students to demonstrate they have acquired the skills and processes basic to those subject areas. Other subject areas can profit from performance-based assessment as well. Students in English can act out a play they have written about the current conflicts in South Africa. Business-law students can debate the issue of punishment for white-collar crime. Third-graders can test the properties of water in its three states: solid, liquid, and gas. Students in history can videotape a *Sixty Minutes* report on the signing of the Emancipation Proclamation. Figure 10.1 shows a group performance and figure 10.2 shows an individual performance.

In order for performance assessment to be authentic, it must be based on real-life experiences and authentic content. Students can perform individually or in groups. They may perform for their classmates or for a larger audience. They may be evaluated by the teacher, their peers, or outside evaluators, which could include teachers, parents, or community members.

The advantages of performance assessment are many. Students create their own performance; they are not restricted by pre-written questions. Although some rote learning may be involved, students develop larger understandings of the issues and concepts while they are preparing their performances. Students are learning in depth; they will remember the issues presented in their performances long after they have forgotten specific facts. Performances boost students' self-esteem and enhance communication skills. Most important, students enjoy the learning that takes place during the preparation and performance. Performance assessments have some limitations as

Fig. 10.1. Group performance

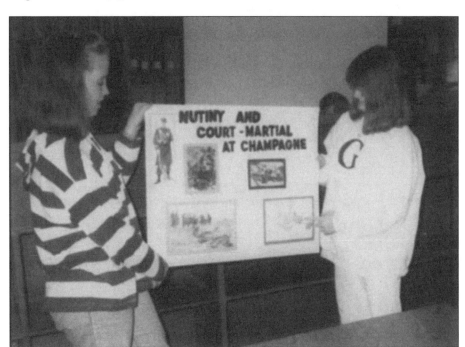

well. They are generally culminating activities; therefore, they must be combined with other forms of assessment to give a clear picture of student progress throughout a unit or semester. Performances require more in-class time and effort on the part of both the students and teachers than do tests or portfolio pieces. It can take days for each student to have a chance to perform. Performances are messy and loud; students are not "in their places" as they write, rehearse, and perform. It is difficult to make performance assessments valid so that they measure the skills and concepts intended and so that the evaluator can generalize about a student's abilities. Research has shown that many samples are needed before such assessments can lead to generalizations.

The most serious limitation of performance assessments is the difficulty of assessing them reliably. Mehrens (1992) has identified four problems with performance-assessment reliability. First, the scores tend to be quite subjective based on who is doing the scoring and what is regarded as important. Writing is the most developed form of performance assessment; with extensive training, evaluators for written work have finally achieved some reliability. Other forms of performance assessment are not as well developed. What is known is that persons who have a vested interest in the scores should not rate the performances. Therefore, teachers should not evaluate the performances of their own students.

Second, Mehrens points out that it is difficult to compare performances to external standards. Performances are often rated on a scale; however, the scale may reveal how well a student performed compared to other students rather than how well the student achieved according to specific criterion-referenced standards.

Fig. 10.2. Individual performance

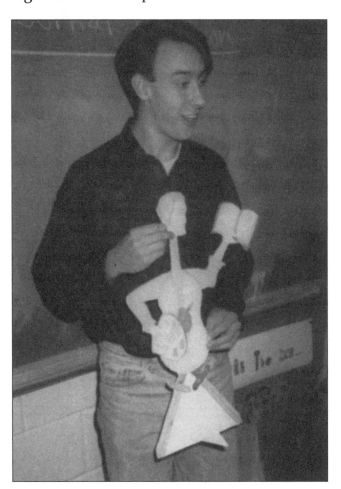

Mehrens also argues that it is extremely difficult to equate performance assignments between classes and from one year to the next. The situations for performances must be changed each year to prevent rote repetitions of supposedly creative interpretations. But the difficulty arises when teachers try to make a situation from one class equal to a different situation in another class or year.

Finally, because many performances are group situations, teachers must wrestle with the problem of assessing the individual versus the group performance. They must decide how to assign an individual grade in addition to the group evaluation.

Despite the limitations, teachers are incorporating performances into their instructional units. Consideration of the skills needed for the performances must be given early in the instructional design process so that teachers can incorporate skills, concepts, materials, and strategies to prepare students for their eventual performance. Students who anticipate a performance tend to be focused and excited about the learning. Performances invigorate the classroom.

Personal Contact with the Student

Because the reliability of assessments is enhanced by increasing the number of samples, teachers may choose to supplement testing, portfolios, and performances with assessments garnered through personal contact with the student. These personal assessments include interviews, questionnaires, and unobtrusive observations. All make the assessment process more interactive, with the students contributing ideas, strategies, and attitudes that may not be obvious to the teacher in other assessment situations. Interactive assessment is intended to discover the conditions that will help a student grow, not simply to document a student's progress to that point (Brozo 1990).

A diagnostic interview (see figure 10.3), already used by reading teachers, can help the teacher understand students' interests and strengths. The teacher can discover if students have a clear understanding of the goals and expectations for a unit. The student can use the teacher as a sounding board to test out new ideas and strategies or to clear up confusing issues. The teacher can conduct a formal assessment interview, recording progress on various criteria and suggesting areas to

Fig. 10.3. Diagnostic interview

pursue, or can use the interview more informally to help the student establish a focus and overcome deficiencies.

Questionnaires can be informal and simple. For example, a teacher might hand each student an index card during the last five minutes of class time. Students write comments in response to a question such as "What is the most important idea that you learned today?" or "How will you use what you learned today to create your final product?" Teachers can also use more formal questionnaires to help students assess their own progress to that point. Although questionnaires provide assessment information about each student, they may actually be more valuable in providing data on the effectiveness of the unit in progress. With such valuable feedback, teachers can make adjustments in content or pace to accommodate students who are having problems.

Observations may be the most powerful form of personal assessment. Students can keep a learning or research log in which they include their successes and frustrations. Teachers can keep a journal with observations about specific students and the class as a whole. Teachers can target a specific behavior and record observations related to that behavior for each student (for example, care with laboratory equipment). Teachers can simply record group dynamics during a class period and review their notes later for insights into how well the groups are functioning. The strength of using student and teacher observations is that they are usually honest representations of the situation; they have not been manipulated by the assessment instrument itself.

Personal contact with the student provides valuable information to the teacher and important feedback to the student throughout the instructional unit. It is a formative assessment strategy that should accompany the summative strategies of tests, portfolios, and performances.

AUTHENTIC ASSESSMENT AS REFLECTION IN ACTION

A shift from traditional assessment to authentic assessment causes changes in teacher and student behavior as well as in the learning environment. Students take a more active role in their own learning. They plan it, carry it out, and evaluate their own progress and success. They reflect on their own performance throughout the learning experience and change their behavior based on their reflections. Students work collaboratively with other students. Finally, students understand the connections between what they are learning and the real world.

Teachers are also more reflective. They use feedback to change what is happening in the classroom. They foster collaboration among students and with other teachers and community members. Teachers use high standards in assessing student work, basing their benchmarks on expected performance outside of school. They expect students to continue learning once they have graduated.

The learning environment of an authentically assessed classroom is more open to resources and technology beyond the classroom and the school (school and public libraries are essential here). Instructional time is flexible enough to allow students to pursue subjects in depth. Students are expected to demonstrate their proficiency through performances or portfolios in addition to testing.

Authentic assessment, with its emphasis on real-life learning and reflection, changes the teaching strategies and content of instructional units. Selecting the type of assessment to be used helps educators continue the instructional design process through the stages of materials selection, activities development, implementation, and evaluation.

ONLINE ASSESSMENTS

Online testing has certainly become an important issue in the K–12 educational environment over the past several years. More and more students are taking courses online, online tests are more readily available, and home schooling is growing in popularity. At this time, much online testing is standardized: Oregon's online standardized tests, given to third, fifth, eighth, and tenth grade students; Idaho's online state testing, which includes multiple-choice exams in mathematics, reading, and language arts for grades two through nine; and South Dakota's comprehensive online tests for third, sixth, and tenth grade students.

However, online learning is moving in the direction of authentic assessment. Distance/online education can offer "rich opportunities for authentic, integrated assessment, which can also be tailored by a learning contract to meet individual needs. Authentic assessments have high validity . . . and as they entail complex tasks with potentially many variables, judgment of student achievement is more likely to be open to larger rather than smaller, discrete tasks. The challenge is for teachers to articulate marking criteria that are sufficiently broad to cover most situations, yet detailed enough that they are useful and provide guidance to students" (Morgan & O'Reilly 1999, 57).

LEVELS OF INVOLVEMENT BY THE SCHOOL LIBRARY MEDIA SPECIALIST AT THE ASSESSMENT OF STUDENT PERFORMANCE STEP

The Initial Level

Although the school library media specialist is not directly involved in instructional planning at this level of involvement, the idea of authentic assessment is new enough to most teachers that the school library media specialist can have a profound impact by building a professional collection of materials for the teachers to consult and by book-talking these during faculty meetings. The school library media specialist can also serve as a clearinghouse for articles on authentic assessment. Particularly interesting articles can be collected and distributed to interested faculty. The school library media specialist may organize a discussion group in which each member reads and reports on an article. By typing and distributing notes from those meetings, the school library media specialist can provide each interested faculty member with a written summary of relevant articles on authentic assessment.

One offshoot of authentic assessment that has received particular attention is portfolios. The school library media specialist can subscribe to a portfolio newsletter, collect portfolio articles, and perhaps contact a school using portfolios to borrow samples to serve as models for interested teachers.

Because authentic assessment involves learning in depth, students often need to use library materials. The school library media specialist at the initial level provides access to these materials and develops the collection based on student needs. Participation in interlibrary loan or a fax network for sharing periodical articles allows the library to meet increased demands caused by authentic assessment.

The following is a list of works on assessment for traditional classrooms and online environments that are recommended for the professional library:

Anthony, R., T. D. Johnson, N. I. Mickelson, and A. Preece. 1991. *Evaluating Literacy: A Perspective for Change.* Portsmouth, N.H.: Heinemann.

Archbald, D. A., and F. M. Newmann. 1988. *Beyond Standardized Testing: Assessing Authentic Academic Achievement in the Secondary School.* Reston, Va.: National Association of Secondary School Principals.

Belanoff, P., and M. Dickson, ed. 1991. *Portfolios: Process and Product.* Portsmouth, N.H.: Heinemann.

Benson, R. 1996. *Assessing Open and Distance Learners: A Staff Handbook.* Churchill Centre for Distance Learning, Monash University, Victoria, Australia.

Danielson, C. and L. Abrutyn. 1997. *An Introduction to Using Portfolios in the Classroom.* ASCD.

Grace, C. and E. Shores. 1998. *The Portfolio Book: A Step-by-Step Guide for Teachers.* Beltsville, Md.: Gryphon House Publisher.Kimball, M. A. 2002. *The Web Portfolio Guide.* Boston: Longman Publishing.

Laffey, J., and J. Singer. 1997. In *Web-Based Instruction,* ed. B. Kahn. Englewood Cliffs, N.J.: Educational Technology Publications.

Mahoney, J., and J. Strickland. 2002. *Power and Portfolios: Best Practices for High School Classrooms.* Portsmouth, N.H.: Heinemann Publications.

National Council of Teachers of English. *English Journal,*

Perrone, V., ed. 1991. *Expanding Student Assessment.* Alexandria, Va.: Association for Supervision and Curriculum Development.

Phi Delta Kappa. *Phi Delta Kappan,*

Race, P. 1989. *The Open Learning Handbook: Selecting, Designing and Supporting Open Learning Materials.* London: Kogan Page.

Rolheiser, C. et al. 2000. *The Portfolio Organizer: Succeeding with Portfolios in Your Classroom.*

Sizer, T. R. 1997. *Horace's Compromise: The Dilemma of the American High School.* 3rd ed. Boston: Houghton Mifflin/Mariner Books.

———. 1997. *Horace's School: Redesigning the American High School.* Boston: Houghton Mifflin/Mariner Books.

Stefanakis, E. H. 2001. *Multiple Intelligences and Portfolios: A Window into the Learner's Mind.* Portsmouth, N.H.: Heinemann Publications.

Stiggins, R. J., E. Rubel, and O. Edys. 1988. *Measuring Thinking Skills in the Classroom.* Washington, D.C.: National Education Association.

Sunstein, B. S., and J. H. Lovell. 2000. *The Portfolio Standard: How Students Can Show Us What They Know and Are Able to Do.* Portsmouth, N.H.: Heinemann Publishers.

Tierney, R. J., M. A. Carter, and L. E. Desai, ed. 1991. *Portfolio Assessment in the Reading-Writing Classroom.* Norwood, Mass.: Christopher-Gordon.

The Moderate Level

At the moderate level, the school library media specialist is more actively involved in the design of the instructional unit. The teacher and school library media specialist co-plan the authentic assessment. If the assessment will be in writing, the school library media specialist offers use of library computers and instruction in word processing for those students who are not experienced. If the assessment is to involve production of audiovisual materials, the school library media specialist assumes responsibility for teaching students production techniques and for helping students produce quality work. If the assessment is to be performance-based, the school library media specialist offers to teach certain performance techniques such as how to make an oral presentation or how to present oneself on camera. The school library media specialist also monitors preparations and rehearsals for certain performance groups while the teacher is involved in assessing the performances of other groups. The support of the school library media specialist frees a teacher to try alternative assessment forms.

A SCENARIO

Joan Winter, a sixth-grade teacher, noticed that her students were oblivious to events happening in the real world. They read the *Weekly Reader,* but none of the news seemed to come alive. She approached the school library media specialist, Valerie Brummer, with her concern.

Joan: I'm looking for a way to get my students involved with what's happening in the world. They don't seem to care about the environment or wars or even people in other places.

Valerie: We can get some current information electronically. What have you thought they might do with the information?

Joan: I don't know. They think that reports are boring.

Valerie: Why don't we have them do their own *Weekly Reader* with a mixture of national, international, and school news?

Joan: I think they'd like that, but I don't know how I'd get it done. They wouldn't know where to start. And I don't think I have the time anyway.

Valerie: Let's use the current *Weekly Reader* as a model. We'll let the students take it apart and look at how each section is done. They can decide which sections to continue and which sections to add. As for the time, let's make this a joint project with the library. I can work with them during library time to collect information and write stories. We have a wonderful computer program that will help them lay out the newsmagazine.

Joan: Oh, that sounds great! You know, I don't want this to be a one-time project. I think they'll get a lot better as the year goes on. I'd like to give them a chance to improve.

Valerie: Why don't we start portfolios for each of the students? We've been talking about trying that anyway. Then we can let the students collect their best stories throughout the year. By the end of the year, the students will be able to see their own progress.

Joan: Yes, I think this unit is going to be exactly what the students need to get them excited about the world around them.

The In-Depth Level

IN-SERVICES

At this level of involvement, school library media specialists provide in-services on authentic assessment strategies. This is especially valuable as teachers shift from traditional, rote-memory tests to more open-ended and authentic assessment techniques. Teachers need extensive in-service training to become comfortable with these new strategies. The school library media specialist can become an expert in assessment and personally conduct the in-service sessions or can plan workshops in which a variety of materials are made available, teachers have the opportunity to work together, and guest speakers are invited to share their expertise.

INSTRUCTIONAL DESIGN TEAM PARTICIPATION

At this level, the school library media specialist helps the classroom teacher design the authentic assessment strategies. In the previous scenario, in addition to suggesting the use of portfolios, the school library media specialist would help formulate the goals for the portfolios based on a knowledge of students' experience with skills and content at other grade levels. Because school library media specialists work with all students in the school, they offer teachers a whole-school perspective.

Perhaps an even greater help to the teachers than designing the authentic assessment strategies is a willingness on the part of the school library media specialist to serve as an evaluator for student work. Because performance-based assessments should be evaluated by someone without a vested interest, the school library media specialist helps the students and classroom teachers by filling that role whenever possible. School library media specialists also evaluate written student products, especially those based on research in the library.

THOUGHT PROVOKERS

1. What are the essential characteristics of authentic assessment?

2. What changes in content and instructional strategies result from a shift from traditional to authentic assessment?

3. What does reflection add to the assessment process?

4. What do authentic tests look like?

5. When are portfolios the most effective assessment strategy?

6. How can the problems of reliability of performance-based assessment be modulated or overcome?

7. A fifth-grade teacher wants every student to understand the causes and results of the Civil War because these will be used to compare the Civil War with the Revolutionary War. How should the teacher assess the students' understanding of these issues?

8. A high school English teacher expects the students to recognize the use of certain narrative techniques dealing with time: flashbacks, foreshadowing, stream of consciousness,

and chronological narrative sequence. How can the teacher be sure that students can recognize these techniques?

(See appendix A for answers.)

REFERENCES

Brozo, W. G. 1990. Learning How At-Risk Readers Learn Best: A Case for Interactive Assessment. *Journal of Reading* 33 (7): 522–27.

Chittenden, E. 1991. Authentic Assessment, Evaluation, and Documentation of Student Performance. In *Expanding Student Assessment,* ed. V. Perrone, 22–31. Alexandria, Va.: Association for Supervision and Curriculum Development.

Diez, M. E., and C. J. Moon. 1992. What Do We Want Students to Know? . . . and Other Important Questions. *Educational Leadership* 49 (3): 38–41.

Herman, J. L. 1992. What Research Tells Us about Good Assessment. *Educational Leadership* 49 (8): 74–78.

Mehrens, W. A. 1992. Using Performance Assessment for Accountability Purposes. *Educational Measurement: Issues and Practice* 7 (1): 3–9.

Meyer, C. A. 1992. What's the Difference between *Authentic* and *Performance* Assessment? *Educational Leadership* 49 (3): 39–40.

Morgan, C., and M. O'Reilly. 1999. *Assessing Open and Distance Learners.* London: Kogan Page.

Murray, J. P. 1990. Better Testing for Better Learning. *College Teaching* 38 (4): 148–52.

Newmann, F. M. 1991. Linking Restructuring to Authentic Student Achievement. *Phi Delta Kappan* 72 (6): 458–63.

Paulson, F. L., P. R. Paulson, and C. A. Meyer. 1991. What Makes a Portfolio a Portfolio? *Educational Leadership* 48 (5): 60–63.

Perrone, V., ed. 1991. *Expanding Student Assessment.* Alexandria, Va.: Association for Supervision and Curriculum Development.

Peters, C. W. 1991. You Can't Have Authentic Assessment without Authentic Content. *Reading Teacher* 44 (3): 590–91.

Portfolio News. Published quarterly by Portfolio Assessment Clearinghouse, c/o San Dieguito Union High School District, 710 Encinitas Blvd., Encinitas, CA 92024.

Vavrus, L. 1990. Put Portfolios to the Test. *Instructor* 100 (1): 48–53.

Wiggins, G. 1989. A True Test: Toward More Authentic and Equitable Assessment. *Phi Delta Kappan* 70 (9): 703–13.

———. 1992. Creating Tests Worth Taking. *Educational Leadership* 49 (3): 26–33.

Zessoules, R., and H. Gardner. 1991. Authentic Assessment: Beyond the Buzzword and into the Classroom. In *Expanding Student Assessment*, ed. V. Perrone, 47–71. Alexandria, Va.: Association for Supervision and Curriculum Development.

ADDITIONAL READINGS

Altieri, G. 1990. A Structural Model for Student Outcomes: Assessment Programs in Community Colleges. *Community College Review* 17 (4): 15–21.

Archbald, D. A., and F. M. Newmann. 1988. *Beyond Standardized Testing: Assessing Authentic Academic Achievement in the Secondary School.* Reston, Va.: National Association of Secondary School Principals.

Ballard, L. 1992. Portfolios and Self-Assessment. *English Journal* 81 (2): 46–48.

Barone, T. 1991. Assessment as Theater: Staging an Exposition. *Educational Leadership* 48 (5): 57–59.

Bradfield-Krieder, P. 1998. Creating a Performance-Based Classroom. *American Secondary Education* 26 (4): 15–21.

Christenson, S. L., and J. E. Ysseldyke. 1989. Assessing Student Performance: An Important Change Is Needed. *Journal of School Psychology* 27 (4): 409–25.

Cizek, G. J. 1991. Innovation or Enervation? Performance Assessment in Perspective. *Phi Delta Kappan* 72 (9): 695–99.

Cooper, W., and B. J. Brown. 1992. Using Portfolios to Empower Student Writers. *English Journal* 81 (2): 40–45.

Frazier, D. M., and F. L. Paulson. 1992. How Portfolios Motivate Reluctant Writers. *Educational Leadership* 49 (3): 62–65.

Fuchs, L. S., and S. L. Deno. 1991. Paradigmatic Distinctions between Instructionally Relevant Measurement Models. *Exceptional Children* 57 (6): 488–500.

Hansen, J. 1992. Literacy Portfolios: Helping Students Know Themselves. *Educational Leadership* 49 (3): 66–68.

Hansen, J. M. 1998. Performance Based Tests Improve Student Learning. *Kappa Delta Pi Record* 34 (4): 124–28.

Hebert, E. A. 1992. Portfolios Invite Reflection—From Students *and* Staff. *Educational Leadership* 49 (8): 58–61.

Heshusius, L. 1991. Curriculum-Based Assessment and Direct Instruction: Critical Reflections on Fundamental Assumptions. *Exceptional Children* 57 (4): 315–28.

Krechevsky, M. 1991. Project Spectrum: An Innovative Assessment Alternative. *Educational Leadership* 48 (5): 43–48.

Maeroff, G. I. 1991. Assessing Alternative Assessment. *Phi Delta Kappan* 73 (4): 272–81.

Mason, R. 1995. Using Electronic Networking for Assessment. In *Open and Distance Learning Today,* ed. F. Lockwood. London: Routledge.

McLean, L. D. 1990. Time to Replace the Classroom Test with Authentic Measurement. *Alberta Journal of Educational Research* 36 (1): 78–84.

Means, B., B. Penuel, and E. Quellmaiz. 2000. Developing Assessments for Tomorrow's Classrooms. *The Secondary Conference on Educational Technology, 2000 Measuring Impacts and Shaping the Future [Proceedings].* Alexandria, Va.

Mitchell, R. 1992. *Testing for Learning: How New Approaches to Evaluation Can Improve American Schools.* New York: Free Press.

O'Brien, C. W. 1992. A Large-Scale Assessment to Support the Process Paradigm. *English Journal* 81 (1): 28–33.

Olson, L. 2002. Idaho to Adopt "Adaptive" Online State Testing. *Education Week* 21 (19): 6–8.

O'Neil, J. 1992. Putting Performance Assessment to the Test. *Educational Leadership* 49 (8): 14–19.

Oregon to Administer Standardized Tests on Computers. 2001. *Electronic Education Report* 8 (9): 7–9.

Paris, S. G. 1991. Portfolio Assessment for Young Readers. *Reading Teacher* 44 (9): 680–82.

Pickering, J. W., and J. C. Bowers. 1990. Assessing Value-Added Outcomes Assessment. *Measurement and Evaluation in Counseling and Development* 22 (4): 215–21.

Portfolios Illuminate the Path for Dynamic, Interactive Readers. *Journal of Reading* 33 (8): 644–47.

Shavelson, R. J., and G. P. Baxter. 1992. What We've Learned about Assessing Hands-On Science. *Educational Leadership* 49 (3): 20–25.

South Dakota Developing Comprehensive Online Tests for Students. 2001. *Curriculum Administrator* 37 (7): 10.

Steinberg, J. 2001. Grilling the Little Ones: Online Testing for Kids. *New York Times* 150: 4–5.

Stiggins, R. J. 1990. Toward a Relevant Classroom Assessment Research Agenda. *Alberta Journal of Educational Research* 36 (1): 92–97.

———. 1991. Assessment Literacy. *Phi Delta Kappa,* 72 (7): 534–39.

Stiggins, R. J., and N. F. Conklin. 1992. *In Teachers' Heads: Investigating the Practices of Classroom Assessment.* Albany, N.Y.: State University of New York Press.

Stiggins, R. J., N. F. Conklin, and N. J. Bridgeford. 1986. Classroom Assessment: A Key to Effective Education. *Educational Measurement: Issues and Practice* 5 (2): 5–17.

Traub, R. E. 1990. Assessment in the Classroom: What Is the Role of Research? *Alberta Journal of Educational Research* 6 (1): 85–91.

Travis, J. E. 1996. Meaningful Assessment. *The Clearing House* 69: 308–12.

Wilson, R. J. 1990. Classroom Processes in Evaluating Student Achievement. *Alberta Journal of Educational Research* 36 (1): 4–17.

Wolf, D. P., P. G. LeMahieu, and J. Eresh. 1992. Good Measure: Assessment as a Tool for Educational Reform. *Educational Leadership* 49 (3): 8–13.

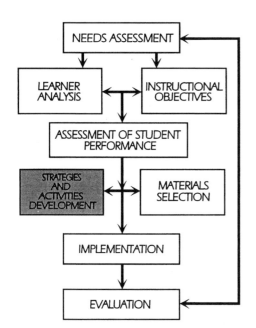

11

Strategies and Activities Development

This chapter provides information to help the reader

- compare content-based and cognitive-based instruction

- understand the dimensions across which instructional strategies and activities vary

- identify learner characteristics relevant to selecting instructional strategies and activities

- understand the impact of the level of the instructional objective on the process of selecting instructional strategies and activities

- select appropriate instructional strategies and activities given learner characteristics and instructional objectives

At some point in the planning process, the teacher must decide on the strategies that will be used to facilitate learning and the activities the students will be involved in during instruction. In the instructional design process used in this book, these strategies and activities are determined after instructional objectives are selected and a learner analysis is conducted. In fact, these two steps are the foundation for the selection of strategies and activities.

CONTENT-BASED VERSUS COGNITIVE-BASED INSTRUCTION

Content-based instruction, as the name implies, puts the content to be mastered at the forefront. The timing and structure of a particular course of instruction is driven by the goal of covering a given amount of content. Cognitive-based instruction is premised on the proposition that each learner interprets the content that is learned based upon what has been learned in the past, and that new learning in turn creates the templates for future learning. For example, during a lecture on erosion, what a seventh-grade student learns will be significantly shaped by knowledge of concepts such as "silt" and "deposit." In turn, the knowledge gained in this lesson will form the template for topics such as water pollution. In addition to emphasizing prior knowledge, advocates of cognitive-based instruction believe that learners use certain strategies to generate their knowledge, *and that these learning strategies are equal to the content in importance.*

Content-based teaching assumes that good students will automatically acquire appropriate learning strategies as a by-product of "good" instruction; cognitive-based instruction has as a goal establishing for each student a set of learning tools that will enable that student to learn independently. The following assumptions of cognitive-based instruction are derived from the work of Jones et al. (1987):

- Instruction should be related to the learning strategies possessed by a student, and there is a high correlation between a student's developmental stage and the strategies possessed.

- Instruction should include the strategies used by the scholars in the content areas.

- The bases of learning are the schemata and instructional enterprises that have been mastered by the student.

- Instruction should encourage students to construct and connect new schemata and instructional enterprises.

- Instruction should encourage independence throughout the acquisition and testing of new learning strategies.

WHAT ARE LEARNING STRATEGIES AND ACTIVITIES?

Students employ *learning strategies* to assist them in acquiring, interpreting, broadening, retaining, and using knowledge. Figure 11.1 presents the stages of learning and sample strategies representing each stage. The strategy of metacognition is also represented as managing the learning process—an important component. These stages and strategies are based upon the works of Tessmer, Jonassen, and Caverly (1989), Snowman (1986), and Cutlip (1988).

If you visit a variety of classrooms, you would see students involved in a variety of *learning activities*. Some students might be listening to a lecture by the teacher, others working at a computer accessing web-based courseware. Students might be working in a small group, role playing or debating. One way to categorize learning activities is by the *action* involved, the *social configuration* used, and the *source of guidance* during the instructional event. Figure 11.2 provides examples for each of these categories. Note that under the category "Source of Guidance," "Teacher" should be broadly interpreted to include the author of instructional materials.

Fig. 11.1. Learning strategies

Getting Ready to Learn	Obtaining the Information		Learning the Information	Managing the Process
Planning	**Attending**	**Organizing**		
Relaxation	Focus	Contrast	Repetition	Metacognition
Anxiety Reduction	Attention	Outlining	Rehearsal	
Goal Setting	Search	Analyzing	Mnemonics	
Concentration		Underlining	Paraphrasing	
		Note Taking	Metaphors	
		Mapping	Exemplifying	
			Analogies	
			Summarizing	
			Hypothesizing	
			Testing	
			Revising	
			Brainstorming	
			Reflecting	
			Reformulating	

Fig. 11.2. Learning activities

Action	Social Configurations	Source of Guidance
Listen	Individual	Student
View	Small Group	Peer Group
Write	Large Group	Teacher
Draw		
Speak		
Sing		
Touch		
Walk		
Run		
Dance		

HOW DO INSTRUCTIONAL STRATEGIES AND ACTIVITIES VARY?

Instructional strategies and activities vary as to the source of reinforcement and guidance during the instructional event, the cognitive environment provided, and the physical environment provided. The instructional team will need to consider each of these variables carefully when selecting strategies and activities.

Source of Reinforcement and Guidance

Who will provide the reinforcement and guidance during the instruction? Will it be the teacher or another adult? Will it be a peer tutor? Will the guidance and reinforcement be contained in the textbook or in an interactive computer presentation? The following are categories of instructional activities and examples for each.

TEACHER-ORIENTED ACTIVITIES

Teacher-oriented activities are those in which the teacher provides the majority of the structure, guidance, and reinforcement.

- *Lectures.* The lecture method, despite the admonishments of practically every methods text, remains widely used and abused, especially at the secondary school level (Kirn and Kellough 1974). There are some learners and performance objectives for which the lecture method is appropriate, and it should not be totally discarded.

- *Field trips.* Although a field trip may also involve other types of learning activities, the majority of field trips consist of activities in which the teacher or some other adult is the main source of guidance.

- *Drills.* Whether the student is standing and reciting or completing a set of problems on a worksheet, the teacher is usually close at hand during drills.

- *Demonstrations.* Demonstrations involve the learner observing the teacher as he or she performs a technique or procedure. This type of activity is often used in conjunction with a lecture.

- *Teacher-led class discussions.* Through questioning and feedback by the teacher during discussions, the learners are led toward the attainment of the performance objective.

GROUP-ORIENTED ACTIVITIES

The main source of structure, guidance, and reinforcement in group-oriented activities is other learners. Structure, guidance, and reinforcement may also be generated internally by the learner and provided by the teacher, but such input is secondary to that received from the group.

- *Problem solving/brainstorming.* This is a specific procedure for the creative solving of problems. Although the teacher may initially direct this approach, learner groups can implement the procedure with minimal assistance. Paired problem solving where students work in pairs and verbalize their attempts to solve math problems has proven to be successful in improving problem-solving abilities (Heiman et al. 1987).

- *Debates.* Debate is a formal group activity if the teacher does not provide the majority of direction.

- *Group discussions.* Group discussion is a free-flowing group activity in which members of the group provide direction and structure in a more or less spontaneous manner.

- *Group projects.* When group projects are conducted, a product is produced. Problem solving and committee work may be involved. The product might include a written report or a non-print product such as a PowerPoint presentation, transparencies, or a poster display.

- *Dramatics.* Groups may be involved in dramatic activities, including role playing, storytelling, plays, and puppet shows. These activities may be performed by themselves or in conjunction with other types of group activities.

STUDENT-ORIENTED ACTIVITIES

In student-oriented activities the individual learner provides the majority of the structure, guidance, and reinforcement.

- *Preparing written presentations.* Written presentations include book or video reports, essays, and reports on events.

- *Preparing oral presentations.* Oral presentations include speeches, storytelling, and puppet shows.

- *Preparing other kinds of non-print presentations.* Non-print presentations can involve paintings, models, and many other kinds of products.

- *Individual assignments without products.* An individual might read, view, listen, or perform some other activity without producing a product. The amount of guidance provided by the instructional material can vary from considerable to virtually nonexistent. The learner can be left alone during the work, or varying amounts of interaction with teachers or peers may occur.

- *Laboratory experiments.* The individual conducts an experiment.

- *Leading a group.* In group leadership, the individual provides the main source of guidance, feedback, and reinforcement to one or more other learners.

Cognitive Environment Provided

What learning strategies are required to be successful in the instructional event selected? Which learning strategies will be supplemented or supplanted by the instruction? How much assistance will be provided in terms of memory aids and prompts, outlining and note-taking help, or paraphrasing and summarizing support?

Suppose a student is studying the Battle of Britain. At one extreme, the student is sent forth to research the topic and locates a chapter in a book on World War II that discusses the battle, its outcome, and the implications. The student uses this chapter as the basis for a presentation on this topic. At the other extreme, the student might be given the same written material with an introduction, outline, and summary added. In addition, each page or two could have been summarized with key ideas outlined. Suggestions for ways in which the material could be presented might also be provided.

The same range of cognitive assistance could be provided in other media. A videotape can be simply a technically adequate rendition of the dissection of an earthworm. The same information could be presented within a different cognitive environment by adding an introduction, illustrative diagrams, pointers, paraphrased steps, inserted questions and answers, and other techniques that supplement and supplant learning strategies. In fact, research has demonstrated that if the instructor simply provides directions that describe the purpose of the video, the students' perception of the content can change (Sharp et al. 1992).

Another example might involve a lecture by the teacher. Suppose that the teacher was lecturing on the causes of the Creek Indian Wars and was pointing out that a major cause was the maintenance of trails by the whites through Creek territories. The teacher could change the cognitive environment by providing an experiential base upon which the students could form a mental model of the concept being taught. The students might write or talk about an example of someone coming into their "territory." This might be a sibling or parent who came into their room uninvited or a rival gang member who invaded their turf.

Physical Environment Provided

The teacher has some control over the physical environment in the classroom, though not as much as is usually preferred. Windows can be shaded or blinds can be removed. Individual workstations can be created. Headphones can help provide background music and can help block out other sounds.

Strategies and activities in which students are employed can take place within a variety of physical environments. See chapter 8 for a detailed description of these environments.

SELECTING INSTRUCTIONAL STRATEGIES AND ACTIVITIES

How does the instructional team select the instructional strategies and activities that will have the greatest probability of success? The possible permutations of guidance sources, cognitive environments, and physical environments are legion. In fact, there is probably no one combination that is clearly the best. The science of instruction is not developed enough for the selection of strategies and activities to be algorithmic. However, the instructional team should plan strategies and activities based upon *the level of learning targeted by the instructional objective, the learner characteristics, and the teacher's judgment as to the range of instructional activities possible.*

Level and Type of Learning Targeted by the Instructional Objective

1. *Associative and discrimination learning.* For performance objectives that involve either associative or discrimination learning, instructional activities involving drills are indicated. As Weinstein and Mayer (1986) point out, repeating information can be highly effective for basic instruction. These can be either teacher-, group-, or student-oriented activities. Games that involve drill and provide a variety of reinforcement can be useful.

   Instructional strategies for this level of learning include using repetition, mnemonics, covert practice, and imagery. Combinations of these techniques can be used effectively. For example, Kulhavy, Peterson, and Schwartz (1986) describe a technique for remembering textual information by associating it with specific locations within a familiar building. They also describe the key-word procedure for learning foreign-language vocabulary. In this procedure, the student associates an English word with the vocabulary word and then forms a visual image that relates the English word to the translation. For example, to learn the Spanish word *pollo,* the student might envision a chicken sitting on a pole or what a Polish chicken might look like.

2. *Concrete concept learning.* Activities that broaden the experiential base of the learner are vital to the acquisition of concrete concepts. As an example, sixth-grade students studying baroque music might encounter the concrete concepts "polyphonic" and "homophonic." A variety of experiences including listening to examples, singing, humming, touching materials of consistent and varied textures, and walking at consistent and varied speeds might be provided. Concrete concepts are strengthened when they are based on a variety of sensory inputs.

   The student should be encouraged to think about the experience and to categorize it in relation to other experiences. In the previous example, the student may place materials with similar textures in boxes. Students might also think of other examples that might be similar to those being experienced.

3. *Defined concept learning.* An introduction to a defined concept might include an experiential activity to reinforce foundational concrete concept schemata. However, the defined concepts themselves are best taught through activities that provide and reinforce the concepts included in the definition, and the relationship of these concepts to each other.

   For example, learning the defined concept "physical weathering" would require the mastery and association of a variety of concepts such as "particle," "exposure," and "disintegrate." Students might read individually or listen to a lecture to obtain the initial information. Reinforcement and practice with the concept might be done in groups and include experiments. Appropriate strategies might include selecting or describing examples of the concept, stating the definition in one's own words, and brainstorming new examples.

4. *Rule learning.* For rules that are a combination of concrete concepts, experiential activities in small groups under the guidance of a peer or the teacher could be beneficial. Rules that consist of defined concepts can be introduced in a variety of activities. Practice and reinforcement should involve both individual and small-group work.

5. *Problem solving.* Experiential activities can be very important in reaching problem-solving objectives. The teacher is important as a source of guidance; group work and peer guid-

ance is also very important. Group problem solving, preparation of presentations, and laboratory experiments are also appropriate to help learners to reach instructional objectives at the problem-solving level.

For rules consisting of defined concepts and for problem solving, the learning strategies are similar. These include brainstorming and hypothesizing, testing, reflecting, and reformulating, and creating metaphors and analogies.

For example, if the instructional objective involved coming up with a rule predicting the relationship between stream flow (direction and velocity) and erosion and deposition, the successful student might hypothesize a relationship between the direction of stream flow in relationship to the shore and the amount of erosion or deposition. The student may then test out the hypothesis by experimentation or by using secondary data. After reflecting on the results, the student may modify the hypothesis to take into account the influence of velocity. During this process, the learner might have employed analogies such as "velocity of stream flow is to erosion as understanding is to tolerance."

6. *Affective instructional objectives.* Appropriate activities for affective instructional objectives include teacher-led discussions, field trips, problem-solving activities, debates, group discussions, and preparation of presentations.

7. *Motor skills instructional objectives.* Demonstrations by the teacher, drills, and preparations by an individual for a presentation involving the skills to be mastered are some of the appropriate activities for teaching motor skills instructional objectives.

Note that no matter what the type or level of learning, there are pre-instructional event strategies that are useful. These include relaxation, anxiety reduction (both physiological and cognitive), goal setting, and concentration.

Learner Characteristics

The following learner characteristics are based on one or more of the learner analysis procedures discussed in chapter 8. Many of the activities prescribed are recommended by the designers of the learner analysis procedures.

1. *Physiological.* Students who need kinesthetic activity can be involved in activities that require touching, walking, running, and dancing. Activities for students who like to eat or drink during learning include both small-group and individual projects. Keep in mind, though, that the learner characteristics and activities must be matched within the constraints of the instructional environment. Also, some students might be irresponsible, which would make some of these activities impossible.

2. *Affective.* For highly motivated students, any type of learning activity can be employed. Even if the student does not prefer an activity, a high degree of motivation should allow him or her to learn. Of course, the teacher should be cautious in assigning too many non-preferred activities to students because even highly motivated learners might get discouraged. Students who are not motivated can be targeted for special attention from the teacher if they are motivated by adult attention. For those motivated by peers, group work may be the answer. In the online environment, it is very important to build in opportunity for peer-to-peer interaction. An online "break room" may be a good idea if the students can work within established guidelines for behavior.

3. *Responsibility.* A learner with a high degree of responsibility should be able to succeed in group and individual activities. Learners who are not responsible should be placed in

teacher-oriented activities, or in a group with an effective leader. Responsibility should be increased whenever possible.

4. *Preference for structure.* Learners who prefer a high degree of structure can be involved in activities such as lectures, drills (any type of seatwork that provides clear directions and few options), and teacher-led discussions. Students who prefer a low degree of structure benefit from activities involving problem solving, group discussions or projects, and individual projects that allow a great deal of latitude.

5. *Working alone or with others.* For students who prefer to work alone, any of the student-oriented activities is appropriate. A group-oriented activity is most appropriate for a learner who prefers to work with peers. The teacher can use a technique such as a sociogram to assist in assigning students to groups. A student will have very definite ideas regarding who is a peer, and merely working in a group might not suffice.

6. *Learning with adults.* Teacher-oriented learning activities are most appropriate for learners who prefer working with adults. However, both group and student-oriented activities might be appropriate if there is an adult nearby to provide direction and reinforcement.

7. *Preference for oral work.* For learners who prefer to tell others what they have learned, activities such as group discussions, debates, preparing oral presentations, preparing non-print presentations, and participating in dramatic presentations are appropriate.

8. *Preference for written work.* Students who prefer to prepare written presentations would benefit from activities that require this.

9. *Preference for mobility.* For learners who prefer mobility while learning, activities such as working on dramatic presentations, preparing non-print presentations, and reading, viewing, and listening in the library media center would be appropriate.

10. *Leadership.* Learners who prefer a leadership role when learning benefit from activities that involve leading a group. Such a group might be a committee, a group of actors, or a group preparing some type of product.

11. *Source of reinforcement.* Students with an external locus of control will benefit from activities in which clear directions and reinforcement are provided. Teacher-oriented activities are indicated. Learners with an internal locus of control benefit from student-oriented activities.

12. *Cognitive.* The foundation of cognitive-based instruction is the premise that learning tools are vital to the success of the instructional venture. An important part of preparing for instruction should be obtaining information on the learning tools a student possesses and making sure that missing or inadequate tools are supplanted or supplemented where possible.

13. *Learning anxiety.* Learning anxiety is a condition that when present to a high degree often hampers the use of a wide variety of learning tools. As an example, highly anxious students will often have a great deal of difficulty locating the important information in a visual display. Anxious learners often will not possess a clear idea of what is to be learned. Summarizing and paraphrasing skills are often not employed adequately by highly anxious students. If instruction is being designed for students who possess a high degree of learning anxiety, care must be taken to build in anxiety-reduction exercises at the start of the lesson and to compensate for the student's inability to apply learning tools throughout the lesson. Strategies and activities for anxious learners include

a. providing for peer tutoring so that the anxious student can work with a supportive friend

b. providing extra time for a student to obtain information and to respond to a question

c. making sure that directions are clear for the student and that, when possible, the directions are in a format that the student may refer to during instruction

d. providing positive feedback whenever possible; keeping negative feedback to a minimum and delivering it positively and privately

e. supplanting the various learning tools (See following recommendations.)

14. *Learning tools.* In chapter 8, the *Learning Tools Inventory* was introduced. The purpose of this inventory is to assist an instructional team to become aware of the learning tools that are missing or weak in a student. Once this is accomplished, the instruction can be designed to both supplant and strengthen these tools. Here are strategies that correspond to each of the tools:

a. *Establishing set.* Activation of background knowledge and relevant schemata can be accomplished by creating concept trees, making lists of terms and definitions, predicting central ideas, creating hypotheses or assumptions about the material to be learned, and checking the veracity of information already possessed. These are all important strategies prior to the lesson. In addition, the learner might recall experiences that are related to the material to be learned.

b. *Structuring information.* Identification of main and subordinate ideas and creation of concept trees, information maps, and complete schemata are all important strategies for structuring information. Of course, outlining and note-taking skills are fundamental. Some learners might benefit from drawing a picture or a diagram.

c. *Locating criterial information.* Learners who are most successful at locating the important information in any medium have a clear idea as to what is to be learned. They are alert, yet relaxed, and are aware that the important information might not be what is most apparent in the presentation.

d. *Generating questions.* Hypothesizing, brainstorming, making predictions, estimating, and creating definitions and rules are all important learning strategies that often involve the generation of questions.

e. *Checking self-perceptions.* The learner may reflect on how the new material has changed what was known previously. The relationship of new concepts to others can be tested. Predictions and hypotheses can be checked and new ones formulated.

f. *Motivation.* Relaxation exercises combined with goal setting and concentration are useful in self-motivation.

g. *Summarizing the lesson.* Paraphrasing the information into the learners' own words is an important strategy. Describing and arranging the most important concepts and their relationship is useful. Diagrams, concept trees, and schemata are tools for summarizing what has been learned and preparing for the next instructional experience.

Information Skills

In his learning and information model, Cutlip (1988, 20–23) lists what he calls information skills. Some of these tools can clearly be seen to be strategies that fall within the categories found in the *Learning Tools Inventory*—for example, formulating questions, note-taking, and underlining. Cutlip goes beyond these and includes text-analysis skills within his model. These skills include structural analysis, text structure, and content structure.

During diagnosis and prescription of learning tools by the teacher, the ability and tendency of the learner to employ both cognitive and information skills are vital tools to assess. In fact, the school library media specialist is probably in the best position to bring the power of learning tools and cognitive-based teaching into the classroom.

LEVELS OF INVOLVEMENT BY THE SCHOOL LIBRARY MEDIA SPECIALIST AT THE STRATEGIES AND ACTIVITIES DEVELOPMENT STEP

The Initial Level

At the initial level, the school library media specialist can assist the teacher at the strategies and activities development step by providing learning materials, facilities, and professional collection materials.

The library media program can be involved in providing a variety of activities. Students can come to the center to perform group and individual activities, and the school library media specialist can maintain an environment that will encourage this type of use. An adequate general and reference collection is essential.

The provision and maintenance of production facilities and equipment with which the students can prepare presentations can be a service of the center's program. Students without access to such equipment are severely restricted as to how to present what they have learned.

Students need to be instructed in the use of the library media center's materials, including the general collection, reference materials, special collection materials, computer programs, production equipment, and so on. The roles of the school library media specialist tend to blur in this case, as providing library instruction to students also serves to provide teachers with a broader range of potential activities for their students.

The following materials are recommended for the professional collection:

Browne, M. N., and S. M. Keeley. 2000. *Asking the Right Questions: A Guide to Critical Thinking Skills.* 6th ed. Upper Saddle River, N.J.: Prentice Hall College Division.

Cook, D. M. 1989. *Strategic Learning in the Content Areas.* Madison, Wis.: Wisconsin Department of Public Instruction.

Cutlip, G. W. 1988. *Learning and Information: Skills for the Secondary Classroom and Library Media Program.* Englewood, Colo.: Libraries Unlimited.

DiVincenzo, J., and F. Ricci. 1999. Group Decision Making. Available at National Education Association Web site: http://www.nea.org [May 8, 2003].

Graham, K. G., and H. A. Robinson. 1984. *Study Skills Handbook: A Guide for All Teachers.* Washington, D.C.: Small Planet Communications.

Hawley, S. H., and R. C. Hawley. 1987. *A Teachers' Handbook of Practical Strategies for Teaching Thinking in the Classroom.* Amherst, Mass.: Education Research Associates.

Lyman, L., and H. C. Foyle. 1990. Cooperative Grouping for Interactive Learning. Available at National Education Association Web site: http://www.nea.org [May 8, 2003].

Rafoth, M. A. 1999. Inspiring Independent Learning. Available at National Education Association Web site: http://www.nea.org [May 8, 2003].

Rafoth, M. A., L. Leal, and L. DeFabo. 1993. Strategies for Learning and Remembering. Available at National Education Association Web site: http://www.nea.org.

Reid, J., P. Forrestal, and J. Cook. 1990. *Small Group Learning in the Classroom.* Portsmouth, N.H.: Heinemann.

Thomas, J. 1988. *Nonprint Production for Students, Teachers, and Media Specialists.* 2nd ed. Englewood, Colo.: Libraries Unlimited.

The Moderate Level

At the moderate level of instructional consultation, the school library media specialist responds to a teacher's request for assistance. Such assistance is usually informal and involves a single step in the instructional design process. At the strategies and activities development step, this assistance can involve 1) helping the teacher select strategies and activities for learners with particular characteristics, 2) designing strategies and activities for a given performance objective, and 3) designing instruction to broaden a given learner's preferences and increase his or her learning-tool repertoire. The teacher may also request that the school library media specialist work with one or more students in preparing a presentation or some other individual or group activity.

The following is a scenario in which a teacher requests assistance from a school library media specialist at this step.

A SCENARIO

Lis Morrill, the school library media specialist at Huntington Elementary, had decided earlier in the year to attempt to move up to the moderate level at the strategies and activities development step. She had always been interested in creating activities and had done a substantial amount of reading on the subject. She prepared a bulletin board for the teacher's lounge that announced professional collection materials on the subject. She put a notice in several of her newsletters announcing the availability of the materials and her willingness to serve as an idea source for activities design. Al Crevling, a newly graduated fifth-grade teacher, has used several of the materials and has decided to ask for assistance with a special problem.

Lis: Good afternoon, Al. What can I do for you today?

Al: I'm looking for the activities idea person. I've read some of the materials that you have here on activities, and I've tried to match up my kids with activities.

Lis: Good for you! How did it work out?

Al: Pretty well. Bob Jackson just thrived as group discussion leader. Seemed to channel all of his natural pomposity in the right direction. For some students, it seemed to work a little too well.

Lis: Oh. . . . How do you mean?

Al: Well, I gave them the choice several times to work in groups or on their own, and each time the new girl, Marda Clemento, has chosen to work by herself. She does great work, but she's such a loner. I'd like to see her mix with the other kids more.

Lis: Well, maybe we should talk to the counselor about this, but you could build in some experiences to help to expand her learning preferences.

Al: Aha! The idea person. Go ahead.

Lis: A start would be to make an assignment where the students work in pairs. Assign Marda to a student who is very outgoing and make sure that they have a grand success. Continue this for a few weeks, and see if she changes her mind. If you do decide to try it, I know where some good group activity ideas can be found.

The In-Depth Level

IN-SERVICES

The strategies and activities development step presents a number of possible in-service topics for school library media specialists. They can introduce the concept of matching learning activities to learner characteristics. New materials and research that pertain to one or more activities can be presented.

INSTRUCTIONAL DESIGN TEAM PARTICIPATION

The school library media specialist can help one or more teachers work through the entire strategies and activities development step. Because this step is linked with several previously performed steps, the school library media specialist who is part of an instructional design team will often have worked on previous steps.

Here is an example of the strategies and activities development step. The instructional design team might have determined the following instructional objective: The eighth-grade general science student will write an original story or create a picture sequence describing the process by which different types of soil are eroded, carried away, and deposited. The product will contain accurate descriptions of the relationship of stream flow, size of particles, stream direction, and deposition. (Rule Learning)

The students have diverse learning styles, and the team has decided that three groupings can be accommodated, as follows:

1. Responsible, low preference for structure, peer-oriented, do not like written work. Some students have strong leadership skills, and most of the students in this group possess the learning tools.

2. Not as responsible, high preference for structure, peer-oriented, do not like written work, few leaders, many with high degree of learning anxiety, low motivation. Many problems with learning tools, particularly establishing set, structuring information, and checking self-perceptions.

3. Responsible, low preference for structure, not peer-oriented, prefer written work, motivated, possess most learning tools, some problems with learning anxiety.

The goal of the school library media specialist at the strategies and activities development step is to help the teachers select strategies and activities for the combinations of instructional objectives and learner characteristics and, perhaps, to provide the teachers with the skills to perform this step more effectively in the future.

At the start of the unit, initial content might be presented to the entire class, probably through the use of lecture and media. The appropriate rules relating to the concepts in the objective can be presented and illustrated at this time. The teacher should provide a clearly written introduction to the lesson and an outline of the information. Learning strategies such as hypothesizing, reflecting, and revising might be covered as part of the presentation.

Students in groups 1 and 2 might be combined and small groups of four to five students formed. After the whole-class presentation, these students can then break into their small groups for activities that include predicting the outcome of various erosion situations, discussing their predictions, testing these in experiments, and revising their hypotheses. The teacher will need to provide these groups with a list of suggested activities and timelines, and monitor these groups carefully to see that students are on task and are reaching the goals of the lesson.

The students in the third group may be allowed to work on their own, perhaps researching a particular question for a written report. Alternatively, they might be members of one of the other groups, serving as information gatherers and report writers.

THOUGHT PROVOKERS

Given the following instructional objectives and learner descriptions, recommend an appropriate learning strategy and activity for each combination of performance objective and learner description (AA, AB, etc.).

Performance Objectives:

A. Given twenty verbs in English, the learner will translate each into Spanish.

B. Write a paragraph comparing and contrasting physical and chemical weathering, including at least three original examples of each.

Learner Descriptions:

A. Low level of responsibility; prefers high degree of structure, working alone, and working with adults; external locus of control. Possesses most learning tools.

B. Highly motivated; prefers working with others, low degree of structure, oral work, and a leadership role. Problems with checking self-perceptions and summarizing.

C. Low motivation; prefers working with others and mobility; not responsible. Very low on learning tools.

(See appendix A for answers.)

REFERENCES

Cutlip, G. W. 1988. *Learning and Information: Skills for the Secondary Classroom and Library Media Program.* Englewood, Colo.: Libraries Unlimited.

Heiman, M., R. Narode, J. Slomianko, and J. Lochhead. 1987. *Teaching Thinking Skills: Mathematics.* Washington, D.C.: National Education Association.

Jones, B., A. S. Palinesar, D. S. Ogle, and E. G. Carr. 1987. *Strategic Teaching and Learning: Cognitive Instruction in the Content Areas.* Arlington, Va.: Association for Supervision and Curriculum Development in Cooperation with the North Central Regional Educational Laboratory.

Kirn, E. C., and R. D. Kellough. 1974. *A Resource Guide for Secondary School Teaching.* New York: Macmillan.

Kulhavy, R. W., S. Peterson, and N. H. Schwartz. 1986. Working Memory: The Encoding Process. In *Cognitive Classroom Learning: Understanding, Thinking, and Problem Solving,* ed. G. D. Phye and A. Thomas, 115–40. Orlando, Fla.: Academic Press.

Sharp, D. L., J. D. Branford, M. Vye, S. R. Goldman, C. Kinzer, and S. Soraci, Jr. 1992. Literacy in an Age of Integrated Media. In *Elementary School Literacy: Critical Issues,* ed. M. J. Dreher and W. Slater, 1–25, 183–209. Norwood, Mass.: Christopher Gordon.

Snowman, J. 1986. Learning Tactics and Strategies. In *Cognitive Classroom Learning: Understanding, Thinking, and Problem Solving,* ed. G. D. Phye and A. Thomas, 243–75. Orlando, Fla.: Academic Press.

Tessmer, M. A., D. P. Jonassen, and D. C. Caverly. 1989. Learning Strategies: A New Instructional Technology. In *World Yearbook of Education 1988: Education for the New Technologies,* ed. D. Harris, 29–47. London: Kogan Page.

Weinstein, C. E., and R. E. Mayer. 1986. The Teaching of Learning Strategies. In *Handbook of Research on Teaching,* 3rd ed., ed. M. C. Wittrock, 315–27. New York: Macmillan.

ADDITIONAL READINGS

Collins, A., J. S. Brown, and A. Holum. 1991. Cognitive Apprenticeship: Making Thinking Visible. *American Educator* (Winter): 6 (11): 38–40.

Connolly, P., and T. Vilardi, ed. 1989. *Writing to Learn Mathematics and Science.* New York: Teachers College Press.

Heward, W., T. E. Heron, and N. L. Cooke. 1982. Tutor Huddle: Key Element in a Class-Wide Peer Tutoring System. *Elementary School Journal* 83 (8): 115–23.

Kahn, E. A., C. C. Walter, and L. R. Johannessen. 1984. Making Small Groups Work: Controversy Is the Key. *English Journal* 73 (2): 63–65.

Lickona, P. 1991. *Educating for Character.* New York: Bantam.

Lyman, L., and H. C. Foyle. 1990. *Cooperative Grouping for Interactive Learning: Students, Teachers, and Administrators.* Washington, D.C.: National Education Association.

Meiser, N. A. 1999. Gifted Students and Cooperative Learning: A Study of Grouping Strategies. *Roeper Review* 21 (4): 315.

Myrick, R. D., and R. P. Bowman. 1981. *Children Helping Children: Teaching Students to Become Friendly Helpers.* Minneapolis: Educational Media Corporation.

Neber, H., M. Finsterwald, and N. Urban. 2001. Cooperative Learning with Gifted and High-Achieving Students: A Review and Meta-Analysis of 12 Students. *High Ability Studies* 12 (2): 199.

Pauker, R. A. 1987. *Teaching Thinking and Reasoning Skills.* Arlington, Va.: American Association of School Administrators.

Peer Research Laboratory. This is not a work but an agency devoted to the concept that every student should have the opportunity to act as tutor. The address is Center for Advanced Study in Education, CUNY, Room 620, 25 West 43rd St., New York, NY 10036.

Pizzo. J. 1982. Small Group Techniques = Big Gains in Reading. *Early Years* (May): 30–31, 73–74.

Presseisen, B. Z., ed. 1988. *At-Risk Students and Thinking: Perspectives on Research.* Philadelphia: Research for Better Schools.

Sweeny, J., and C. M. Reigeluth. 1984. The Lecture and Instructional Design: A Contradiction in Terms? *Educational Technology* 24 (August): 7–12.

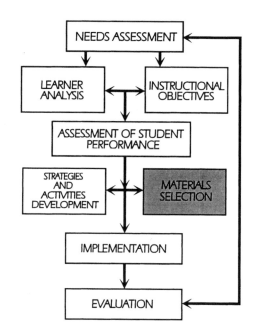

12

Materials Selection

This chapter provides information to help the reader

- understand the steps in the instructional materials selection sequence

- understand the value of including as many of the steps outlined in this chapter as possible when selecting instructional materials

- select and justify a medium when given appropriate information

- learn previewing criteria

- associate learner characteristics with an appropriate media design

- associate levels of learning with appropriate media design

THE PURPOSE OF THE MATERIALS SELECTION STEP

Instructional materials are an essential part of the teaching and learning process. Students spend a large amount of time viewing, listening to, and otherwise interacting with instructional materials.

Hundreds of thousands of titles of instructional materials are available to the teacher. The National Information Center for Educational Media (NICEM) alone boasts a database of 460,000 bibliographic citations covering fifteen media formats. Beginning in the 1960s, the collection of instructional materials in schools has grown dramatically, often assisted by federal programs.

Despite the wide variety of available materials and the advocacy for purchase and use of instructional materials, there is widespread discontent with actual instructional results. Many materials are used only once, if ever, and then left to languish on the shelf.

Instructional materials are synonymous with instructional technology in the eyes of many teachers and administrators. Unfortunately, the misuse of instructional materials and the resultant failure of the materials to live up to expectations have contributed to a lack of acceptance of instructional technology.

Those who have condemned instructional technology because of the failure of any one instructional item have failed to realize that the instructional design process puts the selection of materials at the sixth step in the process. Dashing into the library media center and pulling out an unfamiliar item to use in the next class is putting the materials selection step first or second and will most certainly result in frustration if the teacher expects certain learning to occur. Rejecting instructional technology as a whole on the basis of this kind of experience makes no more sense than throwing out a computer because it fails to operate with a defective CD-ROM.

As stated earlier, the decision involving the instructional materials should be made after considering several sets of information. This information is generated as the result of the instructional objectives step, the learner analysis step, and, to some extent, the assessment of student performance step. *To select instructional materials without considering this information is to invite disaster and to waste the funds used to obtain the materials.*

THE MATERIALS SELECTION SEQUENCE

Within the materials selection step itself are a series of decisions to be made. In general, the more consideration given to various factors in the selection process, the greater the probability that the instructional materials will be effective. This is made evident by considering the following two selection activities. If a teacher opens a publisher's catalog and selects an item at random, the chances that this item will be effective are practically nil. But if an item of instructional material has been tried out with learners and has enabled those learners to reach the instructional objective, the use of the item with similar learners will most likely result in successful learning. Although this contention seems self-evident, much of the instructional materials selection activity that occurs in the schools more closely resembles the former example.

The following are tasks appropriate to the selection of instructional materials once the first five steps of the instructional design process have been completed:

1. selecting the format

2. identifying the materials

3. locating reviews of the materials

4. previewing the materials

5. evaluating the materials with actual learners.

This process can be thought of as putting the materials through sieves of progressively finer mesh until the materials that emerge are the ones most likely to be effective (see fig. 12.1). The main thrust of this chapter will be to consider each of the tasks in this sequence in depth.

Selecting the Format

Given the universe of titles of instructional materials, the first task is to select the most appropriate medium or format. It should be made clear at this point that such a decision is as much an art as a science and is by no means clear-cut. Much of the research in the field of instructional media since the 1960s involved trying to determine which format was most effective (e.g., was a CD-ROM or an online source better?). The results were almost universally disappointing. Much energy has been spent trying to invent an algorithmic approach to selecting a proper format, given a specific objective. The creation of such an algorithm is a tenuous undertaking.

The selection of the format, however, still must be accomplished. And although we do not as yet know enough to make this task algorithmic, categories of information, including research results, can be identified. It must be emphasized at this point that each category must be considered in relation to the others and not in isolation.

The categories of information and their implication for the selection of media are:

1. *Cost.* It is much more fun to talk about selection of instructional materials without reference to real life, but sooner or later the hard realities of the budget enter. Costs of materi-

Fig. 12.1. The selection of instructional materials

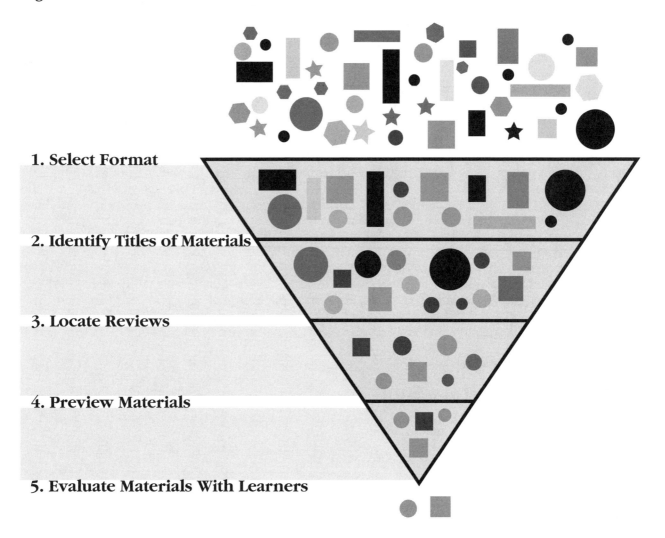

1. Select Format

2. Identify Titles of Materials

3. Locate Reviews

4. Preview Materials

5. Evaluate Materials With Learners

als can range from several dollars to several thousand dollars. There is a correlation between type of format and cost, with DVDs and online databases usually costing more than CD-ROMs and videotapes. However, DVDs and online databases continue to steadily decrease in price, thus making them a more feasible purchase for schools. The person selecting instructional materials with a very limited budget would avoid frustration by choosing the less expensive media. There are qualifications to this generalization, of course. The more expensive media may be available at a low cost from district or state agencies. Materials in these formats can be rented or obtained at a low cost through a licensing agreement.

2. *Equipment availability.* If a school does not own equipment that is compatible with a particular format, then materials in this format must be given a low priority. This is also true if only a few items of the equipment are available and are already overused. As an example, if a school has one laserdisc player and eight VCRs, all else being equal, a videotape would be given priority over a laserdisc.

3. *Learner characteristics.* The characteristics of the learner do affect the selection of format. This relationship can be obvious (deaf students need special materials), and it can be sub-

tle (cost per use for CD-ROMs restricts their use by a single learner, and some learners prefer to work alone). The following learner characteristics can be diagnosed through the use of the instruments discussed in chapter 8 and can be related to certain media.

a. *Preference for structure.* Videotape and PowerPoint presentations tend to be favored by learners who prefer minimal structure. A CD-ROM or computer tutorial would be preferred by those most comfortable with structure. These preferences result less from the inherent characteristics of the format than from the way information has been presented.

b. *Preference for working alone or with a group.* Cost per use is really the most important factor in relating a format to this learning style. Instructional materials for a learner who prefers to work alone would probably be videotapes and audiocassettes, and other relatively inexpensive media. CD-ROMs, DVDs, and online computer programs are more costly per use. The selector must weigh the cost of the instructional material in relation to the number of times the instructional materials will be used, the subjects it can be used for, and the number of students served by its use.

c. *Preference for auditory/visual/tactile/kinesthetic modalities.* For students who prefer, or who are limited to, certain modalities, the most appropriate medium is easy to select. For learners who prefer the auditory mode, the choice of a medium that presents the most important information in this mode, such as an audiocassette or CD-ROM, is obvious. For tactile learners, realia such as kits and puzzles are indicated.

The selection process can be terminated at any point at which teachers or school library media specialists decide that they should produce the instructional materials themselves. Production of in-house instructional materials is most often justified because of a special combination of learner and instructional objective characteristics for which no items can be located.

Identifying the Materials

The production and dissemination of instructional materials is a large and competitive business. As a result, there are many sources of materials and it is often easy to overlook a particular resource in a subject.

The most up-to-date sources of titles are the publishers' catalogs. Because there is nothing in the non-print media analogous to the *Publisher's Trade List Annual*, the school library media specialist would do well to develop a system of classifying the catalogs.

Listings of commercially available titles of instructional materials are often arranged by format, such as *Words on Cassette* (2001). The listings may also be by subject, such as *Applied Science and Technology Index* (2001), or they may be titles of a general collection, such as *Elementary School Library Collection: A Guide to Books and Other Media, Phases 1–2–3, 20th edition* (print and CD-ROM, 2001).

It is beyond the scope of this book to provide an adequate listing and evaluation of sources of instructional materials; suffice to say that this is the task that follows the identification of the most appropriate media.

Locating Reviews of the Materials

Once the teacher has selected a format, or perhaps two, the next task in the selection process is to screen the materials to select those that will be previewed. The screening decision might be based on a description of the material or on actually seeing it.

- *Descriptive information.* Depending upon the source of the material, various amounts of information about it will be available. Some commercial listings provide an annotation of the contents suggesting grade levels, and a technical description including accompanying materials and other details. Some listings of the holdings of system, regional, or statewide media centers contain only the material and format.

  The person selecting the instructional materials should be especially aware of any information that might affect the decision to obtain the resource for preview. Although an item might be in the format sought, for example, CD-ROM, some aspect of the particular item might make it unsuitable (e.g., suitable for PC or Macintosh computers only).

- *Evaluation.* There are sources of evaluation of particular items of instructional materials. These include periodicals such as *Booklist,* which is devoted exclusively to evaluations,

Fig. 12.2. Relationship between format and cost and learner characteristics

FORMAT and COSTS	EQUIPMENT AVAILABILITY*	LEARNER CHARACTERISTICS
Web Courseware (H)		AVIS
Videotape (M)		AVGU
Microcomputer (M)		VIS
FilmStrip (Slides) (L)		V(IG)S
Filmstrip/Cassette (M)		AV(IG)S
Transparency (L)		VGS
Programed Manual (L)		VIS
Simulation/Skill Games (M)		VLT(IG)S
Realia (M)		VKT(IG)U
Audiotape (L)		AI
Study Print (L)		GS

KEY

H = High	(A) Auditory	(V) Visual	(T) Tactile
M = Medium	(K) Kinesthetic	(G) Group	(I) Individual
L = Low	(S) Structured	(U) Unstructured	

* Purchase materials for equipment which is most available

and subject-oriented periodicals such as the *Journal of Science Teacher Education,* which contain reviews as well as other information.

The boom in computers has prompted the publication of periodicals devoted to reviewing computer software. There are also indexes to reviews of instructional materials that do not include the review but do provide information on where the review can be found. Probably the best example is *Media Review Digest.*

Once again, it is beyond the scope of this book to list and describe review sources for instructional materials. A word of caution should be issued about spending too much time searching for reviews of instructional materials. The control of the information is not well established, and many items never get reviewed. Also, the context in which the material was reviewed must be clear. What were the characteristics of the learners who this reviewer assumed were the audience? For what instructional objective(s) was the material reviewed? Unless this information can be ascertained, the review must be used with caution.

Previewing the Materials

As stated earlier in this chapter, as each task in the selection process is performed, the probability increases that the selected materials will contribute significantly to the learner's mastery of the instructional objective. Unfortunately, many teachers and school library media specialists stop when materials have been located and, in effect, guess which materials to purchase. But an important task remains: Obtaining instructional materials for preview.

Anyone attempting to obtain instructional materials for preview must operate under certain constraints. Many producers and distributors are reluctant to provide preview copies. A standard letter stipulating the conditions for preview often helps in obtaining the materials. Responsible actions by previewers, including returning materials on time and in good condition, will also help to persuade producers and distributors to allow previewing.

Once the instructional material is obtained, it should be evaluated according to relevant criteria. If the previewer makes a "go/no-go" decision without specific criteria in mind, there is a good chance that the previewing effort will have been wasted.

Numerous sets of criteria have been published that can be used in evaluating instructional materials. The following criteria have been selected and are for general use. They are not specific to any one format. Rating an item of instructional material on the basis of these criteria should be accompanied by evaluating the item for format-specific characteristics.

I. Appropriateness. The previewer must rate the item of instructional material as to whether it is appropriate for the *learner* and the *instructional objective.*

    A. Learner characteristics. The previewer of an item of instructional materials should have clearly in mind the characteristics of the student(s) who will be using the materials. The previewer should keep the following question in mind: How well does the way that the instructional material is designed match the characteristics of the students who will be using the materials? The following learner characteristics can be diagnosed by one or more of the instruments included in chapter 8.

        1. Auditory/visual/tactile/kinesthetic preference. Although the matching of instructional materials to learner characteristics can be largely accomplished during format selection, a second check should be made during previewing. Occasionally the information content of an item will be unexpected. For example, some videotapes are merely "talking heads." These videotapes would not be appropriate for learners with a preference for learning from iconics (pictures).

2. Experience. For learners from an environment that lacks a variety of experiences, the materials should

   a. use common vocabulary

   b. provide direct experience

   c. require no special training

   d. contain a simple reading level

   e. be introductory in nature

   f. contain clear examples and illustrations

3. Motivation. For learners who tend to be less motivated, the materials should

   a. be attractive

   b. contain provocative examples

   c. contain marked contrasts

   d. be unique

   e. contain activities

   f. contain immediate feedback

   g. show applicability to real life

   h. contain anecdotes and illustrations

4. Need for advance organizers. For students who tend to enter learning situations without a clear idea of what is to be learned, the materials should contain advance organizers such as

   a. outlines or abstracts of the information that will be presented in the presentation (see fig. 12.3)

Fig. 12.3. Example of outline of information to be presented

YOU SHOULD BE ABLE TO:

1. NAME 4 TYPES OF SIMPLE MACHINES.

2. DEFINE EACH MACHINE.

3. STATE A RULE FOR EACH.

4. IDENTIFY AN EXAMPLE OF EACH.

Fig. 12.4. **Example of printed heading**

1. Inclined Plane: A Sloping Surface

    b. points to look for, questions to answer, or problems to solve (given at the start of the presentation)

    c. audio directions to "watch out for" or "attend to" parts of the presentation

5. Inability to structure information. For learners who tend not to be able to structure information as it is presented, the materials should

    a. contain printed or spoken headings of major divisions of content (see fig. 12.4)

    b. provide numbering of points as presented

6. Field dependence. For learners who lack the ability to extract embedded information, the material should

    a. contain verbal directions for finding information

    b. use arrows, circling, and selective focusing

    c. use color for emphasis

    d. contain cartoon-type visuals that reduce irrelevant detail (see fig. 12.5)

    e. use close-ups

    f. contain emphatic repetition

Fig. 12.5. **Example of use of arrows to point out important information**

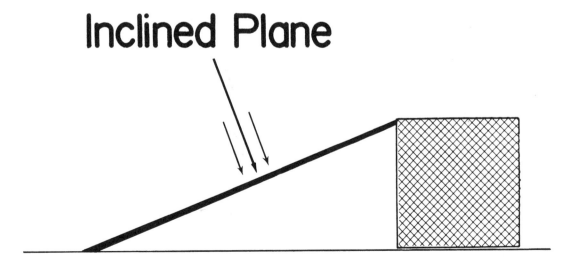

Fig. 12.6. Example of a frame in which the learner is requested to respond

```
SHORTER
LONGER


THE _____        THE INCLINED

PLANE, THE EASIER THE WORK.
```

7. Reluctance to participate. For those learners who do not, on their own initiative, participate in a presentation, the materials should

   a. ask for spoken or written answers to questions given (see fig. 12.6)

   b. ask students to "think" answers to questions given

   c. provide time for note taking

   d. provide time for discussion

8. Need for feedback. For those learners who have difficulty determining on their own whether their answers are correct, the materials should

   a. provide printed or spoken answers to questions (see fig. 12.7)

   b. provide pictorial answers

   c. provide reasons a chosen answer is not correct

9. Information processing rate. For those learners who have slower rates of information processing, the materials should

   a. contain narrative slow enough for understanding

   b. present visuals long enough for information to be received

Fig. 12.7. Example of a frame in which the answer is provided

```
THE ____LONGER____        THE INCLINED

PLANE, THE EASIER THE WORK.
```

10. Difficulty summarizing. For those learners who have difficulty summarizing on their own the information that has been presented, the materials should

    a. provide summary sentences throughout the presentation

    b. require the learner to paraphrase key information

    c. provide an outline of the material at the conclusion

B. Instructional objective(s). An instructional item can also be rated on its appropriateness for reaching a particular instructional objective. There are characteristics of instructional materials that correspond, though not absolutely, to the following types and levels of learning.

1. Associative learning. Instructional materials will have a greater chance of helping a learner reach an associative learning level if the item

    a. contains information that is "chunked," that is, presented in groups rather than all at once

    b. presents the information to be associated in proximity

    c. requires immediate practice

    d. provides immediate feedback

    e. links meaningless to meaningful information (see fig. 12.8)

2. Discrimination learning. A learner will be aided in reaching the discrimination level of learning if the item

    a. emphasizes the distinctive features of the subject

    b. begins with examples that contrast sharply

Fig. 12.8. Example of instructional material that links meaningless to meaningful information

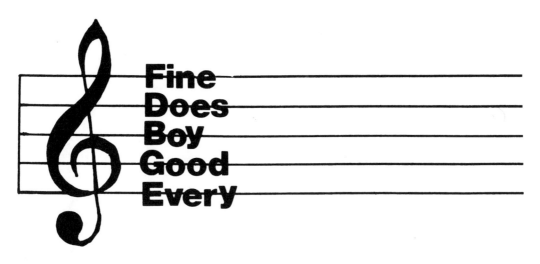

Fig. 12.9. Example of item that introduces criterial attributes at the start

WHICH ONE IS DIFFERENT?

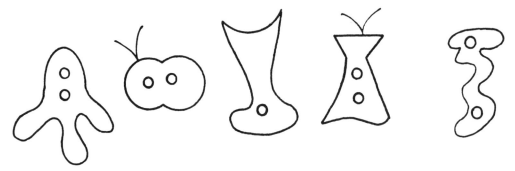

Hint: Count circles

    c. introduces the criterial attribute at the start (learner must understand what serves to discriminate the presented items—is it size, shape, color, or ? (See fig. 12.9.)

3. Concrete learning. This level of learning is aided by materials that

    a. use associations and discriminations that have been previously mastered or are covered in the presentation

    b. show clearly identified examples and non-examples of the concept (see fig. 12.10)

Fig. 12.10. Clearly identified examples and non-examples of a concept

SQUARES

NOT SQUARES

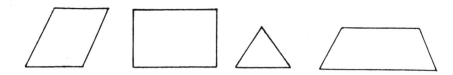

   c.   give sufficient variety to define the concept and to accentuate the criterial attributes

   d.   require the learner to identify examples not covered in the presentation

   e.   provide sufficient examples to form a prototype

4.   Defined concept learning. The defined concept level of learning will be aided by materials that

   a.   contain examples of appropriate concrete concepts

   b.   cover all the concepts within the definition

5.   Rule learning. The rule level of learning is aided by materials that

   a.   contain concepts that have been mastered by the learner or that are covered in the presentation

   b.   provide examples of the rule

6.   Problem solving. The problem-solving level of learning is aided by materials that provide cues to lead the learner through the rule formation

7.   Motor skills learning. Materials that aid in learning motor skills might contain

   a.   a clear rendition of the steps in the sequence

   b.   requirements of practice of the skills

   c.   information to assist the learner in evaluating the performance of the skills

8.   Affective learning. To help change the learner's attitude, the instructional materials should

   a.   be attractive

   b.   feature actors and actresses respected by the learner

   c.   explicitly state the attitude being taught

   d.   use the subjective rather than objective point of view—that is, view the subject through the eyes of the learner

   e.   require participation

II. Authenticity. Because anyone can be a publisher on the Internet, this criterion is particularly important. The question that the evaluator of an item of instructional materials should keep in mind is: Are there inaccuracies in the information that will prevent the learner from reaching the instructional objective? Some characteristics that should be checked follow.

   A. Factual accuracy. Some presentations contain inaccuracies as the result of poor research or production problems. Other presentations have simply become outdated because of the advance of science or technology, the growth of populations, the development of governments, and other factors. The copyright date and date of last update (in the case of a Web site) are good indicators of how current the presentation is.

B. Style. Styles of automobiles, clothing, and other items can date a presentation and be distracting.

C. Objectivity. A presentation should be checked for the way it portrays racial, ethnic, and other minority groups. Is it free of stereotyping, sexism, and racism? Is the material multicultural in viewpoint? The evaluator should also be sensitive to biased presentations of controversial viewpoints. Sponsored materials can be obtained at a low cost, but these materials should be screened carefully in respect to this criterion.

III. Topic Development. The reviewer should consider whether the topic is developed in a well-organized and logical manner. This criterion is critical due to the fact that Web-based materials are often nonlinear. The presentation should stress the main points, be free from excessive extraneous information, and be arranged in a sequence that flows naturally and easily. The overall content and concept development must be related directly to the instructional objectives and the intended audience. Finally, the presentation should arouse and maintain the learner's interest.

IV. Accompanying materials. The instructional materials should be evaluated to determine whether accompanying materials are present and of sufficient quality to enable the learner, in conjunction with the main presentation, to reach the objective. This decision should be based upon information about specific learners and instructional objectives. For some combinations of these, no accompanying materials may be needed; for other combinations, elaborate accompanying materials might be required.

V. Technical characteristics. The evaluator must keep in mind the learner and the instructional objective when judging technical characteristics. The presence of a technical imperfection should not automatically disqualify an item, but if in the evaluator's judgment, the imperfection will prevent the learner from reaching the objective, the item should be rejected. Judgment points include

A. Quality of focus

B. Quality of color

C. Sound quality (Note: For Web-based instructional materials, the quality of sound and video will depend on the level of bandwidth used. The material should be viewed at the lowest bandwidth that can be used by the students.)

D. Redundancy of audio and visual information. An extremely important consideration for multimedia presentations is the nature of the relationship between the media. The effectiveness of different combinations in multimedia presentations is as follows:

1. Same information in both media (listening to CD-ROM of someone reading while reading the same information yourself)—roughly the same effectiveness as the single medium.

2. Different information in each medium (viewing the pyramids on the Internet while listening to an audiocassette discuss ancient Egyptian hairstyles)—substantially less effective than the single medium.

3. Complementary information in each medium (viewing the pyramids on the Internet while listening to a description of the pyramids)—significantly more effective than the single medium.

VI. Physical characteristics. The evaluator should check to determine if the materials

A. Are packaged properly

B. Are durable enough to withstand constant use

C. Are backed by a warranty that provides for replacement of material free of cost

The use of an evaluation form (see appendix G) will assist in the preview process, both in providing structure and in facilitating responses. Ideally, the evaluator should work through the item twice before completing the form. However, time constraints may make this impossible. The appropriateness criterion should be given more weight than the other criteria. Under this criterion, the evaluator considers those characteristics that are relevant to the specific learners and instructional objective(s). No item of instructional materials will receive a perfect rating, especially items for learners who need materials to supplant missing or inadequate learning tools. The school library media specialist and teacher must find the materials that most closely resemble the ideal and decide whether the teacher can make up for the deficiencies during implementation.

As stated previously, the decision may be made at any time in the selection process to produce the instructional materials in-house. The advantage of in-house materials is that, unlike commercial materials, they can be designed specifically for a given learner and instructional objective. The evaluation criteria and the accompanying matching of learner and instructional objective characteristics to the way in which the instructional materials are designed should provide the basis for the design of in-house materials.

Evaluating the Materials with Actual Learners

The last task in the selection process is the evaluation of the instructional materials. This involves trying out the materials with representative learners and determining whether the instructional objective is met. Although this is really the only way a selector of instructional materials can be sure an item will be effective, it is rarely done. Because of resource limitations, most teachers stop at or before the previewing task.

Even if teachers do not evaluate an item before it is used with a large group of students, they should still be aware of the questions posed in the evaluation process:

• How many students reached the objective?

• Were certain enabling objectives not reached?

• Is there a commonality among students who did not reach the objective? Are they of the same learning style?

• What teacher behaviors could be implemented to compensate for the deficiencies in the materials? (See chapters 13 and 14 for more information on this.)

LEVELS OF INVOLVEMENT BY THE SCHOOL LIBRARY MEDIA SPECIALIST AT THE MATERIALS SELECTION STEP

The materials selection step presents one of the best opportunities for school library media specialists to become involved in helping teachers at all levels because materials selection is seen by many teachers as falling within the traditional role of the school library media specialist. Also, school library media specialists are often more comfortable and better prepared to deal with teachers in this area.

The Initial Level

The school library media specialist can help the teacher obtain effective instructional materials at this level by obtaining and maintaining materials, facilities, and equipment.

The school library media specialist can maintain a collection of instructional materials. This includes processing, storing, and circulating the materials. At the initial level, the collection is built with a minimum of communication with the teachers. The school library media specialist makes an educated guess as to the appropriate materials based on whatever knowledge of the learners and instructional objectives is at hand. The best that can be said for this practice is that it might be better than having no collection at all or having materials selected through an approval-plan arrangement in which collection development decisions are made by sources outside the school.

The school library media specialist can maintain a previewing area for teachers. A production area with appropriate equipment and supplies can be established and maintained as an activity at the initial level.

Professional collection materials that will help teachers implement the materials selection step can include materials that explain the instructional materials selection procedure. Information sources such as lists of resources and indexes to reviews might be included.

The Moderate Level

A school library media specialist can provide moderate-level assistance throughout the entire selection process. This can include assistance in selecting the format, locating titles, obtaining materials for preview, and evaluating materials. The school library media specialist can also produce instructional materials for the teacher as well as help the teacher produce the materials.

The following is a sample interaction between the school library media specialist and the teacher at this level.

A SCENARIO

This conversation takes place in the library media center between Adrienne Lipscomb, the school library media specialist, and Diane Zeilner. Diane is a first-year teacher of eighth-grade science.

Diane: I appreciate your setting up this time for me to come and talk to you. I'm trying to keep ahead of my classes in planning, but it isn't easy.

Adrienne: No, it isn't. Especially for someone who is new to the school and trying to learn all the logistics! What are you working on now?

Diane: The solar system unit. I'm excited about it because there have been so many discoveries made recently, but I'm concerned about finding materials.

Adrienne: You think that because so many of these discoveries have been made recently, materials won't be available?

Diane: Yes, and I'm teaching the unit in three weeks. I want to do a good job, but I'm close to panic.

Adrienne: Have you thought about what you want to cover in the unit?

Diane: Yes. The text presents the names of the planets, distances from the sun—the usual—and the kids need to know that, but I want to concentrate on the new discoveries.

Adrienne: If I were one of your students, what would I be able to do when the unit is completed?

Diane: I have my objectives right here (hands Adrienne a sheet of paper).

Adrienne: I wish everyone who came looking for materials was
(scanning as well prepared. Now tell me a little bit about your
the paper) students.

Diane: Well, they don't seem motivated. Most of them are reasonably well behaved, but the information I give them seems to fly right by. They sure were interested in my description of dissecting the pig in zoology, though!

Adrienne: Sometime I would like to talk to you about learning styles. Right now, it sounds as though your students need instructional materials that motivate, direct attention, and call for participation. Let me keep your objectives for a few days. I'll come up with a few suggestions of materials we can get our hands on quickly. Let's plan on meeting Thursday, same time. Why don't you try gathering as many Internet sites of the recent explorations as possible.

Three weeks is not a long time to obtain instructional materials that are not a part of the library media center's collection, but it is certainly not unusual for a school library media specialist to be given this short notice. In fact, to a school library media specialist who has practiced for any length of time, "I'm teaching the lesson on ___ this afternoon. Do you have any materials?" is not an unfamiliar query. Although the first response that comes to mind is often to pull one's hair out, this question is a request for help.

This is the highest level at which some teachers will ever interact with the center, and nothing the school library media specialist can do will change this. Many other teachers, however, will change their behavior if they are shown that the more lead time they provide, the better the materials that can be obtained.

The In-Depth Level

IN-SERVICES

The tasks involved in selecting and evaluating instructional materials are the basis for many possible in-service presentations by the school library media specialist. These might include the following:

- *Demonstrations of the capabilities of a selected format.* This could involve a familiar format such as the overhead transparency and involve the demonstration of reveals, overlays, and the simulation of motion. State-of-the-art media can be demonstrated as the materials and equipment become available to the teachers. These can include computer presentations, interactive video equipment, and CD-ROM technology and software.

- *Demonstrations and displays of selected items from the collection.* Sometimes new materials are not used because faculty members are not aware of them. The school library media specialist might emphasize all the materials on a certain topic, such as decimals, or might emphasize a certain format, such as CD-ROMs.

- *The use of acquisition tools.* The school library media specialist can introduce tools that are available in the school and from the district media center.

- *Policies and procedures for obtaining materials* for rent or preview through the center, as well as avenues for obtaining free materials.

- *Evaluations of instructional materials* for students with particular learning styles and for particular levels of learning.

INSTRUCTIONAL DESIGN TEAM PARTICIPATION

Instructional design team participation at this step involves working with one or more teachers through all the tasks in the materials selection step. The interaction at this level has two purposes: 1) to obtain effective instructional materials, and 2) to improve the teachers' abilities in this area. The degree to which either one of these purposes is stressed over the other depends upon what the school library media specialist is trying to accomplish at the time.

An example of how these tasks might be carried out for a particular combination of instructional objectives, group of learners, and logistical constraints is given below.

Instructional objective: Given a description of the life requirements of a hypothetical organism, the learner will select a planet in the solar system that would provide those living conditions.

Learners: Eighth-grade general science students. Highly visual; prefer to learn in groups but not to lead; not highly motivated; with tendencies not to organize in advance, structure, locate, participate, or evaluate.

Logistical constraints: A limited budget for purchase or rental. More VCR equipment than any other kind, but computers for CD-ROMs and DVDs available.

Possible sequence of tasks:

1. *Select format.* The fact that the learners are highly visual tends to rule out audiotapes and transparencies. Their need for structure, participation, and feedback indicates that realia, study prints, and textbook-type manuals might not be appropriate. Costs and equipment constraints place videotapes as a secondary choice. A CD-ROM or Web-based instructional module might be the appropriate choice. If an appropriate item is not available, it can be purchased at a moderate cost.

2. *Locate materials.* The school library media specialist and teacher(s) begin the search for resources in the library media center's collection. The search can be extended to the local public library, other schools, the system's materials, and regional and state holdings, until enough materials have been located.

3. *Preview materials.* On the basis of the descriptive information, time limitations, and budgetary constraints, the school library media specialist decides which titles beyond those available locally should be obtained for preview. The copyright date, if available, is especially important to note for a topic such as this. The materials are previewed on the basis of format-specific characteristics and previously determined criteria for the instructional objective and learner characteristics. If CD-ROMs are previewed, format-specific questions would include the following: Is it appropriate for the age level? Is it user-friendly and interactive? Does it include the information required?

    a. *Appropriateness.* For this audience and stated objectives, the evaluator would look specifically for interesting yet simple visuals, a simple vocabulary, and advance organizers that both arouse interest and let the learner know what is to be learned. For the last objective, a presentation that uses a space traveler's point of view and begins by stating, "Let's visit each planet and see what it would be like to live there" would be appropriate.

        The audiotape should prepare the learner for certain information: "As we visit each planet, think about how hot and cold it gets during an average day."

        The information should be structured in the presentation. The videotape could be structured around a series of questions. For example, the first section could contain the title "What Is a Planet?" The videotape would then be structured around the relative locations of the planets, for example, "1. The Inner Planets."

        The presentation should help the learner locate the important information in the visual. This assistance can be provided through the audiotape: "Notice the swirls on the surface of Jupiter. These swirls are an indication of the high surface winds of up to 800 miles per hour."

        The presentation should require the learner to participate. Example: "If you were standing on the equator on Mars at noon during a typical summer day, you would most likely a) freeze, b) burn up, c) neither freeze nor burn up."

        The presentation should provide feedback to the learner. Example: "The average high temperature at the equator during the summer on Mars is close to room temperature. You would neither freeze nor burn up."

    b. *Authenticity.* In selecting materials for a topic such as the solar system, the selector must be especially careful that the information is not so dated that it is no longer accurate. Even if the item does not contain any factual inaccuracies, the evaluator should check to see if critical recent discoveries have been included.

c. *Topic development.* Because the instructional objective is concerned with the planets and characteristics of the planets having to do with the maintenance of life (atmosphere, temperature, nutrient availability, etc.), these should be covered. An item that deals with the sun, asteroids, stars, or other extraneous topics should be rated lower.

d. *Accompanying materials.* Accompanying materials necessary to help the specific learners reach the objective should be included.

e. *Technical qualities.* The videotape should not contain visual or audio imperfections that will prevent the learners from reaching the instructional objective.

f. *Physical characteristics.* Because these materials will probably be used with a small group of students at a time, they should provide clear directions for operating the equipment.

THOUGHT PROVOKERS

1. Given the following instructional objective, select the most feasible and least feasible format for the following learner groups and logistical constraints: The learner will describe ways animals prepare for winter during autumn.

   a. Very restricted budget. Highly tactile learners; like to work in groups; prefer unstructured learning.

   b. Bountiful budget. Highly auditory learners; prefer working alone on structured learning tasks.

   c. Limited budget. Visual and auditory learners; no strong individual or group preferences; prefer structured learning.

2. Locate at least three materials in the format you selected for a, b, and c in question 1.

3. Find reviews of these resources.

4. Obtain and preview one item according to the criteria described in this chapter. If you cannot obtain the actual item, use an item you can obtain. *Before you look at the materials,* define a learner group and an instructional objective. Evaluate the material using this information.

(See appendix A for answers.)

REFERENCES

Applied Science and Technology Index. 2001. New York: H. W. Wilson

AV Marketplace. 2001. New York: R.R. Bowker.

Barron, Ann E., and Karen S. Ivers. 1998. *Internet and Instruction: Activities and Ideas.* 2nd ed. Englewood, Colo.: Libraries Unlimited.

Baule, Steven M. 2001. *Technology Planning for Effective Teaching and Learning.* 2nd ed. Worthington, Ohio: Linworth Publishing.

Book Report. Worthington, Ohio: Linworth Publishing.

Booklist. Chicago: American Library Association.

Branch, Robert Maribe, and Mary Ann Fitzgerald, ed. 2001. *Educational Media and Technology Yearbook.* Englewood, Colo.: Libraries Unlimited.

Bucher, Katherine Toth. 1998. *Information Technology for Schools.* 2nd ed. Worthington, Ohio: Linworth Publishing.

Children's Software and New Media Review. Alexandria, Va.: Association of School and Curriculum Development.

Elementary School Library Collection: A Guide to Books and Other Media, Phases 1–2–3. 2001. Williamsport, Pa.: Brodart.

Evans, G. Edward. 2000. *Developing Library and Information Center Collections.* 4th ed. Englewood, Colo.: Libraries Unlimited.

Farmer, Leslie S. J., and Will Foster. 1999. *More Than Information: The Role of the Library Media Center in the Multimedia Classroom.* Worthington, Ohio: Linworth Publishing.

Gillespie, John J., and Ralph J. Folcorelli, 1998. *Guides to Collection Development for Children and Young Adults.* Englewood, Colo.: Libraries Unlimited.

Homa, Linda L. (ed.); Schreck, Ann L.; Hoebener, Maureen. 2001. *Elementary School Library Collection: A Guide to Books and Other Media.* Williamsport, Pa.: Brodart.

Kovacs, Diane. 2000. *Building Electronic Library Collections: The Essential Guide to Selection Criteria and Core Subject Collections.* New York: Neal-Schuman.

Library and Information Science Abstracts (LISA) database. New York: R.R. Bowker.

Library Journal. New York: R.R. Bowker.

Library Talk. Worthington, Ohio: Linworth Publishing.

Mason-Robinson, Sally. 1996. *Developing and Managing Video Collections: A How-To-Do-It Manual for Librarians.* New York: Neal-Schuman.

McKenzie, Jamie. 1999. *How Teachers Learn Technology Best.* Worthington, Ohio: Linworth Publishing.

Media and Methods. Philadelphia, Pa.: American Society of Educators.

Media Review Digest. Ann Arbor, Mich.: Pierian Press.

Miller, Elizabeth B. 2001. *Internet Resource Directory for K-12 Teachers and Libraries, 2000–2001.* Englewood, Colo.: Libraries Unlimited.

NICEM Audiovisual Database. Albuquerque, N.M.: National Information Center for Educational Media (NICEM).

Only the Best: The Annual Guide to the Highest Rated Educational Software and Multimedia. (2000–2001). Alexandria, Va.: Association of School Curriculum and Development.

Reese, Jean. 1999. *Internet Books for Educators, Parents, and Students.* Englewood, Colo.: Libraries Unlimited.

School Library Journal. New York: R.R. Bowker.

Schrock, Kathleen, ed. 2000. *The Technology Connection: Building a Successful School Library Media Program.* Worthington, Ohio: Linworth Publishing.

Seamon, Mary Ploski, and Eric J. Levitt, 2001. *Web-Based Learning: A Practical Guide.* Worthington, Ohio: Linworth Publishing.

Software Encyclopedia: A Guide for Personal, Professional, and Business Users. 2001. New York: R.R. Bowker.

Van Orden, Phyllis J., and Kay Bishop. 2001. *Collection Programs in Schools: Concepts, Practices and Information Sources.* 3rd ed. Englewood, Colo.: Libraries Unlimited.

Video Librarian. Seabeck, Wash.: Video Librarian.

Wood, Irene, ed. 1997. *CD-ROMs for Kids: Booklist's Best Bets.* Chicago: American Library Association.

Words on Cassette. 2001. New York: R.R. Bowker.

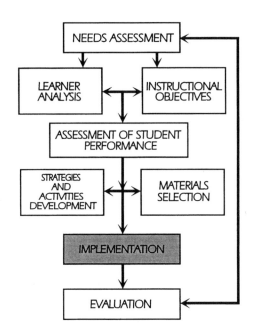

13

Implementation

This chapter provides information to help the reader

- learn activities a teacher can implement to compensate for a learner's deficiency in learning tools

- identify at least one teacher activity for each level of learning

- learn the parts of a lesson plan

- design compensating teacher activities when there is a mismatch between an item of instructional material and a learner group

- understand learners' environmental preferences

The information provided in chapters 7 through 12 is designed to help the school library media specialist help teachers design needs assessments, establish instructional goals and delineate instructional objectives, analyze learners, design student performance assessments, and develop instructional materials and activities. These steps can be characterized as the planning stage of the instructional design process. This chapter deals with the implementation step, which can be thought of as the "doing" phase of the instructional process (Armstrong, Denton, and Savage 1978). The chapter will also cover planning teacher activities.

During the actual instructional event, the teacher usually plays the role of both educator and manager. This chapter will help the school library media specialist help the teacher implement the role of educator and manager in three ways: 1) by providing information on the teacher's general instructional activities as well as advice on media use, 2) by providing information on classroom management, and 3) by linking the learning styles described in chapter 8 with the classroom environment.

THE PURPOSE OF THE
IMPLEMENTATION STEP

Many seemingly foolproof instructional projects that look promising in the design stage fail in implementation. It is extremely important that the instructional consultant and teacher(s) work together to ensure that implementation of the unit is not beyond what the teacher is able or willing to do. It is imperative to carefully explore the role of the teacher in the implementation of the instruction being designed.

During the design of the instruction, it is critical that the impact of the implementation of the instruction on the limited resources available be considered (Tessmer and Harris 1990). Every change in instruction requires resources, and unless these are available the instruction is likely to become "orphaned" and never used again (Tessmer and Harris 1990, 16). As an example, a science lesson that involves donation of film and loaning of a camera by a local photography store may be very successful but not sustainable. What facilities and equipment are required? Is there special lighting, space, or ventilation required? What support staff are required to implement the instruction? Is the administrator aware of the costs of the implementation, and has this person's support been gained? Finally, are resources available for the inevitable revisions that must be made?

THE TEACHER'S INSTRUCTIONAL ACTIVITIES

Whether the instruction involves individuals or large or small groups, and whether the instructional materials used are a textbook or a multi-media online approach (or solely the teacher in a face-to-face environment), the teacher usually has a role as the facilitator of instruction. Although totally self-contained instructional packages do exist, the vast majority of materials and activities require some instructional intervention on the part of the teacher in the implementation of the instruction.

In chapter 8, eight learning tools were identified. Students who possess these tools will be much more effective and efficient learners:

- Establishes a "set" for learning

- Structures information into a format that aids learning

- Locates the important information presented during the learning event

- Asks questions of himself or herself during the learning event

- Checks to see if answers to self-generated questions are correct

- Processes information rapidly

- Is motivated to learn

- Paraphrases and summarizes what is to be learned during and after the learning event

In implementing instruction, part of a teacher's activity repertoire should be to compensate for student learning tools that are missing or inadequate. A continuing goal of instruction also should be to strengthen these learning tools. This is particularly true if some or all of the instruction occurs online. Students who do not possess these learning tools are at particular risk in the online environment.

The Teacher as the Medium

If the teacher serves as the main controller of the instructional event, as during a lecture or demonstration, actions can be taken to ensure that students who lack one or more of the tools are provided compensatory instruction. Compensatory activities include the following:

- Providing for learner readiness by outlining the main points to be covered (Hoover 1982) and discussing and reviewing previously learned and related material.

- Using appropriate note-giving techniques that structure the information. The teacher can provide the major outline headings and make it a practice to indicate where the information being discussed belongs.

- Using aids to help the student "zoom in" on the information. These include video cameras during a demonstration, the use of oversized models, changes of voice quality for important points, and so on.

- Questioning a wide range of students during the presentation. Too often, only the students who raise their hands are called upon. These students need to be reinforced, but it is also important to make sure that all students are participating. This can be done by calling on students who have not raised their hands and by requiring everyone to respond to certain questions in writing during the presentation. Hoover (1982) recommended that the teacher be aware of nonverbal signals from students as indicators of participation. These include nods of the head, chuckles, and facial expressions. Harris (2000), in her article "Batting 1,000: Questioning Techniques in Student-Centered Classrooms," provides successful questioning strategies for student-centered classrooms.

    Hunkins (1972) delineated two types of questions: "centering" questions, which cover material presented up to the point of the question, and "expansion" questions, which lead to the point to be presented next. Hunkins suggests that the teacher systematically use expansion questions that represent increasingly higher levels of learning. If the students are unable to answer an expansion question, then a series of centering questions is used in combination with information to provide the basis for the correct answer.

    Yule (1985) suggests pacing methods for distance-learning students. Some techniques include short-term regular assignments, tutorial letters, and videotape usage.

- Providing feedback to a student's response. As much as possible, the teacher should help a student understand why an answer is not correct. The teacher should also attempt to develop a variety of verbal responses to correct answers. The student will respond more positively to a comment if it is one that has not been used repeatedly (Armstrong, Denton, and Savage 1978).

- Varying the pace of the presentation. Information should be presented at a rate appropriate to the learner. For a given student, the presentation rate should also change within the presentation. Generally, the fastest rate should occur at the start and finish of the presentation (Hoover 1982). The teacher should use students' responses to questions as a continuing monitor for pacing.

- Paraphrasing and summarizing the important points during and after the presentation. The teacher can periodically stop during a lecture and help students paraphrase the main points. At the conclusion of the presentation, the main points can be summarized by the teacher with help from the students.

For learners who possess all the learning tools, the use of these activities would make for an intolerable and probably ineffective presentation by the teacher. Conversely, if these actions are not taken for learners who do not possess the tools, the presentation will also be intolerable and ineffective. The teacher needs to know the students and design the instruction accordingly. This design could well include instructing students in smaller groups while the rest of the students are engaged in alternative activities. In this way, the teacher can tailor the approach to the learning tool deficiencies of the smaller group.

The Teacher's Role in Student-Led Group Projects

Group work by students often poses a dilemma for the teacher. Many group projects begin with great enthusiasm but have disappointing results. Although many students prefer group work to individual work, they also often lack crucial learning tools. If some or all of the instruction occurs online, there will likely be a strong dose of group or peer-oriented work. Online instruction naturally includes instructional assistance by peers, often whether the teacher plans this interaction into the online lesson or not. If the majority of the instruction will occur online, it is probably a good idea to make sure that a structure is in place that will encourage successful group work.

Teachers can build compensating activities into group work. The following are suggestions for helping students who are doing group work but who also are deficient in the learning tools.

- Provide specific, clearly stated goals for group.

- Make sure the group has a leader who possesses the requisite learning tools.

- Provide an outline of activities and information to be collected.

- Provide an example of the product to be produced.

- Make a list of questions to answer and include regular checks to see if the answers are adequate.

- Make "mini" assignments and provide immediate feedback.

- Build a summarizing activity into the assignments so that the generated information can be synthesized into a coherent form.

The Teacher's Role in Using Instructional Packages

IN FACE-TO-FACE INSTRUCTION

Some teachers believe that packaged instructional materials are a waste of money and do not really teach. A significant cause of this negative feeling is that these instructional materials are too often perceived, and used, as self-contained learning packages. The teacher's role, in the view of many, is to plug in the machine, turn it on, and turn it off. Unfortunately, very few instructional materials are designed to be effective if used in this manner. Most seem to have been produced under the assumption that the students would possess all of the learning tools. The teacher must compensate for weakness in the materials by retaining control of instruction in order to ensure that the learners who lack one or more of the learning tools are provided a reasonable chance of success. This will require that the teacher

- know which learning tools the students do not possess to an adequate degree

- be familiar with the instructional materials and the learning tools needed to be successful with them

- intervene before, during, and after the materials are used as necessary to compensate for deficiencies

Intervention involves activities the teacher would have undertaken for a given set of instructional objectives if the instructional materials were not used. As an example, consider the following situation.

> *Instructional objective.* Learn the uses of several simple machines, for example, wedge and inclined plane.

Instructional material. A videotape that contains several good examples but that has very complex visuals. For instance, the wedge is illustrated in a scene of a man splitting wood. The man is wearing a brightly colored checked shirt and is surrounded by trees with many-colored leaves.

Students. A group of learners who have a great deal of difficulty locating embedded information. (In this case the important information is the wedge in the log.)

As a compensating activity, the teacher could stand by the screen and point out the wedge or stay seated and say, "Notice the wedge. The wedge is the machine," or do both. If the video is projected on a screen, the teacher could use a laser pointer to assist in pointing out the criterial information.

As this example illustrates, compensating activities do not have to be complex or difficult. It is vital, however, that teachers realize that using instructional materials often involves their providing compensating instructional activities.

The Online Environment Accessibility in Distance Education (ADE) is a project focused on helping teachers develop accessible online learning materials for people with disabilities and on raising awareness about the need for accessibility in online learning. One can learn more about ADE by visiting their Web site (http://www.umuc.edu/distance/odell/cvu [May 8, 2003]); a handbook and faculty training guidelines are also available. For additional information call (301) 985-7602.

Increasingly, instructional materials can be accessed online. For students who do not possess one or more of the learning tools to an acceptable degree, the teacher may design a front-end activity that introduces the content to be mastered and assists the student in locating the important information. The teacher could insert online self-tests and quizzes to provide chunked feedback for those students who need it. In the ideal instructional setting, these interventions would be inserted only for the students who would benefit from them.

TEACHER ACTIVITIES AND LEVELS OF LEARNING

Based upon the work of Fleming and Levie (1978), several instructional propositions can be advanced that correlate teacher activities to specific levels of learning. The following are but a few of the many included in their work, which is recommended as a professional collection choice.

I. Associative learning

    A. Make information meaningful.

        1. Use rhyming.

        2. Have students generate relational phrases (e.g., Every Good Boy Does Fine for notes on the musical scale).

        3. Use concrete versus abstract words.

        4. Have students generate relational images (e.g., Helen sitting on a mountain = Helena, Montana, for states' capital cities).

    B. Provide for repetition and practice.

    C. Provide information to be learned in chunks (e.g., in learning the Russian translation of a list of forty nouns, present them eight at a time).

II. Discrimination learning

    A. Point out differences.

    B. Make sure the learner is familiar with the attributes in which the objects to be discriminated will differ.

III. Concept learning

    A. Provide a clear definition using familiar vocabulary (e.g., "A desert is a land deficient in moisture that supports little or no vegetation." The learner must understand *deficient, moisture, supports,* and *vegetation.*).

    B. Provide examples and non-examples of the concept.

        1. Choose examples in which the non-criterial attributes vary widely (e.g., in teaching the concept "square," show squares that are big, small, red, blue, striped, and tilted).

        2. Choose examples in which the criterial attributes are as obvious as possible (e.g., a simple line drawing of a square).

    C. When presenting the examples, say the name.

IV. Rule learning

    A. Make sure that the concepts included in the rule are understood.

    B. Provide for practice with the rule.

V. Problem solving

    A. Provide a structure conducive to solving the problem.

    B. Provide guidance for recording information, testing hypotheses, and managing the learning situation in general.

CLASSROOM MANAGEMENT

Information Management

In any learning situation, a certain amount of information is generated. If a teacher attempts to instruct on several different levels in response to a variety of learner characteristics, the control of information becomes more difficult. In any instructional situation, the teacher must keep track of the information to be presented and the output from the learner.

KEEPING TRACK OF THE MATERIAL TO BE PRESENTED

Traditionally, when instruction involves a presentation by the teacher to a group of students, a lesson plan is used. There are many formats for lesson plans, often varying with the methodology employed. The lesson-plan format provided below can be used with varying group sizes and methods.

Preliminary information:

1. Primary instructional objective

2. Description of important schemata including enabling objectives (having the instructional enterprise on hand can be helpful)

3. Learner group (brief description of learner group and reference to more detailed information)

4. Test results (reference to pretest and self-test results)

Summary of instructional event:

5. Motivating activity (includes providing for learner readiness, e.g., advance organizers)

6. Description of experiences (For a lecture, this might include an outline; for an individually performed laboratory experiment, logistical information and points to look for.) (Henson, 1988)

7. Provisions for participation (key questions to ask and particular student responses to watch for)

8. Materials needed

9. Summarizing activities (How will the lesson be "wrapped up"?)

Evaluation:

10. Testing and feedback (provisions for testing achievement of the objectives and actions to be based upon these results)

In learning situations where instruction is totally individualized, each learner will have a separate prescription form especially designed in accordance with learning styles and instructional content needs. The Systematic Approach to Reading Improvement (SARI) program developed by the Northern California Program Development Center is an example of such an approach (Phi Delta Kappa, 1978).

KEEPING TRACK OF STUDENT OUTPUT

In a traditional classroom where all students are taking the same test, a simple gradebook-type management system is possible. As instruction moves toward individualization with pretests, self-tests, and posttests, more sophisticated methods of dealing with student output are required. Many an innovative program in which excellent instructional strategies were employed has failed because the teacher was overwhelmed by student output.

Among the instructional support systems available today are computer-based student information management systems (SIMS). Typically, these systems address four major areas: student records, scheduling, attendance, and progress. Selection of the most suitable software system is critical to the successful implementation of SIMS. Today, a few hundred to a few thousand dollars buys multi-megabytes of SIMS software capability. In view of the long-term impacts that a system can have, it is critical that its selection results from a carefully considered evaluation process.

If the school has access to one or more of the emerging online platforms, such as WebCT or Blackboard, these contain useful student information management systems. WebCT allows the instructor to maintain a gradebook where each student can see his or her current grade information. Tools such as dropboxes allow the teacher to establish date windows during which the student can submit work, with notification provided to the student that the assignment was received. Even if all of the instruction occurs in the classroom, platforms such as these can be used to assist in the management of student information.

Management of the Physical Environment

As was pointed out in chapter 8, there has been a developing awareness that students vary in their preferences regarding environmental conditions. Even if the teacher has little or no control over the physical environment, it is probably a good idea to determine which students are particularly susceptible to extremes in the environment. There are some minor actions the teacher can take to help match students' preferences to the environment. *Learning Style Inventory Manual* (Dunn, Dunn, and Price 1981) provides information on several learning styles and environmental factors and suggestions for matching the learning styles with an appropriate environmental design. The learning styles and corresponding environments include

- *Preference for time of day.* If possible, according to the authors of the LSI manual, learners should undertake the most strenuous learning at their preferred time of learning. Although such matching might be difficult at the secondary level, a primary teacher could find it possible.

- *Temperature preference.* Once again, room temperature is out of the control of many teachers. (If one teaches in the South in August with no air-conditioning, one can only hope that the learners prefer warmth!) For small-group work and individual work, however, students can often be placed in preferred environments.

- *Light preference.* Learners who prefer light can be placed near windows or other illumination. For learners who prefer a darker environment, the teacher can use plants to shade the light, use dividers to block light, or let younger children bring in large boxes to build learning spaces.

- *Noise-level preference.* Students who prefer sound can be provided background music and group-learning opportunities.

- *Design of learning area.* Students can be allowed to design their classroom environment as far as possible. Some might prefer the desks in rows. Others might prefer a more informal atmosphere including wall decorations, plants, and beanbag chairs.

Management of the Instructional Event

CREATING ORDER

If one studies the classrooms where learning consistently occurs, a common characteristic is that order prevails. *Order* does not mean that the students are seated quietly in rows doing seatwork but rather that there are rules for social participation and academic work (Doyle 1986). Such rules are particularly important when an attempt is being made to diversify the instructional strategies. If students are working in groups, it is imperative that the rules for interaction have been established and made known to all.

Evertson and Emmer (1982), in a study of effective and noneffective classrooms, found that effective teachers developed rules and procedures, communicated information, and organized instruction *at the earliest point possible in the year.* These actions are particularly important when dealing with students who have problems staying on task and who disrupt the learning of others. Petty (1989) advances the viewpoint that a "behavioral curriculum" should be designed and taught along with the subject-area curriculums.

It is important at this point to remind the reader that the purpose of the instructional design process is to create instruction that is relevant to the learners and to match it with their learning styles. If the teacher has planned the unit and lesson and is confident of the subject matter, and if the probability of success for each student is high, many of the causes of classroom behavior problems will be removed. But problems will occur in implementing any lesson, no matter how well the content is designed. Teachers need to have at their disposal a repertoire of classroom skills to ensure the optimum implementation of the planned instruction.

These recommendations also apply to online instruction. It is particularly important to provide a feeling of "order" in an online class. Students, particularly if they are new to online instruction, are vulnerable to feelings of isolation, confusion, and anger. A "Start Here" icon on the Home Page of the class linked to well-ordered information about the class and getting started successfully is strongly recommended.

MOTIVATING THE STUDENT

Henson (1988) points out that motivating students is both a complex undertaking and critical to long-term success in the classroom. A positive attitude toward the learning experience is a combination of students' attitudes toward themselves, toward the teacher, and toward the subject matter. Henson (1988, 271) argues that although many of these attitudes are brought into the classroom, the profile of teachers who motivate their students to learn is emerging. Such teachers show a real interest in the subject they are teaching and in the students in the class. The teacher uses positive humor and an enthusiasm for teaching.

USING THE IMPLEMENTATION TOOLS

There is no magic recipe for the successful management of the classroom. As pointed out previously, entering the teaching and learning event with a tightly planned lesson that matches the instructional needs and the learning styles of the students is certainly the foundation for success. Jones and Jones (1990, 255–75) provide a suggested list of actions from which the teacher can choose to help ensure that the implementation of the instruction is successful.

A. Giving Instructions

1. Give precise directions

2. Describe the quality of the work expected

3. Vary the approach to giving instruction

4. Employ attending and listening games

5. Positively accept students' questions about directions

6. Place directions where students can refer to them

7. Have students write out directions before beginning

8. Give directions immediately prior to the activity they describe

B. Beginning a Lesson

1. Select and teach a "cue" for getting students' attention

2. Do not begin until everyone is paying attention

3. Remove visual and auditory distractions before beginning the lesson

4. Start with a highly motivating activity

5. Hand out materials to help the students organize their thoughts and focus their attention

C. Maintaining Attention

1. Arrange classroom so that students do not have backs to the speaker

2. Strive for a seating arrangement that does not discriminate against any students

3. Use random selection in calling on students

4. Complete the question before calling on a student

5. Wait at least five seconds before answering a question or calling on another student

6. Use games that encourage attentive listening

7. Ask students to respond to their classmates' answers

8. Model listening skills by paying close attention when students speak

9. Vary instructional media and methods

10. Ask students to think about the question for a while before answering

D. Pacing

1. Watch for nonverbal cues that students' attention is waning

2. Break activities into short segments

3. Vary the style as well as the content of the instruction

E. Seat work

1. Make seatwork diagnostic and prescriptive

2. Develop a specific procedure for obtaining assistance

3. Establish a clear procedure for what to do when seatwork is completed

4. Monitor seatwork by moving around the room

5. Work through the first several problems with the students

6. Spend considerable time in presenting and discussing material before assigning seatwork

7. Relate seatwork directly to material presented before it

8. Provide short segments of seatwork

9. Have students work together during seatwork

F. Summarizing

1. Ask students to keep a journal of the things that they have learned

2. Have students use drama to summarize what they have learned

3. Have students create learning displays

4. Display student work

5. Provide frequent reviews

6. Use tests as tools for summarizing

G. Feedback and Evaluation

1. Help students view evaluation as part of learning

2. Tell students the criteria by which they will be evaluated

3. Relate feedback to goals and objectives

4. Provide immediate and specific feedback

5. Ask students to list factors that contributed to their success

6. De-emphasize comparisons between students and their peers and de-emphasize grades as feedback

H. Instructional Transitions

1. Arrange for efficient movement

2. Post a daily schedule

3. Have material ready for next lesson

4. Do not relinquish students' attention until clear instructions are given for the next lesson

5. Develop transition activities

LEVELS OF INVOLVEMENT BY THE SCHOOL LIBRARY MEDIA SPECIALIST AT THE IMPLEMENTATION STEP

The Initial Level

At the initial level, the school library media specialist provides materials, facilities, and equipment to help the teacher do a better job.

The library media center can be used at times for instruction. This might involve students working individually or in small groups. The school library media specialist can maintain a pool of equipment that teachers and students can check out for instructional use. The school library media specialist will need to be familiar with purchase procedures and keep up with the changes in the field, including maintenance.

The school library media specialist can obtain and maintain computer software that will assist the teacher in managing instruction. Professional collection materials can be obtained that will provide teachers with information to help them carry out the implementation step more effectively. The following are recommended titles.

Armstrong, D. G., et al. 1978. *Instructional Skills Handbook.* Englewood Cliffs, N.J.: Educational Technology Publications.

Briggs, L. J., K. L. Gustafson, and M. H. Tillman, ed. 1991. *Instructional Design: Principles and Applications.* Englewood Cliffs, N.J.: Educational Technology Publications.

Curwin, R., and A. Mendler. 1989. *Discipline with Dignity.* Alexandria, Va.: Association for Supervision and Curriculum Development.

Dick, W., et al. 1990. *The Systematic Design of Instruction.* 5th ed. Glenview, Ill.: Scott, Foresman.

Dunn, R., and K. Dunn. 2001. *Teaching Students through Their Individual Learning Styles: A Practical Approach for Grades 7–12.* Reston, Va.: Reston.

———. 2001. *Teaching Students through Their Individual Learning Styles: A Practical Approach for Grades 3–6.* Reston, Va.: Reston.

Fleming, M., and W. H. Levie. 1993. *Instructional Message Design.* 2nd ed. Englewood Cliffs, N.J.: Educational Technology Publications.

Grossnickle, D., and W. Thiel. 1987. *Promoting Effective Student Motivation in School and Classroom.* Reston, Va.: National Association of Secondary School Principals.

Jones, V., and L. Jones. 2000. *Comprehensive Classroom Management.* 6th ed. Boston: Allyn and Bacon.

Knirk, F. G. 1989. *Instructional Facilities for the Information Age.* Syracuse, N.Y.: ERIC Clearinghouse on Information Resources.

National Council of Teachers of English. 1999. *Substitute Teachers' Lesson Plans: Classroom Tested Activities from the National Council of Teachers of English.* Urbana, Ill.: National Council of Teachers of English.

The Moderate Level

At the moderate level many school library media specialists currently perform the implementation-step activity of delivering equipment upon request. Setting up a delivery system with the actual delivery performed by student assistants often results in more efficient equipment use because it helps minimize the "my computer or VCR" syndrome.

The school library media specialist can assist the teacher at the implementation step by providing advice on specific teaching strategies. The following scenario depicts such an interaction.

A SCENARIO

Adrienne Walton, the school library media specialist, and Bill Shapero, the eleventh-grade history teacher, are staffing the concession stand for the basketball game. Bill has been at South High School for a number of years and has usually taught the higher-level history, government, and social studies classes. There has been a shift in demographics in the city and there are fewer higher-level classes. This year, for the first time in more than ten years, Bill has two sections of eleventh-grade American history for noncollege-track students. There are rumors that he is having problems with his classes.

Bill: What a slow night. But, I can use the calm after today.

Adrienne: Rough day?

Bill: Yes. It's those two classes that I was stuck with this year. I'm supposed to teach them American history. It goes in one ear and out the other.

Adrienne: Where do you seem to have the most problems?

Bill: During my lectures. I did try to adapt the lectures to this level, but it hasn't helped.

Adrienne: What sort of adaptations did you do?

Bill: Mainly, I reduced the amount of material I try to cover in each lecture. I realize that some of these kids have trouble taking a lot of information in at one time.

Adrienne: That was a good move. Other than that, your approach remains about the same as for the honors sections?

Bill: Yes. I follow the same outline—just cover less material. I try to spice up the lectures with anecdotes. You know, make it seem more real.

Adrienne: One problem with using the same information-delivery approach with these classes that you use with your honors sections is that these students probably don't have the same learning tools.

Bill: Learning tools?

Adrienne: Yes. Do students from these classes and your usual classes seem equally ready to learn?

Bill: No.

Adrienne: Do they take the same-quality notes?

Bill: No!

Adrienne: Do you think, at the conclusion of a lecture, that both groups equally review, on their own, the material that was covered?

Bill: No way! I think I see what you are aiming at. But they should know how to do these things. This is high school!

Adrienne: But many of our students don't. For a lecture to be really successful with these students, these learning techniques have to be built in.

Bill: Give me a "for instance."

Adrienne: Okay. A good practice would be to provide the outline for the notes on the board or overhead projector. The students could be shown the whole outline before the lecture begins. Then the outline could be covered up and parts revealed as they're taught in the lecture. Another idea might be to break the lecture into short parts and involve the students in group activities between the parts. Come by the center tomorrow, and I'll show you some materials I have on this.

Note that this is a moderate-level interaction. The school library media specialist is concentrating on this step only. She is also being careful not to overwhelm the teacher, who is evidently having a great deal of trouble. Ideally, she would work through the entire instructional design process with him. Given the learners and instructional objectives, the lecture method is probably not appropriate. But teachers, like any humans, often are very resistant to change. Although Bill Shapero is probably ready for some change because of the difficulties he is facing, proposing too much might lose him altogether.

Adrienne Walton might also not be ready to enter the in-depth level at this point. Perhaps she has limited resources. She might not judge her skills as developed enough. By interacting in the manner depicted in this scenario, she is making a solid contribution by helping the teacher teach more effectively.

The In-Depth Level

IN-SERVICES

There are many topics involving the implementation step around which an in-service may be built. These include:

- *Equipment operation.* An in-service on equipment operation would have the goal of familiarizing faculty with the use of selected kinds of equipment. An opportune time for such an in-service is when a new type of equipment is purchased by the school.

- *Equipment use.* There are many tricks of the trade beyond the simple operation of the equipment. The in-service can include PowerPoint techniques, computer projection devices, effective uses of VCRs and laser disc players, advice regarding audience placement, and so on. Simple troubleshooting of equipment malfunctions is another good topic.

- *Teacher activities.* Specific techniques for a given level of learning is a useful topic for an in-service on teacher activities.

- *Compensating activities.* Demonstrating activities to compensate for deficiencies in instructional materials is a topic that will benefit teachers. Another possible in-service topic is compensating activities in general—that is, integrating compensatory activities into the whole range of teacher interactions with students.

A SCENARIO

Correy Anderson, a third grade teacher, stopped by the library to ask Jo-Anne Doah a question.

Jo-Anne: Hi, Correy, what can I do for you today?

Correy: Jo-Anne, I have been thinking. I have a classroom with a very wide range of skills. I have just begun using an online learning package to teach multiplication skills, but many of my students just cannot learn from the package—they don't have the right "tools" to comprehend it. I would like for the package to be useful for all of my students.

Jo-Anne: I understand, Correy, and I believe I have a solution. I am conducting an in-service next Tuesday after school on precisely this subject—modifying online learning packages for all levels of students. It will begin at 4:00 in the SLMC and should last about an hour. Can you come? I think this will help you with your problem.

Correy: Sure, that is perfect! See you then—and thanks, Jo-Anne.

INSTRUCTIONAL DESIGN TEAM PARTICIPATION

The school library media specialist at the in-depth level can work with one or more teachers in implementing instruction. This might include helping the teachers design teacher activities based upon the previous steps in the instructional design process. It could include actually co-teaching a lesson with one or more teachers.

The following scenario describes the process of designing implementation activities for a teacher using a videotape that is not fully appropriate for a set of learners.

A SCENARIO

Ken Ramer, the school library media specialist, is working with Bill Cabelerri, a science teacher, in developing instruction for a group of students who have not performed up to expectations. They have already conducted a learner analysis, using the *Learning Tools Inventory.* This technique was chosen because of Bill's description of his class's symptoms (see chapter 8).

They are currently designing a unit on the seasons. The particular lesson they are designing in this example is on autumn. After performing the needs assessment and instructional objectives steps, they came up with the following results:

Goal: The student will know about autumn.

Goal-elaboration statement: This knowledge will include typical weather, plant behavior, and plant changes.

Primary instructional objective: The learner will describe the driving force behind plant and animal behavior during autumn. (Problem Solving)

Enabling objectives:

• The learner will compare the environmental characteristics of autumn and winter. (Defined Concept Learning)

• The learner will describe and give examples of classes of animal behavior during autumn. (Defined Concept Learning)

• The learner will describe types of changes in plants during autumn. (Concrete Concept Learning)

Ken and Bill agreed that these learners needed large amounts of teacher guidance, were group oriented, and were visual learners. They rated the learners very low using the *Learning Tools Inventory;* therefore, they judged the learners as being lacking in many learning tools.

They located and evaluated a videotape. They rated the presentation very low in appropriateness because it did not tell the students in advance what was to be covered, did not structure the information, and did not require participation. However, because the presentation did contain the information corresponding to the instructional objectives and a variety of visual information, and was the only material available in the collection on this topic, Ken and Bill decided that the presentation should be used along with compensatory activities. They wrote a plan for this as follows.

Learner/teacher activities:

- Increasing motivation. Students will imagine being an animal in a given environment. For example, "You are a squirrel, and it's fifteen degrees with three feet of snow on the ground. You are hungry. What do you do?" If the student says, "I would go to my nest and eat nuts," the teacher might ask, "Where did the nuts come from?" The purpose of the activity is to illustrate the difficulty of surviving in adverse climates, and to interest the learner in finding out more about the topic.

- Ensuring learner readiness. The learners will be told in advance what they are expected to learn. The teacher will write the objectives on the board and explain each briefly.

- Providing a clear structure. The teacher will introduce the videotape and will put an outline of the main points on the overhead projector:

  I. Characteristics of autumn

  II. Characteristics of winter

  III. Animal behavior

      A. Migration

      B. Hibernation/increased eating

      C. Camouflage

      D. Food storage

      E. Change in diet

  IV. Plant changes

      A. Color change

      B. Reduced liquids

      C. Plants go to seed

(Space was left under each entry so that Bill could enter additional information.)

- Providing appropriate pacing and pointing out important information. As the videotape presentation proceeds, the teacher will stop the tape, if necessary, and verbally and physically point out the important information, referring to the outline.

- Requiring student participation. The teacher will instruct the learners to take notes at critical points in the presentation. The teacher will also stop the presentation and ask questions such as "What is the field mouse doing?" "What are the advantages of storing food?" and "What are the advantages of a plant shedding its leaves before winter?"

- Providing feedback. The teacher will respond to the students' answers and review if necessary.

- Paraphrasing and summarizing the important information. The teacher will fill in the outline on the overhead with the main points as the presentation proceeds.

- Synthesizing the information. Following the presentation, the teacher will refer to the primary instructional objective and have the students attempt to write a statement describing the reason for animal behavior and plant changes during autumn. The teacher will employ guidance by using "centering" questions, if necessary,

THOUGHT PROVOKERS

1. A teacher asks you for help in designing a field trip for a science class of eighth-grade students deficient in the learning tools. The topic for the field trip is glaciers. The teacher complains that field trips teach nothing—the students pay no attention as information is pointed out, and they do not behave well. Describe and justify at least three activities you would recommend to the teacher to increase learning on the field trip.

2. Describe an appropriate teaching activity for helping students learn the names of the Great Lakes and their locations.

3. Describe examples that you would recommend for teaching the concept "under."

(See appendix A for answers.)

REFERENCES

Armstrong, D. G., J. J. Denton, and T. V. Savage, Jr. 1978. *Instructional Skills Handbook.* Englewood Cliffs, N.J.: Educational Technology Publications.

Doyle, W. 1986. Classroom Organization and Management. In *Handbook of Research on Teaching* (3rd ed.), ed. Merlin C. Wiltrock, 392–491. New York: Macmillan.

Dunn, R., K. Dunn, and G. E. Price. 1981. *Learning Style Inventory Manual.* Lawrence, Kans.: Price Systems.

Evertson, C. M., and E. T. Emmer. 1982. Effective Management at the Beginning of the School Year in Junior High Classes. *Journal of Educational Psychology* 74 (4): 485–98.

Fleming, M., and W. H. Levie. 1978. *Instructional Message Design: Principles from the Behavioral Sciences.* Englewood Cliffs, N.J.: Educational Technology Publications.

Harris, R. L. 2000. Batting 1,000: Questioning Techniques in Student-Centered Classrooms. *Clearing House* 74 (1): 25.

Henson, K. T. 1988. *Methods and Strategies for Teaching in Secondary and Middle Schools.* New York: Longman.

Hoover, K. H. 1982. *The Professional Teacher's Handbook.* Boston: Allyn and Bacon.

Hunkins, F. P. 1972. *Questioning Strategies and Techniques.* Boston: Allyn and Bacon.

Jones, V. F., and L. S. Jones. 1990. *Comprehensive Classroom Management: Motivating and Managing Students.* 3rd ed. Boston: Allyn and Bacon.

Petty, R. 1989. Managing Disruptive Students. *Educational Leadership* 46 (6): 26–28.

Phi Delta Kappa. 1978. *Educational Planning Model, Phase II.* Bloomington, Ind.: Phi Delta Kappa Center for Dissemination of Innovative Programs.

Tessmer, M., and D. Harris. 1990. Beyond Instructional Effectiveness: Key Environmental Decisions for Instructional Designers as Change Agents. *Educational Technology* 10 (7): 16–20.

Yule, R. M. 1985. The Problem of Pacing a Student Learning at Home. *Programmed Learning and Educational Technology* 22 (4): 315–19.

ADDITIONAL READINGS

Bowen, C. 2001. A Process Approach: The I-Search with Grade 5: They Learn! *Teacher Librarian* 29 (2): 14.

Brueggeman, M. A. 2001. Creating Highly Motivating Classrooms for All Students (book review). *American Secondary Education* 29 (4): 79. (Book by Margery B. Ginsberg and Raymond J. Wlodkowski.)

Bullock, T., and K. Hesse. 1981. Six Ways to Teach Reading. *Today's Education: Social Studies Edition* 70 (2): 58–61.

Bycura, D., and P. W. Darst. 2001. Motivating Middle School Students: A Health-Club Approach. *The Journal of Physical Education, Recreation and Dance* 72 (7): 24.

Chuska, K. R. 1995. *Improving Classroom Questions.* Bloomington, Ind.: Phi Delta Kappan.

Comprone, J. J. 1988. Classical "Elementary Exercises" and In-Process Composing. *Freshman English News* 17 (1): 5, 11–13.

Concept Web. 2002. *Scholastic Scope, Teacher's Edition* 50 (18): T-5.

Duffy, G. G., L. R. Roehler, and G. Rackliffe. 1986. How Teachers' Talk Influences Students' Understanding of Lesson Content. *Elementary School Journal* 87 (1): 3–14.

Hall, V. 2001. Management Teams in Education: An Unequal Music. *School Leadership and Management* 21 (3): 327–41.

Heinich, R., M. Molenda, and J. D. Russell. 1982. *Instructional Media and the New Technologies of Instruction.* New York: John Wiley.

Henak, R. M. 1984. *Lesson Planning for Meaningful Variety in Teaching.* Washington, D.C.: National Education Association.

Intermediate Grades: What Makes Intermediate-Grade Students Want to Read? 2002. *Reading Teacher* 55 (6): 568.

Joyce, B., et al. 1999. *Models of Teaching.* 6th ed. Boston: Allyn and Bacon.

Lasarenko, J. 1996. Teaching Paraphrase, Summary, and Plagiarism: An Integrated Approach. *Exercise Exchange* 41 (2): 10–12.

Macrorules for Summarizing Texts: The Development of Expertise. Technical Report No. 270. *Reading and Communication Skills,* 40.

Maguire, S., and S. Edmondson. 2001. Student Evaluation and Assessment of Group Projects. *Journal of Geography in Higher Education* 25 (2): 12–14.

Peterson, D., J. Kromrey, and J. Borg. 1990. Defining and Establishing Relationships between Essential and Higher Order Teaching Skills. *Journal of Educational Research* 84 (2): 5–12.

Vargas, M. F. 1985. Developing an Immunity to Sophomoric Plagiarism: Notetaking Skills. *English Journal* 74 (2), 42–44.

Weinstein, C. E., and R. E. Mayer. 1983. The Teaching of Learning Strategies. *Innovations Abstracts* 5 (32): 4–7.

Weinstein, C. E. et al. 1989. Helping Students Develop Strategies for Effective Learning. *Educational Leadership* 46 (4): 17–19.

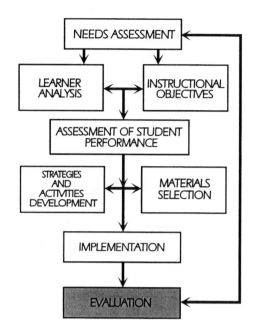

14

Evaluation

This chapter provides information to help the reader

- understand formative evaluation

- understand the three levels of formative evaluation

- compare the phases of formative evaluation

- given appropriate information, isolate the problem step or steps in the instructional design sequence

The term *evaluation* as used in education can be interpreted in a variety of ways. Chronbach (1963) described three types of evaluation.

- *Evaluation of the individual student.* This type of evaluation includes assigning grades and assigning to levels within courses, and can include the type of pre-instruction diagnostic testing called learner analysis (Schuncke 1981).

- *Evaluation for administrative decisions.* Administrative decisions can include comparing instructional approaches, comparing schools, and evaluating teachers.

- *Evaluation to improve a lesson, unit, or course.* This kind of evaluation, often called formative evaluation, has as its goal the improvement of instruction. It will be the focus of this chapter.

THE PURPOSE OF FORMATIVE EVALUATION

Formative evaluation involves assessing the results of each step in the instructional design process to improve the results of the process. Although the evaluation step is placed last in the model, it is an ongoing process. The school library media specialist as instructional consultant in effect asks these questions for each step: Did carrying out the step lead to effective instruction? and How can the step be carried out better? This type of evaluation makes the instructional design process constantly improving, based upon evaluation of results. Improving instruction has always been important, but if a Web-based approach is involved, constant quality improvement is particularly important. Online instruction is still in its infancy and many of the decisions made in the design of a particular unit will, upon application of the unit, need to be modified.

Romiszowski (1981) has delineated three levels of formative evaluation:

1. *Evaluation that will result in changes for current students.* A teacher might have used a videotape for instruction during the first day of a unit and discovered that the students had a

great deal of trouble structuring the information due to the complexity of the presentation. The next day, instead of using part 2 of the tape as planned, the teacher might employ more compensating activities. In another example, a teacher who is teaching a course that is largely Web based might find that the information in the "Start Here" section of the course is leading to confusion on the part of some of the students. The teacher immediately adapts the directions.

2. *Evaluation that will result in changes for the next group of students going through the lesson.* A teacher might have found that the essay questions used on the unit test were ambiguous. The next time the unit is taught, the questions can be reworded. The analysis of the test items might demonstrate that the students had particular trouble with a certain concept and the teacher might add more and varied examples of that concept to the unit.

3. *Evaluation that will result in changes in the way future instruction is designed.* The instructional design process can be implemented in many ways. Evaluating the results of the process can lead to different actions the next time the process is employed. For example, a teacher might decide to put more emphasis on learner analysis the next time instruction is designed because a new learner analysis tool became available.

If all instruction were perfect, no evaluation step would be necessary. However, the science of instruction is still barely beyond its infancy. Whatever levels of changes result from the evaluation process, formative evaluation is vital to the instructional design procedure.

Questions to Be Answered in Formative Evaluation

Of course, the main questions to be answered during a formative evaluation are: Were all instructional objectives met to criterion? and, Are the students ready to learn more? If the answer to either or both of these questions is no, then third and fourth questions arise: At which step(s) in the instructional design process did the problem occur? and, How can the step(s) be improved?

Posner and Rudnitsky (1978) employed a useful analogy in this area. They compared the formative evaluation procedure to the troubleshooting done by a television-repair person. The first action taken is to plug in the set and see if it works satisfactorily. If it does, then the evaluation is complete. If not, then the repair person attempts to locate the problem component and service it.

No matter how tightly instruction is planned, there will be consequences that are not related to the instructional objectives. Posner and Rudnitsky (1978) called these consequences "side effects," in contrast to the learning specified by the instructional objectives, or "main effects." These side effects include beneficial learning. For example, a learner may, in learning a list of spelling words, correctly generalize the rule for forming the plural of words ending in f or fe. The evaluator should be sensitive to any learning of this type that has occurred, especially if a further lesson is planned that can capitalize on this learning.

Often, however, the side effects of planned instruction can be counterproductive. These misunderstandings can involve incorrect concept and rule generalizations and can interfere with subsequent learning. Aikenhead (1979) suggested that the evaluator analyze test results to ascertain what was learned incorrectly, as well as which instructional objectives were mastered.

Information to Be Collected

The important information to be collected at the evaluation step is that which will help in deciding how to improve instruction. The information collection process must be efficient, and the collection of useless information must be minimized. In conducting an evaluation, the following information should be considered:

- results of assessment of instructional objectives

- results of attitude questionnaires

- results of conversations with students

- comments of experts in the subject matter

- comments of impartial observers (Gagne and Briggs 1974)

If the instruction was delivered using a platform such as WebCT, the teacher will have information available on the student's behavior during instruction, including number of times a page is visited, self-tests taken, number of discussions posted and responses given, chat questions and responses, and so on.

PHASES OF FORMATIVE EVALUATION

The conscientious designer of instruction will endeavor to prepare the best possible product before using the product with learners. However, it is difficult, if not impossible, to initially produce high-quality instruction right off the drawing board. The instructional designer therefore should choose the minimum number of students for the initial implementation of instruction.

Dick (1977), in addressing this problem, described a three-phase process for implementing and evaluating instruction.

1. *Phase 1 (one-to-one evaluation).* At this phase, the instructional design has just been completed. Materials are in rough form (e.g., a Power Point presentation is still in outline form). The school library media specialist or teacher selects one to three students who represent the group for whom the instruction is being designed. (For a homogeneous group of learners, one student would suffice. For a heterogeneous group, three might be required.) The materials are shown to the teacher and others who teach the same subject. The teacher or school library media specialist meets with the students and works through the outline. The students are encouraged to ask questions and make comments. The teacher or school library media specialist records problem areas in the presentation.

2. *Phase 2 (group evaluation).* At this phase, the instruction is developed further, but still not in a polished form (e.g., an instructional game may be designed, but the parts are made out of paper rather than card stock, or a Web-based module has been created but graphics are not yet created.). The teacher selects a group of eight to twenty-four students, preferably at random. Pretests and posttests are given, learning time is carefully monitored, and student comments are encouraged. On the basis of this information, the instruction is revised for the third phase.

3. *Phase 3 (field testing).* In the third phase, the instruction is close to final form. The instruction is implemented with the entire class or classes. Information on learning time, attitudes, and performance is again collected through instruments and observation.

Dick and Carey (1978) advised that the three-phase approach be used primarily when developing instructional materials. Russell and Blake (1988) also advocate considering the evaluation of instructional materials as a process separate from evaluation of learners. While there is little doubt that evaluation at all three phases would result in better instruction, resource constraints preclude this in most cases.

At minimum, an instructional consultant should recruit another person to act as a sounding board as each step is designed and to evaluate the results of the instruction. Often, if the consultant explains the plan, problems can be spotted before they occur in implementation. Many benefits can accrue from taking time to reflect on the strengths and weaknesses of the instruction and how it can be improved.

EVALUATING EACH STEP AFTER INSTRUCTION

Whether the instruction has involved one to three students, as in phase 1, or all of the students, each step in the instructional design process should be considered in the evaluation. Because time is often at a premium, the steps at which problems occurred should receive the most attention during evaluation.

Aikenhead (1979) suggested looking for extremes in the data collected to assist in pinpointing the problem steps. These extremes might involve test items on which virtually all students were correct or incorrect. Do these items correlate with a particular instructional objective? Other "flags" are materials and activities that received a large amount of negative feedback from students or observers. In evaluating Web-based instruction, the teacher should be particularly sensitive to areas of the instruction that generate a large volume of e-mail from the students asking for clarification or assistance.

In order for the evaluation process to achieve improved instruction, the evaluators must strive to minimize ego involvement. The teacher is not being evaluated, nor is the instructional process being graded. The instructional process is being evaluated to make the instruction more effective, not to place blame for failure to reach instructional objectives.

Evaluating the Needs Assessment

The needs assessment step is vitally important in the design of instruction but is seldom carried out in a systematic manner. Thus teachers often attempt to teach what has already been learned or what is not needed. Unfortunately, this step is also often overlooked when evaluating instruction. Teachers often jump to evaluating steps 5 through 7—strategies and activities development, materials selection, and implementation—and begin by asking questions such as whether they used the correct PowerPoint slides or provided enough reinforcement. The first question that should be asked, however, is Was the correct content chosen?

The following questions should be considered in answering this larger question:

- Were various sources of content considered?

- Was a rationale for selecting the content established?

- Were instructional goals clearly stated?

- Were the learners' previous accomplishments correctly identified? (This question is especially pertinent if the teacher used intuition for this decision.)

- Was the content prioritized for instruction? Did this prioritizing bear up in practice?

- Were information skills included in the needs assessment?

- Were affective needs considered?

- What are the implications for this step the next time this lesson is planned?

Evaluating the Learner Analysis

Instruction that is implemented without considering the characteristics of the learners involves a gamble that the activities and materials will be effective. Unfortunately, this step is often skipped. If a learner analysis is attempted, it should be evaluated in terms of appropriateness and effectiveness. The following questions should be asked in evaluating learner analysis:

- Was a learner analysis attempted?

- Was the method of conducting the learner analysis appropriate for the students? Was the method selected in order to achieve specified goals? Was the method chosen because of the availability or ease of use of instruments?

- If the method chosen involved student participation, did this procedure appear valid and reliable?

- Were learners analyzed individually or by groups?

- Did the method yield information to assist in the design of materials and activities?

- What are the implications for this step the next time this lesson is used?

Evaluating the Instructional Objectives

Designing adequate instructional objectives is a problem for many teachers. Consequently, many times disappointing results of instruction can be traced back to this step. In evaluating the instructional objectives step, the following questions should be considered:

- Were the instructional objectives derived from goal-elaboration statements rather than from goals alone?

- Did the objectives clearly state an observable learner behavior?

- Could it be ascertained who was to perform the behavior?

- Were the objectives correctly identified according to type and level of learning?

- Were appropriate schemata created for concepts and rules?

- Were enabling objectives established for each primary objective? Were these adequate?

- Were entrance skills delineated? Did the students possess them?

- Was an instructional enterprise created? Did it make sense?

- Was a teaching sequence of objectives established? Was it appropriate?

- What are the implications for this step the next time the lesson is used?

Evaluating the Assessment of Student Performance

The results of assessments of student performance often form the core of the information used in the evaluation process. Therefore, the assessment procedure should be evaluated carefully.

- Was the assessment procedure based upon the instructional objectives?

- Were all instructional objectives assessed?

- Was the type of assessment used appropriate for the instructional objectives?

- Was a wide range of assessment procedures used?

- If a Web-based teaching platform was used in the instruction, were the assessment capabilities of the platform used appropriately?

- What are the implications for this step the next time this lesson is used?

Evaluating Strategies and Activities Development

The process of selecting the strategies and activities the students engage in during instruction should be evaluated, as well as the effectiveness of the activities.

- Were instructional objectives considered in the selection of the strategies and activities?

- Were learner characteristics considered in the selection of the strategies and activities?

- Did the learners spend the majority of the time on task?

- Was the interaction of the student with peers and teacher beneficial?

- Was the match of strategies and activities with learner characteristics and instructional objectives employed in the lesson appropriate?

- What are the implications for this step the next time this lesson is used?

Evaluating Materials Selection

Materials are a vital part of the instructional process. The evaluator should assess not only the effectiveness of the materials but also the process by which the materials were selected.

- Were materials selected on the basis of the instructional objectives?

- How was the format selected?

- Was a range of titles sought?

- Were reviews consulted?

- Were materials previewed?

- Were learner characteristics considered in the selection of the materials?

- Were the materials tested with small groups of students?

- During use, did the materials seem to be appropriate for the learner characteristics? Did the students respond to the materials? Were they involved?

- In Web-based instruction, was there an effective method of assisting the students to have a successful entrance into the instruction? For example, several tutorials could be embedded within the online course to assist students in understanding how to navigate the course, use e-mail, post information on the discussion board, chat with others, submit assignments, and so forth.

- What are the implications for this step the next time the lesson is used?

Evaluating the Implementation

The implementation step is especially difficult to evaluate. The teacher's own behaviors are often the focal point, and it is difficult to maintain objectivity. The quality of the other steps in the process so influences what happens at this step that it is often difficult to separate the classroom behaviors of the teacher from the output of the prior steps. For example, if inappropriate instructional materials were selected and used, should the ensuing problems be attributed to poor selection of materials or to inadequate implementation activities that failed to compensate for the inadequate materials?

The purpose of evaluating the implementation of instruction is to remove problems. Ideally, the problem should be traced to as close to the beginning of the instructional design process as possible. Although defects in all of the steps previous to the implementation of instruction can be, at least partially, remedied during implementation, it is usually more efficient to correct the problem in the earlier steps rather than trying to fix it in implementation. For example, if instructional materials are not effective, then selecting more appropriate materials would be preferable to designing compensatory activities.

- During teacher-led instruction, did the teacher compensate for students' learning deficiencies?

- When using instructional packages or Web-based instruction, did the teacher compensate for students' learning deficiencies?

- Did the teacher prepare and use an adequate teaching plan?

- Were the results of tests recorded systematically?

- Was the classroom environment designed to match learner characteristics?

- Was sufficient order maintained to enable learning to take place?

- If Web-based instruction was used, did the teacher respond in a timely and appropriate manner?

- What are the implications for this step the next time this lesson is used?

Evaluating the Evaluation

The instructional design process is not complete until the evaluation step itself has been evaluated. These questions should be considered:

- Was an evaluation of any kind attempted?

- Was a wide range of information sources considered?

- Were all steps in the process considered?

- Were the steps that contained problems emphasized?

- Were recommendations for solutions to the problems formulated?

- Were personalities left out of the evaluation process as much as possible?

- To what extent did the intervention by the school library media specialist as instructional consultant alter the instruction by the teacher? What were the results of this intervention?

- What are the implications for this step the next time this lesson is used?

LEVELS OF INVOLVEMENT BY THE SCHOOL LIBRARY MEDIA SPECIALIST AT THE EVALUATION STEP

The Initial Level

Many teachers' evaluation skills are in need of a great deal of strengthening. At the initial level, the school library media specialist can assist by providing various resources including equipment and materials.

The key to an effective evaluation is collecting the appropriate information, and the school library media specialist can assist in this effort by obtaining and maintaining a computer and appropriate software for information management. Because student attitudes play an important role in evaluation, the center can establish a file of instruments that can be used to determine attitudes.

Professional collection materials can be obtained that will provide teachers with information to help them carry out the evaluation step more effectively. Several of the works recommended in earlier chapters include information on evaluation that would help teachers improve their skills. The following are recommended titles.

Bailey, G. D. 1983. *Teacher-Designed Student Feedback: A Strategy for Improving Classroom Instruction.* Washington, D.C.: National Education Association.

Briggs, L. J., K. L. Gustafson, and M. H. Tillman, ed. 1991. *Instructional Design: Principles and Applications.* 2nd ed. Englewood Cliffs, N.J.: Educational Technology Publications

Carter, E. W. 2002. Doing the Best You Can with What You Have: Lessons Learned from Outcomes Assessment. *The Journal of Academic Librarianship* 28 (1/2): 36–41.

Cullen, R. 2002. An Action Plan for Outcomes Assessment in Your Library. *Journal of Academic Librarianship* 28 (3): 164–66.

Dick, W., et al. 2000. *The Systematic Design of Instruction.* 5th ed. Glenview, Ill.: Addison-Wesley.

Gagne, R. M., L. J. Briggs, and W. W. Wager. 1992. *Principles of Instructional Design.* 4th ed. Fort Worth, Tex.: Harcourt, Brace, and Jovanovich.

Gallini, J. K., and D. D. Barron. 2001. Participants' Perceptions of Web-Infused Environments: A Survey of Teaching Beliefs, Learning Approaches, and Communication. *Journal of Research on Technology in Education* 34 (2): 139–56.

Hernon, P. 2002. Editorial: The Practice of Outcomes Assessment. *Journal of Academic Librarianship* 28 (1/2): 1–3.

———. 2002. Outcomes Are Key But Not the Whole Story. *Journal of Academic Librarianship* 28 (1/2): 54–56.

March, J. K., and K. H. Peters. 2002. Curriculum Development and Instructional Design in the Effective Schools Process. *Phi Delta Kappan* 83 (5): 379–81.

Mukhopadhyay, M., and M. Parhar. 2001. Instructional Design in Multi-Channel Learning Systems. *British Journal of Educational Technology* 32 (5): 543–56.

Shambaugh, R. N., and S. G. Magliaro. 2001. A Reflexive Model for Teaching Instructional Design. *Educational Technology Research and Development* 49 (2): 69–92.

Sherry, L., et al. 2001. Assessing the Impact of Instructional Technology on Student Achievement. *T.H.E. Journal* 28 (7): 40–43.

Summers, L., et al. 2002. Building Instructional Design Credibility through Communication Competency. *TechTrends* 46 (1): 26–32.

Ward, D. 2000. Evaluation: How Are We Doing? *School Planning and Management* 39 (11): 4.

The Moderate Level

The evaluation step essentially consists of troubleshooting activities in which problems in the instructional process are identified and removed. Many of the interactions portrayed in the scenarios in earlier chapters included evaluation activities.

If the school library media specialist is perceived as someone who is willing to listen and provide objective feedback, teachers will often take advantage of this opportunity. In fact, a significant part of the instructional consultation role at the moderate level will involve acting as an evaluation expert, listening to symptoms, and helping the teacher diagnose problems in instruction.

The school library media specialist who fills this role often finds it difficult to keep on track and not alienate the teacher. Teaching is a high-stress occupation, and many teachers like to vent frustration by griping. To serve as an effective troubleshooter, the school library media specialist must cut through the symptoms to find the problem. It is always tempting to get caught up in gossip and waste the limited time available. As more schools begin to move some of the curriculum into an online environment, the level of stress on the faculty can increase dramatically at the onset of this transformation. Often these teachers are asked to move their materials online with little technical or time support. Evaluation of the results of this effort is particularly important and the school library media specialist can play a crucial role in assisting in the evaluation. The school library media specialist faces a particular challenge in providing this assistance and not being ensnared in the emotional response of the teacher to the change in instructional delivery method.

In order to accomplish the task, the school library media specialist will need to use a wide range of communication skills, including the verbal and physical facilitating skills discussed in chapter 5. The school library media specialist often has only a limited amount of time to gather enough information to make a tentative diagnosis. This is often analogous to practicing medicine at the scene of a large disaster. Some hints for conducting informal evaluations follow:

- Be careful not to imply that the teacher's activities were at fault. The teacher might have done a poor job of planning and implementing instruction, but a defensive teacher will often spend more time defending actions than improving performance.

- Try to steer the teacher away from symptoms and toward problems. A complete description of all of the misbehavior that took place during the showing of a videotape is not necessary. Why did the students misbehave? Was the videotape introduced? Did the students know what they were to learn from the tape? Did the teacher point out important information during the showing? Were participation activities designed?

- Work back as far as possible in the instructional design process. Remember, the materials and strategies and activities are built on needs assessment, learner analysis, and instructional objectives. Rebuilding a house on a weak foundation is often wasted effort.

- Avoid making a snap diagnosis. Evaluation at the moderate level is very difficult because of time restraints. Be cautious, and don't be afraid to say, "I don't know." When first attempting this level of interaction, be content to offer suggestions for minor changes rather than for sweeping course revisions. (For example, "Many students will pay closer attention if they have a set of questions to answer from the videotape.")

The In-Depth Level

IN-SERVICES

Most teachers need a great deal of training in evaluation, and there are many topics on which the school library media specialist can implement an in-service in this area. This is an area, however, in which the school library media specialist must proceed with caution. Unless the traditional perception of the school library media specialist has been altered, an in-service on evaluating instruction may not be well received. In a study by Turner (1983), principals preferred involvement by school library media specialists in the other seven steps to involvement in this step.

In-services in the evaluation area are important, however. School library media specialists who desire to move to this level at the evaluation step should build a foundation through activities at the prior levels. They should become familiar with the literature, make this information available to the teachers, publicize their availability for informal assistance, and build a core of teachers with whom such interaction has taken place. With this background, an in-service will have a much greater probability of success.

An excellent opportunity for the school library media specialist to become involved at this level occurs in schools that adopt a Web-based teaching platform that includes a variety of methods to gather assessment information. As an example, if the history department in a high school uses a Web-based module to teach the Civil War, the school library media specialist may do an in-service with the teachers to demonstrate how the data collected by the platform can assist the teachers to determine whether the students visited the number of pages that they would need to in order to master the content.

INSTRUCTIONAL DESIGN TEAM PARTICIPATION

One advantage of working at the in-depth level with an instructional design team is that the evaluation phase of instructional design is much more likely to be effective. At the moderate level, the school library media specialist must often guess at what has gone on in planning the instruction or must spend a great deal of time trying to find out. If the school library media specialist has been consulted in planning and implementing the instruction, then problems in the system will be more easily located.

Even with enlightened teachers who have systematically planned instruction and included the school library media specialist as part of the design team, there is often the tendency to shortchange the evaluation step. An important role of the school library media specialist is to emphasize the importance of the evaluation and revision process. The school library media specialist in the role of consultant can help to emphasize the atmosphere of objectivity and the need to evaluate instruction rather than people.

THOUGHT PROVOKERS

1. Why would instructor-presented instruction be difficult to evaluate at phase 1 (one-to-one evaluation) or phase 2 (group evaluation)?

2. What might be some symptoms of problems at the instructional objectives step?

3. What might be some symptoms of problems at the learner analysis step?

4. What might be some symptoms of problems at the strategies and activities step?

5. An American Government teacher approaches you, the school library media specialist, and mentions that students who are using the newly-implemented online module on the branches of the U.S. government are scoring very poorly on the quiz even though the information is presented in the charts that are part of the material. What are the steps in the instructional design process that should be recommended by you to be analyzed?

(See appendix A for answers.)

REFERENCES

Aikenhead, G. S. 1979. Using Qualitative Data in Formative Evaluation. *Alberta Journal of Educational Research* 25: 117–29.

Chronbach, L. J. 1963. Evaluation for Course Improvement. *Teachers College Record* 64: 672–83.

Dick, W. 1977. Formative Evaluation. In *Instructional Design: Principles and Applications*, ed. L. J. Briggs, 311–36. Englewood Cliffs, N.J.: Educational Technology Publications.

Dick, W., and L. Carey. 1978. *The Systematic Design of Instruction.* Glenview, Ill: Scott, Foresman.

Gagne, R. M., and L. J. Briggs. 1974. *Principles of Instructional Design.* New York: Holt, Rinehart and Winston.

Posner, G. J., and A. N. Rudnitsky. 1978. *Course Design: A Guide to Curriculum Development for Teachers.* New York: Longman.

Romiszowski, A. J. 1981. *Designing Instructional Systems.* New York: Nichols.

Russell, J. D., and B. L. Blake. 1988. Formative and Summative Evaluation of Instructional Products and Learners. *Educational Technology* 28: 22–28.

Schuncke, G. M. 1981. The Uses and Misuses of Evaluation. *Clearing House* 54: 219–22.

Turner, P. M. 1983. Levels of Instructional Design Involvement by the School Media Specialist: Perceptions of Selected School Principals. *International Journal of Instructional Media* 11: 11–26.

Wang, M. C. 1976. The Use of Observational Data for Formative Evaluation of an Instructional Model. *Instructional Science* 5: 365–89.

ADDITIONAL READINGS

Bennett, P. G. 1999. From Secondary School Blues to Lifelong Learning?—Aspects of the Retrospective Re-Evaluation of Formative Educational Experience by Adults. *International Journal of Lifelong Education* 18 (3): 155.

Branch, R. M., et al. 1999. Evaluating Online Educational Materials for Use in Instruction. *ERIC Digest,* ED-99-CO-0005.

Carlson, E. R. 1995. Evaluating the Credibility of Sources: A Missing Link in the Teaching of Critical Thinking. *Teaching of Psychology* 22 (1): 39.

Cennamo, K. S., and J. D. Ross. 2000. Strategies to Support Self-Directed Learning in a Web-Based Course. Paper presented at the Annual Meeting of the American Research Association: Teacher Education. April 24–28.

Clark, D. B. 2000. Evaluating Media-Enhancement and Source Authority on the Internet: The Knowledge Integration Environment. *International Journal of Science Education* 22 (8): 859.

Criswell, J. R., and S. J. Criswell. 1995. Modeling Alternative Classroom Assessment Practices in Teacher Education Coursework. *Journal of Instructional Psychology* 22 (2): 190.

Desmarais, L., et al. 1998. Evaluating Learning and Interactions in a Multimedia Environment. *Computers and the Humanities* 31 (4): 327.

Epler, D. 1991. Using Evaluation: To Bring School Library Resource Center. . . . *Emergency Librarian* 18 (3): 8.

Garcia, J. C. 2001. An Instrument to Help Teachers Assess Learners' Attitudes towards Multimedia Instruction. *Education* 122 (1): 94.

Grossen, B. J. 2002. The BIG Accommodation Model: The Direct Instruction Model for Secondary Schools. *Journal of Education for Students Placed at Risk* 7 (2): 241.

How to Evaluate Educational Software. 2000. *Curriculum Review* 39 (7): 15.

Hurwitz, C. L. 1999. A Teacher's Perspective on Technology in the Classroom: Computer Visualization, Concept Maps and Learning Logs. *Journal of Education* 181 (2): 123.

Maslowski, R. and A. Visscher. 1999. Formative Evaluation in Educational Computing Research and Development. *Journal of Research on Computing in Education* 32 (2): 239–55.

Morgan, W., and C. M. Wyatt-Smith. 2000. Improper Accountability: Towards a Theory of Critical Literacy and Assessment. *Assessment in Education: Principles, Policy & Practice* 7 (1): 123.

Perrenoud, P. 1998. From Formative Evaluation to a Controlled Regulation of Learning. *Assessment in Education* 5 (1): 85.

Repman, J. 2002. Information Literacy and Assessment: Web Resources Too Good to Miss. *Library Talk* 15 (2): 12.

Sadler, D. R. 1998. Formative Assessment: Revisiting the Territory. *Assessment in Education: Principles, Policy & Practice* 5 (1): 77.

Wager. J. C. 1983. One-to-One and Small Group Formative Evaluation. *Performance and Instruction* 22 (5): 5–7.

Welch, M. 2000. Descriptive Analysis of Team Teaching in Two Elementary Classrooms: A Formative Experimental Approach. *Remedial & Special Education* 21 (6): 366.

Zucco, C. M. 1998. Evaluating Mathematics Videotapes for Use in the Classroom. *Mathematics Teacher* 91 (4): 348.

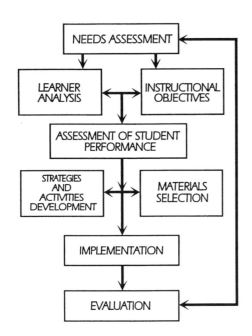

15

Conclusion

THE FUTURE OF THE PROFESSION

There continue to be both pessimistic and optimistic views of the future of the school library media profession. Pessimists point to a chronic shortage of school library media specialists and of faculty to prepare the next generation of professionals. They point out cases in which professionals are replaced by clerical staff as a result of budget reductions or inability to fill the position. Faced with a shrinking resource base, we are unsure of our place in an era of accountability. Others point out that the role has been further diluted by the assignment of information technology duties that are time consuming and in actuality, clerical.

There have also been examples that reinforce an optimistic view of the profession during the years since the second edition of *Helping Teachers Teach.* With the advent of the World Wide Web, the profession of librarianship experienced a renaissance of its public reputation. School library media education programs in many universities became the first program to "go online," helping to alleviate the severe shortage of professionals.

The greatest cause for optimism is the fact that school library media specialists are in the right place at the right time to play a significant role in the transformation of teachers that must occur as K–12 education is impacted by the revolution in telecommunications and information technologies. If school library media specialists step forward armed with the competencies to serve as instructional consultants, there is a bright future ahead. If we do not or can not, a dim future looms.

We must, both as individual school library media specialists and as a profession, determine our roles and communicate these roles to our principals, teachers, students, parents, and others. No one in the school has greater potential to have an impact on the learning of children and young adults. We must demonstrate our ability to make this impact.

YOUR ROLES AS A SCHOOL LIBRARY MEDIA SPECIALIST

Since there is never enough time, energy, and money to do everything you want to do, it is especially important to make the effort to consider carefully your roles as a school library media specialist. Consider the needs of your students and faculty, your own preferences and competencies, and the resources available to you. Make a commitment to improve your program in one or more of the role areas. Communicate this commitment and publicize the results.

If you have worked through chapters 1 through 14, you should have a clear idea of your roles as a school library media specialist, can determine your levels of involvement in instructional design consultation, and possess the skills and desire to increase this involvement.

Actually, there is a good chance that you are feeling overwhelmed and far from competent in the area of instructional consultation. Although a goal of this book was to avoid esoteric terminology, a lot of new information was presented. If you were unfamiliar with the instructional design process before you began, it is natural for you to be unsure of your competence in this area at this point.

The cure for this doubt is the continued acquisition of information and practice. Reread sections of this book while you use the information. Look at appendix H, which is a unit developed by a team using this procedure, but also read or view the materials recommended in each chapter. Most important, try to put the instructional design process into practice as soon as possible.

The next time you plan an information skills lesson or a literature presentation, try using the steps in the process. If you choose to increase your involvement in the area of helping teachers teach, do not expect a smooth path. There will be rebuffs, failures, and times when progress seems impossible. Try not to get discouraged. Know that there are teachers who need your help even though they may not always come forward. Use the levels approach to set goals you are likely to accomplish.

Don't hesitate to begin instructional consultation because you cannot immediately initiate a large-scale project. Keep in mind the major point of the levels approach: All instructional consultation is valuable. Whether you begin building a professional collection where none existed before or plan and carry out an in-service for your teachers, you are helping teachers teach and children and young adults learn.

A

Answers to Thought Provokers

CHAPTER 1

1. As any school library media specialist can tell you, there is an extremely large universe of potential activities from which you could have chosen. Perhaps you saw the school library media specialist reading the classic *Make Way for Ducklings* to a group of kindergarten students. Maybe the students were creating their own adventure story using a hypertext software package. Perhaps the school library media specialist was ordering a children's story on CD-ROM. In each case, you probably correctly identified the activity as falling within the reading, viewing, and listening program function.

   Perhaps you saw the school library media specialist setting up a stack of CD-ROM readers and connecting these to a local-area network. Maybe the high school library media specialist was leading a discussion on the role of perception of language in the classification of concepts. Some might have pictured the information professional teaching an English class about the use of an online biographical dictionary. Each of these school library media specialists was performing activities that fall under the category of providing information skills.

   Some readers might have imagined a school library media specialist making PowerPoint slides on the parts of an atom, which the chemistry teacher would use later on in the week. Others might have seen the school library media specialist discussing possible videotape titles with the first-grade teacher. Both of these actions are carried out to help the teacher teach and fall under that program function.

   Perhaps the activity visualized did not fit clearly under one program function but spilled over onto several. For example, you might have seen the school library media specialist maintaining a VCR. This activity could be in support of teachers in their instruction, but the same piece of equipment could be used to show a video of Briggs's *Snowman*. There are many activities that cross over the boundaries created by the model. In fact, the school library media program is at its most powerful and efficient state when activities simultaneously impact across the three functions—for example, when the school library media specialist develops a unit with the social studies teacher on the use of the Internet as a political weapon and when the students read and discuss an online ebook.

   Finally, there were some activities envisioned that did not fit under any of these program functions. Some might have seen the school library media specialist collecting lunch money in homeroom. Some might have seen him or her sponsoring the cheerleaders or the yearbook. Perhaps the school library media specialist was on hall patrol or monitoring a study hall. The school library media specialist is a member of the school community and, as such, is obligated to carry out certain activities as part of being a "good citizen." Unfortunately, too often these activities that fall outside of the three program functions take up a disproportionate amount of the school library media specialist's resources. One powerful aspect of a model is that it shows clearly when this is happening.

The actual model you end up with is not as important as the process of thinking through your philosophy of the functions of the school library media program. Rather than wait until someone asks you, "What are the purposes of the school library media program?" take some time to think this through. Establish your own personal vision and let others know about it. (See Roland Barth's *Improving Schools from Within* in the References section of chapter 1.)

CHAPTER 2

1. a.   Step: implementation. Level: moderate.

   b.   Step: materials selection. Level: in-depth.

   c.   Step: all steps, but concentrating on the learner analysis step. Level: in-depth.

   d.   Step: assessment of student performance. Level: initial. The school library media specialist is helping the teachers assess their learners.

   e.   Step: needs assessment. (The school library media specialist is helping the teacher decide on the content to be covered in the unit on community helpers.) Level: This is the moderate level because there is interaction involved.

2.   There are very many activities that can be performed at either end of the three dimensions of instructional consultation. A possible activity is to purchase CD-ROMs that teachers can use to make instructional materials. Notice that there is no interaction involved. In this example, the school library media specialist decided unilaterally that teachers might need these raw materials and made them available. The purpose was not to provide guidance to the teachers and increase their skills. It was presumed that they knew how to use the materials, or that they would learn on their own. Only one step was targeted. Therefore, this activity is at the far left of two dimensions, and almost completely to the left of the third.

Targeting the same step, materials selection, the school library media specialist might have decided to plan and conduct an in-service on creating PowerPoint presentations and burning them onto a CD. At the conclusion of the in-service the participant might be able to use the basic principles of design to create a PowerPoint presentation. In this example, the school library media specialist would have extensive interaction with the teachers in planning, teaching, and following up the in-service. The purpose of such an in-service is to enhance the teachers' skills and, perhaps, to change their attitudes toward the use of self-produced instructional materials. This activity, therefore, would fall on the right of the first two dimensions and still target only one step.

Carrying out the second of the previous two examples would require significantly more resources from the school library media specialist. Expertise in designing visuals and in using the equipment would be required. Adequate supplies and equipment would need to be available to meet the demands engendered by a successful workshop. In addition, there would need to be a foundation of trust on the part of the teachers that the time spent in an in-service given by the school library media specialist would result in useful skills.

Both of these examples of instructional consultation by the school library media specialist can help teachers. The first example requires many fewer resources, with commensurate impact and recognition. A successful in-service requires a significant effort, and success is likely to bring more work. It also brings recognition of the library media program as providing essential instructional support and as helping the teachers teach better.

CHAPTER 3

1. If you or the school library media specialist you interviewed is typical (i.e., overworked and overwhelmed!), the completed ICAC could seem a bit disappointing. The highest levels will probably be at the materials selection and implementation steps. Our traditional role has been to provide materials to teachers, which these two steps represent.

    Remember that although helping teachers teach is an important role, it is only one of three (see fig. 1.2). Given the many constraints under which school library media specialists labor, increases in involvement will be slow. The trick is to keep the vision in mind and one's feet on the ground.

2. Target areas exist for those steps at which the in-depth level has not been reached. The target area for each of these steps is the next highest level. As higher levels are implemented, it will quickly become apparent that improvement within a level that has already been reached could be targeted. For example, if a professional collection has been established (initial step), the materials for any one step could be evaluated and improved.

3. Of course, there is no single answer to this question. The following is one possible plan:

    I. Goal statement. Build a collection of professional materials that will enable teachers to determine instructional content most effectively.

    II. Objectives statement

    A. Systematically select at least five resources on the topic.

    B. Begin collecting exemplary units from other schools and establish a file that includes at least five units.

    III. Things to do

    A. Collect (or locate online) publishers' catalogs from likely sources such as the National Education Association, Phi Delta Kappa, and American Society for Curriculum and Development.

    B. Conduct an online literature search for articles and other materials.

    C. Preview and review materials.

    D. Contact school library media specialists at other schools to discuss a unit-sharing plan.

    E. Circulate a form among teachers that requests the identification and location of exemplary units.

    F. Set up a file including circulation policies and procedures.

    G. Obtain and process materials.

    H. Evaluate by keeping track of circulation figures and informal comments of faculty.

    IV. Resources required

    A. One hundred fifty to four hundred dollars for materials.

    B. Ten to thirty professional hours, depending on sophistication of results expected.

    C. Five to ten clerical hours.

    D. Shelving space (three feet), and two file drawers for all formats of materials.

For readers who are completely new to the concept of instructional design, this question might prove to be too much. If you are not satisfied with your answer, try again after reading chapter 7.

4. Each person's vision will be, and should be, unique. What is your ideal program? How will you help improve the effectiveness of teaching? Now that you have covered the first three chapters of this book, your vision will probably include some in-depth instructional consultation activities. Remember that a vision is dynamic and that as you progress through the remainder of this book, this vision should develop. Keep it in a pocket of your mind and bring it out occasionally to look at. Let it inspire, not discourage, you.

CHAPTER 4

1. Such a display can range from a simple block-letter heading to a computer graphics bonanza. What is chosen in a particular school should depend upon the teachers and the resources of the school library media specialist. Figure A.1 is a sample.

2. For most teachers, the book talk should be kept short and to the point. Stress what the work can do for the teacher and the amount of time required for use. If special indexes or content outlines have been prepared, these should be pointed out. The following is the first part of a talk that introduces a volume of a journal that contains articles on learning styles.

Did your mother ever come into a room in which you were perfectly comfortable and say, "Put on a sweater, it's cold in here"? The environment in which we function best varies for each of us. And this variety includes not only temperature but lighting, seating, noise level, and many other factors.

Matching learning and teaching styles is an area where a lot of research and development is taking place. I have here a collection of articles, some of which contain information that can be readily used by the classroom teacher. [If appropriate, several of the best articles could be described here.] This volume of *Theory into Practice* on learning styles will be in the professional collection. I have annotated what I consider to be the most useful articles—print and online. Let me know what you think, and if you want me to order any materials mentioned on this topic, let me know that, too. Thanks, and put on your sweater, I'm cold.

CHAPTER 5

1. Does a real need seem to exist for this level of activity at this step? Have teachers requested it? Have there been new developments at the school that call for this level at this step? What is the principal's attitude? What resources are required to move up to this level? What competencies do I have in this area? What competencies are required? What is my attitude toward this step and level?

Fig. A.1. Example of a display poster for the teachers' lounge

2. Such a poster should emphasize a certain activity that is being offered by the library media program at this step and level. Because the materials selection step is so detailed, specifying the activities you are offering to carry out would avoid teachers requesting something that cannot be accomplished.

3. Not only did you probably feel neglected and frustrated during the first conversation, but the quality of the communication was probably poor. School library media specialists are often so busy that they try to do several things at once. As a result, they sometimes neglect to attend to others properly. Being conscious of these skills may help to correct this.

4. There are several ways in which this statement could be opened. This is one: "When you used the videotape on Africa last, what did you see as its good and bad points?"

5. The temptation sometimes, especially at the end of a particularly trying day, is to respond negatively to someone's request for help and understanding. In this case, a cutting remark about working smart instead of hard might be on the tip of the tongue, but something like "You certainly work hard to make your class the best that it can be!" might be a better way to begin your response.

6. One example of an accurate paraphrase: "This PowerPoint presentation is technically well prepared, but for some reason, it doesn't teach what you wanted it to."

7. One example of accurate summarizing: "I think we can come up with something that is easier and more effective than your having to draw the diagrams on the board. After I look at the sample diagrams, I'll give you some different approaches to choose from."

CHAPTER 6

1. Most school library media specialists will probably feel most comfortable in the role of helper or partner. Most teachers are used to regarding themselves as self-sufficient in the classroom, for better or for worse. There is little history of a presence in the school of an expert consultant. In addition, most school library media specialists lack the training that would make them an expert in most of the steps in a systematic process of planning, implementing, and evaluating instruction. Being there and providing nonjudgmental assistance is probably the most comfortable (and effective) role. (Actually, this role is probably effective for the vast majority of instructional consultants in business and industry as well. A true partnership for enhancing instruction just has to function better than a relationship that involves an expert dictating pedagogy!)

2. Of course Teacher 2 is correct. Skill in group dynamics is crucial to the success of the school library media specialist as a member of an instructional design team. Tact, especially at the end of a long, hard day, is an invaluable aid. In this case, the school library media specialist needs to avoid putting down Teacher 1 without losing the useful thought Teacher 2 has brought to light. Perhaps a response might be, "The whole problem of selecting computer materials today is difficult. When I see a title that looks relevant—which isn't very often—I am tempted to get it right away. So many programs, however, just don't work, and in order to get the best use of our limited funds, we should try to preview first." This could be followed up by asking Teacher 2, "What would be the most important thing a computer program should do?"

3. It is difficult to predict the answer to this one. Depending upon the learning style of the teacher, for example, an unstructured approach employed during the workshop could be perceived as good or bad. Do these responses validate the tips given under "Designing a Successful In-Service"?

4. Some comments are easily dealt with in designing an in-service. If the teacher liked participation, or didn't like the fact that evaluation was not incorporated as part of the session, these details can be incorporated or remedied. More difficult to deal with are the factors beyond the control of the school library media specialist. If the teacher wanted to be paid for the time, or wanted to attend a conference in another city, not much can be done directly.

5. Because the most effective in-service will be one to which teachers come voluntarily, publicity is crucial to success. Possible methods include two or three waves of flyers or e-mail notices letting the faculty know what they will gain from the in-service; posters in high

teacher-traffic areas; a drawing for a prize to be given away at the end of the in-service (this prize could be a box of cookies or a book donated by a publisher); a word-of-mouth campaign started by people you trust to be enthusiastic and prolific in their contacts; and a "good word" at a meeting by an opinion leader (head teacher, principal, or department head).

6. It is so good to have the principal excited about your conducting a workshop that it is tempting to say, "Sure, bring them all on!" As you might have experienced, though, it takes just one or two people who do not want to be at a workshop to really mess it up. The social studies teachers in this case seem to be candidates for disgruntled attendees. Perhaps this school library media specialist might suggest a very small voluntary workshop (limited equipment availability is a good excuse). A second workshop just for the social studies teachers can be proposed at the same time.

CHAPTER 7

1. a. Source: an established standard. Example: Each ninth-grader should be able to perform basic mathematical computations in order to pass the ninth-grade state competency test.

   b. Source: comparisons with what is being taught somewhere else. Example: Parents of students in the enrichment program say that their children ought to be able to program a computer because similar students are doing this in a neighboring city.

   c. Source: anticipating learning that will be needed in the future. Example: A curriculum committee decides that, because the percentage of new jobs in the service area will increase, students should have instruction in basic human relations in the tenth grade.

   d. Source: asking the population to be taught. Example: When asked what she would like to study in a multimedia class, a student replied, "I would like to learn how to make a video (using photographs) with music to give to my grandmother as a present."

   e. Source: using unsolicited requests from the students. Example: A group of students approached their American history teacher and said, "We would like to study more about wars and battles."

2. a. Using sources and situations external to the group to be taught has the advantage of efficiency because a list of previously formulated goals is a convenient starting point. The disadvantage of this approach is that sometimes the group for which the standard goals were developed is sufficiently different from the target group that this content is not warranted. Goals on commercially available lists, in order to appeal to a wide market, sometimes tend to be too general for use at the classroom level.

      Determining instructional content based on what the learner states is desired has the benefit of helping to motivate the students. Negative aspects of this approach include the time and resources required to collect and interpret the student responses. Also, this process would tend to fragment the curriculum because these perceptions would seldom be expressed in a logical order.

   b. The small-scale needs assessment procedure described in chapter 7 can use as the inputs in phase 1 information from any of the sources. In practice, sources external to the students would tend to predominate. This is due to the widespread use of the Internet as the primary source of content and to the difficulties inherent in using student-generated content in lessons.

3. It is important when you begin to use the small-scale needs assessment procedure that you understand it is an ideal but can be used in a practical way with a variety of clients. Some teachers will comment that the only goals they must include are stated in the textbook, and that they believe these goals, as stated, are needs. Aside from explaining the needs assessment procedure, you cannot do much as an instructional consultant in this case. Perhaps if a teacher realizes that the content selected is either inappropriate or has already been mastered, a change in perception will occur. Remember, this needs assessment procedure is a tool that represents a philosophy. There is considerable leeway within the philosophy to permit modification of the tool.

The following is an example of the application of the small-scale needs assessment procedure by an elementary school library media specialist. This school library media specialist is working with the third-grade math teacher to develop a unit on linear measurement for the advanced and gifted class. The teacher has stated that although there are a number of introductory concepts that need to be covered, the children should also be challenged to learn higher-level material and to learn on their own from sources outside of the classroom.

I. Phase 1. Generate a list of possible goals.

A. Sources of information

1. The textbooks for grades 3–6.

2. State competency requirements for measurement for grades 3–6.

3. Several instructional material items (all formats) from the system media center.

B. Persons involved

1. Third-grade math teacher

2. Gifted-education adviser for system

3. School library media specialist

4. Students

C. Actions. The teacher talked with the students about measuring things and asked them what they would like to learn on the topic. The teacher and the school library media specialist studied the materials from part A and brainstormed a list of topics. The gifted-education specialist joined them, and the three of them modified the list.

D. Output. Students should

1. know why we need measurement systems, including finding and describing incidents where measurement was critical

2. understand that measurement systems are arbitrary, including the creation of their own measurement system

3. know the units for measurement of length in the metric and English systems

4. know the tools for measuring short and long distances

5. know how to change from one unit to another within systems (e.g., feet to inches or centimeters to millimeters)

6. know how to estimate length in both metric and English forms of measurement

7. know how to add and subtract in metric and English forms of measurement

II. Phase 2. Rank goals in order of importance. The math teacher and the gifted-education specialist ranked the goals separately and then reconciled their rankings through discussion. Their final ranking was 1, 2, 6, 3, 4, 5, 7.

III. Phase 3. Determine the extent to which goals have been reached. The teacher studied the results of the previous year's achievement test in the area of linear measurement. Members of the team spoke with several of the students. They decided that for the large majority of the students, goals 3, 5, and 7 had already been reached and therefore were not instructional needs.

IV. Phase 4. Prioritize needs. The entire team considered the needs in light of the previously stated priority, materials and time required, and the complexity of the material. The final priority ranking was 1, 2, 6, 4.

Note that designing instruction for the individual student is the ideal. If teachers are designing instruction for groups, compromises have to be made. What about the few students who had not reached goals 3, 5, and 7? The team made the assumption that this type of student could easily catch up on the basic skills missed, but does this put them at risk?

4. The information skills to be taught in a given unit should be selected to facilitate the acquisition of the content, should compensate for learning deficiencies associated with learner characteristics, and should match the number of sources and amount of guidance provided by the instructional experience.

In the preceding case, the content, for the most part, is high level and the information skills should match that level. These students should have few, if any, learning deficiencies. The teacher has stated an expectation that the students be required to use a range of sources outside of the classroom. Based on this information, the school library media specialist carries out the following needs assessment.

I. Phase 1. Generate a list of possible goals. The content selected for this unit and the expectation of the teacher required all categories of information skills. Students would need to locate, process, use, and create information. The school library media specialist, using a variety of sources of information skills as well as experience, created a list of possible goals. Students should

A. understand what information is being sought and be able to state this as a purposeful task. Examples: "I need to find an example of where the act of measuring distance saved someone's life"; "I need to find an example of a measuring system saving a great deal of money"; "I need to find three examples of linear measurement systems."

B. understand the process of selecting the important concepts and combinations of concepts on which to search for information.

C. be able to determine the most appropriate resources (print, non-print, or Web-based) to search for a given information task.

D. be able to select the important information—that is, that which pertains to the use of linear measurement in real life or to linear measurement rather than to volume or weight.

E. be able to paraphrase and summarize the important information regarding linear measurement.

F. be able to formulate original generalizations.

II. Phase 2. Rank goals in order of importance. The school library media specialist met with the teacher and discussed the possible goals. They were ranked by the two as 5, 4, 6, 3, 2, 1.

III. Phase 3. Determine extent to which goals have been reached. The school library media specialist, teacher, and gifted-education adviser used achievement test results and their experiences with these children to formulate their conclusions as to content previously mastered. They determined that many of the students had, through instruction and experience, mastered goals 1–4. For them, no instruction in these would be necessary.

IV. Phase 4. Prioritize needs. Because there was a substantial minority who the team believed did not possess the knowledge and skills for goals 1–3, these could not be assumed for the entire class. It was decided not to teach these lower-level information skills but to make available a great deal of guidance to compensate for deficiencies in this area. Examples of this guidance:

A. The teacher would make available a list of questions to use in guiding the students in their search for information regarding examples of linear measurement having an impact in everyday life.

B. The teacher would make available a list of the resources that might be used to find the information.

C. Students would be allowed to form pairs to work through the information gathering.

D. The goals selected for instruction were, in priority order, 5, 4, and 6.

CHAPTER 8

1. Were you different from your partner? Perhaps you differ in characteristics other than the ones this procedure addresses.

2. Did you find it frustrating to judge some of these characteristics? Because many of these processes take place at a barely conscious or subconscious level, they are hard to quantify.

For a learner at either end of the continuum, quantification will not be as difficult, and it is for these learners that designed instruction is most important.

3. There is no research to back up any proposition that a particular category of learner characteristics is most important. The proponents of a particular learner analysis procedure, of course, believe that the learner characteristics measured by their process are important.

   Would a learner who prefers to work alone and is forced into a group project suffer more or less than a learner who processes auditory information slowly and is forced to learn from a fast-paced computer program? There is no doubt that the amount of instruction that does not match the characteristics of the learners is monumental. At this point, making teachers aware of the categories and beginning the process of identifying *any* characteristic and matching instruction to it is sufficient. Rather than spend a great deal of effort trying to think of which characteristic is the most important, let the teacher decide which one can be accommodated within the teacher's comfort level. Success with one characteristic will lead to efforts to deal with others.

4. This statement typifies the reaction of some educators to the idea of learner analysis and reflects a real lack of understanding of the types of learner characteristics. As Keefe points out, physiological and affective characteristics are the result of genetic coding and personality development, and are often resistant to training. This does not mean that students shouldn't be encouraged to work in environments that do not match their preference. The self-discipline reflected in the ability to do so is important for success in many aspects of life. However, students who are forced to do so will expend valuable energy resources coping with what is for them an adverse learning environment.

   Cognitive characteristics, conversely, are internal controls and are more amenable to training, as with the development of critical thinking skills. However, the use of materials and activities that are severely mismatched to the learner's cognitive abilities will most likely result in failure to learn rather than a strengthening of cognitive abilities.

   The primary purpose of the materials and activities employed should be to help the student master the instructional content. Using materials and activities that do not match students' learning characteristics on the grounds that it is good for them is not only bad teaching, it can be damaging.

CHAPTER 9

1. a. intellectual skills

   b. motor skills

   c. intellectual skills

   d. intellectual skills

   e. affective/attitudinal

2. There are many possible instructional objectives for each of the goals stated in question 1. What follows is a possible instructional objective for each, and the goal-elaboration statement, if needed.

   a. Goal elaboration statement: The student should be able to add two mixed numbers and end up with a sum of one mixed number. The student should understand that when adding mixed numbers, if the simple fractions add up to an improper fraction, then the improper fraction must be changed to a mixed number and the whole-number portion added to the sum of the whole numbers of the original mixed numbers. The student should not only be able to carry out the procedure but should understand that a whole is being created each time the numerator equals the denominator.

Primary instructional objective: Given twenty pairs of mixed numbers, the learner will find the correct sum, expressed as a mixed number, for at least eighteen of the pairs.

b. Primary instructional objective: Given four regulation horseshoes and standing the regulation distance from the pole, the learner will toss the horseshoes so that no horseshoe is more than four feet off the line formed by the two poles. Also, at least two of the horseshoes will be within two feet of the target pole.

c. Goal-elaboration statement: The student should be able to recognize vowels and consonants and recall the rule for adding suffixes to words ending in *y* when the *y* is preceded by a consonant or a vowel. The student needs to understand what a suffix is and the common uses of suffixes. The student should be able to apply the rule.

Primary instructional objective: Given twenty words, ten ending in (consonant) *y* and ten in (vowel) *y* and a suffix for each, the learner will correctly add the suffix to at least eighteen of the words.

d. Goal-elaboration statement: The student should recognize the major works of art created during the Renaissance and know the name of the artist who created each piece of art.

Primary instructional objective: Given ten computer printouts of paintings and sculptures by Renaissance artists, the learner will recall the correct title of the work and the artist for at least nine of the examples.

e. Primary instructional objective: During Select-a-Club Week, at least 20 percent of the students in general biology will choose the Biology Club as one of the two clubs chosen.

3. a. Defined concept learning.

b. Associative learning.

c. Problem solving.

d. This can be either concrete concept or defined concept learning. If the learner had formed a prototype of *mammal* from experience but had not been provided with or had not established a definition, then the learning would probably be at the concrete level. If the learner possesses and understands a definition of *mammal* as well as a prototype, then the learning has most likely occurred at the higher level of defined concept.

e. Discrimination.

f. Rule learning. This designation assumes that there is understanding of place value and of the concept of division as repeated subtraction, and that the student is not just blindly following a procedure that uses division facts. It is possible, and quite common, for students to arrive at a correct quotient with no more understanding than if they were doing the same operation with a computer.

g. Rule learning. Again, this behavior can occur as a result of a much lower level of learning if understanding is not present. In fact, if the verbs are ones that have been seen conjugated before, the learning might be at the associative level.

    h.   Defined concept learning (see comment in g).

    i.   Defined concept learning.

    j.   Associative learning.

4. Figure A.2 illustrates one possible instructional enterprise to achieve the stated goal.

5. There are many of the enabling objectives in this instructional enterprise that would probably be considered entrance skills. It is especially important in mathematics to include these in the instructional enterprise design so that they can be acknowledged and pretested if necessary. As indicated in figure A.2, the enabling objectives for reducing fractions, changing improper fractions to proper fractions, and adding whole numbers are assumed to have been previously mastered. This would probably also be the case for the numerator and denominator enabling objectives. In this case, the instruction would be targeted on teaching the recognition and understanding of like denominators and the understanding and the use of the role for adding fractions with like denominators.

If this instruction was not part of a sequence in which the learner's possession of the entrance skills had been established, it probably would be beneficial to have some type of assessment technique to ensure that the entrance skills had been obtained. A possible order of instruction would be to teach the defined concept of like denominator first, providing a variety of concrete experiences. The move into adding these fractions would be natural once this concept had been mastered.

CHAPTER 10

1. Authentic assessment measures student achievement throughout the process of learning. The assessment must be based on authentic content—important concepts that relate to the real world, are appropriate for the developmental level of the student, and require a high level of thinking. During authentic assessment, students must apply what they have already learned and think analytically and creatively to develop new understandings that measure up to the achievement standards that have been set. Throughout the process of authentic assessment, both students and teachers reflect on their achievements and progress.

2. When teachers and students shift from traditional to authentic assessment, both content and instructional strategies change. Of course, the scope of the changes depends on the original learning situation. The content of the authentic-assessment classroom is ideas and concepts, not simple facts. Students can see that the content is connected to real life. The climate is intellectually stimulating because students are grappling with issues, finding information on their own, and pursuing subjects in greater depth. Students in the authentic-assessment classroom develop responsibility for their own learning. Teachers are coaches; they facilitate but do not dictate what students are learning. As students direct their own learning, teachers can concentrate on teaching thinking strategies and information skills instead of lecturing on content-specific facts. Both teaching and learning are collaborative.

3. Reflection by both teachers and students makes the assessment process and the learning itself more interactive and personal. Students begin to see themselves as learners able to evaluate their own strengths and weaknesses. Consequently, many students identify for themselves the areas in which they need to work. Teachers use reflection to appraise students' progress, both individually and collectively. In addition, teachers assess their own instructional plans and teaching strategies. They identify changes to make, initiate them,

Fig. A.2.

INSTRUCTIONAL ENTERPRISE*

Goal: The student will know how to add fractions with like denominators.

Goal Elaboration Statement: The student will understand what each part of a fraction represents. The student will be able to recognize that two fractions have like denominators and to arrive at the fraction or whole/mixed number that represents the sum of the fractions.

Primary Instructional Objective: Given ten pairs of fractions, each pair having like denominators, the student will calculate the sum and reduce it to its simplest form. (Rule Learning)

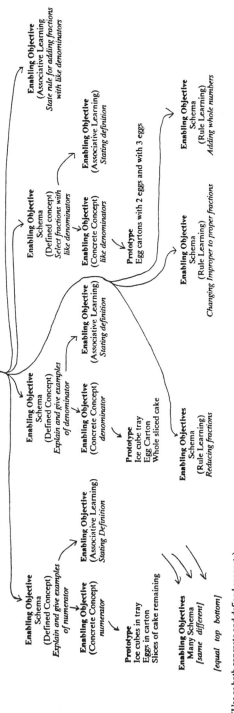

(Use as both concrete and defined concepts)

Prototypes   (Associative learning of definitions)

* This instructional enterprise leaves the schema clusters for *reducing fractions, changing improper to proper fractions,* and *adding whole numbers* in an underdeveloped state. These are assumed to be entrance skills.

and then analyze their effect. Through reflection, teachers become learners and learners become teachers.

4. Authentic tests measure authentic content. Rather than calling for rote memorization of isolated facts (the "right" answers), authentic tests require students to use the facts in a thoughtful way and in a real-life context. In other words, authentic tests extend rather than interrupt the learning process.

So what does an authentic test look like? Can it have matching, true-false, and multiple-choice questions? If those questions simply require students to parrot memorized information or can be answered by guessing, they are not authentic. If, however, the teacher constructs the questions so that they require new thinking (matching the function of body systems in one organism with the parts of an entirely different organism, for example), then they are authentic. Probably short-answer and essay questions are easier to make authentic than are the more quickly graded matching, true-false, and multiple-choice questions. An interesting variation of authentic testing is to allow students to write their own questions or problems (within some guidelines) and then answer or solve them.

All authentic tests must involve depth rather than breadth. The general rule is to ask a few questions that require substantial thinking and real understanding of the important issues, rather than asking abbreviated or superficial questions on every fact covered during the unit.

5. Portfolios can be the most effective assessment strategy when schools are interested in measuring students' achievements in areas not tied to specific classes. Students may be asked to demonstrate proficiency in a number of areas: writing an autobiography; reacting to personal reading; compiling a resume or writing an essay on career goals; analyzing a critical societal issue; performing a scientific experiment or writing a scientific essay; completing an extensive, thoughtful research project; creating an artistic project; and using mathematics to solve a practical problem.

Portfolios are also extremely effective in subject areas that depend on the development of a sequence of skills—foreign languages, mathematics, and writing, for example. Because portfolios are compiled over time, students see their progress in learning and feel rewarded for their success along the way. They may be more likely to participate actively throughout the learning process, which is so important for these sequential classes.

Finally, portfolios will be successful as an assessment technique in any class in which the teacher expects students to display and use their knowledge. Students get excited about the opportunity to compile their best work, especially if they have been allowed to complete a variety of projects, not just tests, to demonstrate their achievements.

6. Reliability problems with performance-based assessment can be modulated by preparing assessment rubrics that describe carefully the behaviors and understandings that would be considered outstanding, average, and poor. If the descriptions are specific enough, evaluators will have a clear picture of what to look for.

Student performances should be rated by several evaluators, but not by the teacher for that class. The evaluators should be carefully trained so that their standards are the same and the scores are reliable no matter who evaluates which students. As part of the training, evaluators should have the opportunity to see a model of the standard that is expected from the students.

Because it is so difficult to equate performance situations, teachers should be careful to work through each performance assignment before giving it to the students. Teachers will be able to detect gross inequalities at that point. In addition, evaluators should be careful to rate each performance according to the rubric for that situation and not compared to situations from other classes or years.

The reliability problem caused by individual versus group performance could be partially overcome by having students within the group evaluate the contributions of each group member. Students are generally thoughtful and honest in such reflective evaluations. Another alternative is to rate individuals according to their written supportive material (notes, outlines, scripts, drawings), and rate the group on the whole-group performance.

Obviously, performances are difficult to evaluate. Setting the expected standard of performance early in the unit focuses the learning process for students and teachers. This clear vision of the expected outcomes increases the number of students who achieve the performance standard and enhances the reliability of the evaluators in assessing the performances.

7. Because the teacher wants students to understand the causes and results of the Civil War well enough to use that knowledge in a comparison to the Revolutionary War, the assessment must provide students with the opportunity to both develop and display their understanding. This is a fairly high-level objective for fifth-grade students; therefore, the students must be required to do more than simply list causes and results. A variety of higher-level assessment techniques can be used: a learning log in which students write their own judgments about the causes and results as they discover them throughout the unit; a soapbox speech in which each student picks a cause or result and tries to convince the class of its primary importance; a diary of someone alive at the time, looking at the causes and later the results from a personal perspective; a class newspaper with headlines and feature articles on each cause and result. The important aspect of the assessment, no matter which technique is used, is that it matches the instructional objectives and stimulates students to probe the issues thoughtfully in order to reach new understandings.

8. If the teacher wants students to recognize literary techniques, then the assessment must include practice in that skill. Because recognition is a low-level instructional objective, the teacher can use simple assessment. For example, the teacher could provide written excerpts from literature or videotaped excerpts from television, and the student could identify the literary techniques used. One would hope that this low-level instructional objective is part of a larger unit with high-level instructional objectives. The culminating assessment activity for the unit might require students to deepen their knowledge about the manipulation of time in literature by employing each of the literary techniques in their own creative writing.

CHAPTER 11

Possible strategy and activity prescriptions:

AA: Short segments of drill are performed individually under close supervision of teacher. Constant feedback and a variety of reinforcement by teacher. Use of the key-word procedure.

AB: Student organizes and leads an activity with other students that involves creating a story or poem with the vocabulary words. Teacher needs to check several times to see if the vocabulary is correct as used.

AC: A tutee works with a competent and strong peer tutor who uses games that involve considerable drill and reinforcement.

BA: Student uses multimedia demonstration of types of weathering. Individual students experiment under the supervision of the teacher or parent volunteer. Students are guided by the teacher in a note-taking exercise.

BB: Student participates in a whole-class introduction of concepts that is led by the teacher. Student leads a group project to create a play depicting the life of a rock undergoing physical and chemical weathering. Teacher needs to check in periodically to see if poetic license is in check.

BC: Teacher leads in a presentation of concepts. Teacher guides structuring activities involving note-taking and outlining. Teacher uses cartoon story of a family of mice whose home is being washed away during a thunderstorm. Teacher closely supervises games involving brainstorming examples of the concepts.

CHAPTER 12

1. Remember that the selection of a format is not a cut-and-dried procedure. Many people involved in selecting instructional materials believe it is preferable to think of this step as eliminating clearly unsuitable media. Given the information provided in question 1, the following conclusions are possible:

   a. Most feasible media: simulation games, realia, and study prints. Least feasible media: videotapes and computer programs.

   b. Most feasible media: computer programs, CD-ROMs, DVDs, and audiotapes. Least feasible media: simulation games and videotapes.

   c. Most feasible media: programmed manuals with illustrations, audiotapes. Least feasible media: Computer Web quests and rented or borrowed videotapes and CD-ROMs.

CHAPTER 13

1. Field trips are probably the most abused of all teaching activities. They often deteriorate into social events, and little of the hoped-for learning occurs. This is not surprising because field trips are seldom as tightly designed as are regular classroom experiences. Because the real world offers a much wider range of stimuli than does the classroom, it is little wonder that intended learning outcomes seldom occur. The teacher can develop a wide range of activities to increase the effectiveness of the field-trip experience.

   The teacher can set instructional objectives for the field trip and communicate these to the students. For example, "When we are finished with the field trip, you should be able to describe at least three kinds of evidence of glacial action." Providing students with a clear idea of their responsibility will serve to direct attention to the appropriate stimuli.

   The teacher can make sure that the concepts necessary for the objectives have been mastered. For example, students should be able to identify striations—parallel marks left on rocks by glaciers. Unless students can recognize the critical information, they will not be able to relate key concepts and understand the rules relating these concepts.

   The teacher can break the students into groups with questions to answer at each stop in the field trip. (The students could be required to take a picture that would answer a question such as How deep is the topsoil in this area?) If a student is looking for information that will answer a specific question, there will be little time for nonproductive activity. Providing a digital camera for each group gives a means for recording and presenting the information.

The teacher can provide an opportunity for synthesizing the information gathered on the trip by having each group show the digital pictures and answer the questions. (The students might have taken a picture of the side of a road-cut to demonstrate depth of topsoil.) As each group reviews the pictures in preparing for its presentation, the information is reinforced. The concepts and generalizations are reinforced again during the presentation.

2. The Great Lakes from left to right (west to east) on the map are Superior, Michigan, Huron, Erie, and Ontario. The first letters could be made into an acronym (SMHEO). The students could be directed to make up a mnemonic sentence (e.g., Some men have eggs only).

3. The teacher could show a number of objects that are clearly under other things (e.g., a dog under a bridge, a dog under a table, shoes under a bed, and a kite under a cloud). The important thing is to show a variety of situations in which one object is clearly under the other. For a more sophisticated group of students, discussions of nontraditional uses of *under* might be employed. What does "under the weather," "under suspicion," or "under a cloud" mean? The students could be asked to discuss and perhaps draw their prototype of the concept "under."

CHAPTER 14

1. An integral part of instructor-presented instruction should be the interaction between teacher and students. This give-and-take would be difficult to achieve with the small number of students involved in phases 1 and 2.

2. Establishing instructional objectives, identifying type and level of learning, and arranging the objectives into a hierarchy is a complex process. Therefore, there are many possible problems and attendant symptoms. These can include a teacher's complaining that all the students seem to learn is facts; a teacher's complaining about the difficulty of planning strategies and activities; a teacher's commenting that the students are always complaining that they aren't sure of what will be covered; a teacher's commenting that his or her instruction just seems to wander; and poor performance on higher-level learning tasks (e.g., "These students don't know how to think!" Were any problem-solving instructional objectives ever identified?).

3. Comments by students such as "It's always too cold in here," "I'd rather work by myself," or "Listening is such a pain!" might indicate a mismatch between learner and instructional approach. Another symptom might be evidence that a student has not learned from an instructional item that is clearly appropriate in terms of content. Poor performance by a student who normally does well working individually but has been involved in a group project is a symptom that calls for consideration of the learning preference-activities match.

4. The symptoms of problems at the strategies and activities step might well be identical with those of answer 3. The task of the instructional consultant is to determine whether the symptoms are the result of a lack of diagnosis (or an incorrect diagnosis) of learning styles or the result of a mismatching of strategies and activities to correctly diagnosed learner characteristics. If a teacher mentions that some of the students always seem to miss the point in a videotape presentation, the consultant might inquire if the teacher has used a

learner analysis instrument with these students. If the answer is yes and the results seem valid, the problem probably is with the lack of compensation for missing learning strategies. If the answer is no or if the results of the method used seem suspect, the consultant can suggest action at the learner analysis, strategies and activities, materials selection, and implementation steps.

5. Actually, there might be a problem with almost all of the steps in the process. Assuming that the content was selected based on knowledge of the students' needs and that the quiz was the result of well-designed performance objectives, the learner analysis, materials selection, and implementation steps would be prime candidates for evaluation.

   As an example, was a learner analysis conducted that identified the students who might have a special problem with extracting information from visuals? At the materials selection step, was the content presented logically with appropriate organization? If the module was "imported" by the teacher, did he or she insert information into the module that called attention to the important concepts to be covered?

B

Instructional Consultation Assessment Chart (ICAC)

INSTRUCTIONAL CONSULTATION ASSESSMENT CHART (ICAC)

IN-DEPTH							
MODERATE							
INITIAL							
NO INVOLVE-MENT							
	NEEDS ASSESSMENT	INSTRUCTIONAL OBJECTIVES	LEARNER ANALYSIS	ASSESSMENT OF STUDENT PERFOR-MANCE	STRATEGIES AND ACTIVITIES DEVELOPMENT	MATERIALS SELECTION	IMPLEMEN-TATION	EVALUA-TION

Name of Teacher,_____
Department, or
School

Time Span (Previous_____
Week, Month, Year, etc.)

Comments_____

_____

_____

The use of the instructional consultation activities chart (ICAC) is intended to provide the school media specialist with a graphic representation of the amount of instructional consultation that he/she is performing with a particular teacher(s). ICAC results can serve as a basis for identifying areas of the media center program in which more resources are needed.

RECOMMENDED PROCEDURE:

1. Identify the teacher(s) that is the subject of the instructional consultation that is to be graphed. (This can be a single person, a group of teachers, or even an entire school.)

2. Select the time span in which you are considering your activities. (This could be the previous week, month, or year.)

3. For each step in the instructional design consultation process, mark the level that represents your interaction with the selected teacher(s). (Refer to the detailed description of the steps if necessary.)

C

Excerpt from a Policies and Procedures Manual

II. BEVERLY PUBLIC SCHOOLS LIBRARY MATERIALS SELECTION AND ADOPTION POLICY

The libraries of the Beverly Public School System are committed to raising the level of student academic achievement by enhancing and expanding library services in Beverly schools. Services are provided that promote and encourage children and young adults to love and appreciate reading and good literature, create capable and critical users of information and technology, and encourage critical thinking as well as teach reading and comprehension skills.

Responsibility for Selecting Media

The School Committee delegates the selection of school library media center materials to the professionally trained employees of the school system. Selection of these materials should involve many people: administrators, teachers, supervisors, and school library media specialists. The responsibility for coordinating the selection of the school library media center materials and making recommendations for purchase rests with professionally trained school library personnel.

Objectives for Selecting Media

The primary objective of the Beverly Public School System's library media centers is to enrich and support the instructional program of the school. The school library media program makes available, through the school library media collection, a wide range of materials on varying levels of difficulty with a diversity of appeal compatible with the different needs, interests, and viewpoints of students and teachers.

To this end the responsibility of the school library media program is as follows:

- To provide school library media that will enrich and support the curriculum, taking into consideration individual needs and the varied interests, abilities, socioeconomic backgrounds, and maturity levels of the students served.

- To provide school library media that stimulates the growth in factual knowledge, literary appreciation, aesthetic values, and ethical standards.

- To provide a background of information enabling students to make intelligent judgments in their daily lives.

- To provide materials on opposing sides of controversial issues so that students may develop, under guidance, the practice of critical thinking and critical analysis of all media.

- To provide materials representative of the many religious, ethnic, and cultural groups in our nation and the contribution of these groups to our American heritage.

- To place principle above personal opinion and reason above prejudice in selecting school library media of the highest quality in order to assure a comprehensive collection appropriate for the users of the school library media center.

Criteria for Selecting School Library Media

Individual learning styles, the curriculum, and the existing collection are given consideration in determining the needs for library media in individual schools.
Materials considered for purchase are judged on the basis of the following criteria:

- Purpose—Overall purpose and its direct relationship to instructional objectives and the curriculum

- Reliability—Accurate, authentic

- Quality—Writing or production of merit

- Treatment—Clear, comprehensible, skillful, convincing, well-organized, unbiased

- Technical production—Audio and visual clear and well-crafted

- Construction—Durable, manageable, attractive

- Special features—Useful illustrations, photographs, maps, charts, graphs, and so on.

- Materials shall be selected for their strengths rather than rejected for their weaknesses.

Procedures for Selecting and Maintaining the School Library Media Collection

The school library media professional, in conjunction with teachers and administrators, will be responsible for the selection of materials. In coordinating this process, the school library media specialist will:

- Use reputable, unbiased, professionally prepared selection criteria.

- Judge gift items by standard selection criteria and, upon acceptance of such items, reserve the right to incorporate into the collection only those meeting these specified criteria.

- Purchase duplicates of extensively used materials.

- Weed worn, obsolete, and inoperable items continuously from the collection.

- Purchase replacements for worn, damaged, or missing materials basic to the collection.

- Evaluate expensive sets of materials and items procured by subscription carefully and purchase only to fill a specified need.

Procedures for Reconsideration of Materials

Occasional objections to some materials may be voiced by the public despite the care taken in the selection process and despite the qualifications of persons selecting materials.
If a complaint is made, the following procedures should be observed:

1. The building principal, in conjunction with the school library media specialist will inform the complainant of the selection procedures.

2. The building principal will invite the complainant to file his or her objections in writing and send the complainant a copy of the form *Request for Reconsideration of School Library Media Material* for submitting a formal complaint to the materials review committee.

3. The special committee (which will be composed of central administrators, building principals, teaching staff, and parents named by the superintendent) will:

   - Re-examine the challenged material.

   - Survey appraisals of the material in professional reviewing sources.

   - Weigh merits against alleged faults to form opinions based on the materials as a whole and not on passages isolated from context.

   - Discuss the material and prepare a written recommendation within 30 days to the superintendent and School Committee.

4. The School Committee will, based on the recommendation of the superintendent, make a final decision regarding the materials and deliver the decision in writing to the complainant and appropriate staff members.

http://www.bhsonline.org/library/policies.html

D

Materials Publicizing
Helping-Teachers-Teach Role

The first item is a brochure (see page 258) created by Donna Baumbach, Professor, University of Central Florida, to distribute to teachers, particularly new teachers.

The second item is the first page of a newsletter (see page 260) created by Augie Beasley, Cheryl Foster (library media specialists), and Carol Buchanan (medai assistant) at East Mecklenburg High School, SOuth Carolina.

Teaching for the First Time?

Feel like you're carrying a heavy load?

There's Help!

Instructional Technology/Educational Media
University of Central Florida
College of Education
Department of Educational Services
Orlando, FL 32816

(407) 275-2153

You don't have to be alone your first year of teaching--or the second, or third, or ever!

There's help available each and every day right in your school media center. The media specialist is a member of your instructional team! And he (or she) is ready, willing, and trained to help!

Here are some of the things your media specialist can do to help you. They can:

-- suggest instructional materials to help you teach
-- provide materials in your subject area in a variety of formats to help all kinds of learners
-- help you produce your own instructional materials like transparencies, slides, videotapes and computer programs
-- locate materials for you from sources outside the media center and outside of the school
-- work with you to teach students to locate, utilize, analyze and produce information
-- provide opportunities for exhibits and displays
-- keep you informed of new materials and new trends
-- work with small groups of students
-- adapt materials to students with special needs
-- bring you information about the newest technologies for instruction and information
-- locate information for you and for your students
-- plan units and lessons with you
-- talk to students about media center materials and encourage life-long learning
-- provide media equipment and instruction in its use
-- promote and support instructional programs
-- place materials on reserve for your classes

Here are some things you can do to help your media specialist to help you! You can:

-- promote the use of the media center by your students
-- model effective use of the media center
-- invite the media specialist to your department or grade level meetings
-- use many types of materials and select the type best suited for your purpose
-- participate in the selection of new materials and in the decisions to discard old materials
-- schedule the use of the media center by small groups, large groups, and individuals
-- send students to the media center with a clear understanding of the purpose for their visit
-- ask for materials you can't find
-- offer to serve on the media advisory committee
-- keep the media specialist informed of your assignments that call for the use of the media center and its materials
-- make your needs known well in advance whenever possible

You're never alone when you have a media specialist! Visit your media center soon! Tell them the UCF Educational Media program sent you!

MEDIA SPECIALISTS--Helping Teachers Teach!

VOL. X, NO. 10   **EAST MECKLENBURG HIGH SCHOOL, CHARLOTTE, N.C.**   FEBRUARY 1992

Utilizing Your Overhead Projector

The overhead projector is the most used and abused piece of audiovisual equipment in the presentation inventory. The machine is easy to operate, and transparencies are easy to produce; but the user needs to follow guidelines in using an overhead projector and in designing visuals. All too often, poorly designed transparencies become an impediment instead of an aid to communication.

However, the overhead projector can be a powerful presentation tool. Remember, people are visually oriented. We learn 11 percent by listening, 83 percent by sight and the 6 percent by our other senses. We remember 20 percent of what we hear and 50 percent of what we see and hear. Using overhead projectors, we show and tell -- a perfect combination for learning.

To use an overhead projector effectively, you need to know some transparency design fundamentals. Most of us do not have the time, money, skill or patience to use many of the production methods shown in audiovisual textbooks. Also, we must work with what the school has,

or what the school can afford for transparency production. In these days of budget cutbacks, the best transparency is the simplest and least expensive to produce.

Before designing a transparency, ask yourself, what is its objective? What is the concept I wish to visualize? Can it be done with a single transparency? Are overlays needed? Is color necessary? What transparency production equipment do I have? The following guidelines are applicable to all transparencies. Follow them and your presentation will sparkle. More important,

you will communicate your message -- before a classroom or an audience of 500.

> *Lettering is not needed on every transparency.
> *Limit words to seven per line. Limit the number of lines to 7.
> *Allow 1 1/2 times the letter height between the lines.
> *Keep the visual simple. Limit it to one main point, idea, or comparison.
> *Use color for a specific purpose. Do not overuse.
> *Use lower case letters instead of all upper case letters.

Please see **Overhead** on page 3

Dateline: February

Feb. 1--**U.S. SUPREME COURT** held its first session in 1790, Chief Justice John Jay presiding.

Feb. 2--**GROUNDHOG DAY.**

Feb. 8-23--**WINTER OLYMPICS** in Albertville, France.

Feb. 14--**VALENTINE'S DAY.**

Feb. 14--**SALMON RUSHDIE,** author of **The Satanic Verses,** given death sentence by Ayatollah Khomeini in 1989 because of book's content. Threat of death continues despite Khomeini's death.

Feb. 16-22--**BROTHERHOOD/SISTERHOOD WEEK.** But honor it all 52 weeks this year.

Feb. 17--**PRESIDENT'S DAY.**

Feb. 22--**REPUBLICAN PARTY,** made up of anti-slavery elements of the Whigs and Democrats, founded in 1854. First presidential candidate who made it to the White House? Lincoln, in 1860.

Feb. 25--**VIOLETA CHAMORO** became leader of Nicaragua in a free election this day in 1990 due to a broad-based coalition that wanted to end fighting between the Contras and Daniel Ortega's group.

Feb. 29--**LEAP YEAR.**

E

Student Learning Styles — A Survey

WICHITA PUBLIC SCHOOLS
MURDOCK TEACHER CENTER
670 North Edgemoor
Wichita, Kansas 67208

LEARNING STYLES ANSWER SHEET

Name _____ School _____ Grade _____ Date _____

Instructions:

Read each statement carefully and decide which of the four responses agrees with how you feel about the statement. Mark out the number of the response on the answer sheet.

Sample Statement:

I would rather do school work in the morning than in the afternoon.

On the answer sheet, there are four possible responses ranging from "MOST LIKE ME" to "LEAST LIKE ME." Decide which response best describes the way you feel about the statement and mark out that number in the parentheses. Respond to the sample statement here by marking out the one response that best describes your feelings.

	MOST LIKE ME			LEAST LIKE ME
1.	(4)	(3)	(2)	(1)

Explanation of Response:

If you are the sort of person that rises early and enjoys working before noon you would probably respond by marking the (4). If you start slowly and usually begin to work better later in the day you probably would respond by marking the (1). If you are somewhere in between, then your response should be a (3) or a (2) depending on where you think you fit. You cannot make a mistake because there is no right or wrong answer; only the way you feel about the statement. There are 45 statements on the three pages to which you will be asked to respond. Mark your answers on the answer sheet the same way you did for the sample statement. You may have all the time you want so please respond to every statement.

Learning Styles Answer Sheet

MOST LIKE ME	LEAST LIKE ME		MOST LIKE ME	LEAST LIKE ME		MOST LIKE ME	LEAST LIKE ME
1. (4) (3) (2) (1)		*	16. (4) (3) (2) (1)		*	31. (4) (3) (2) (1)	
2. (4) (3) (2) (1)		*	17. (4) (3) (2) (1)		*	32. (4) (3) (2) (1)	
3. (4) (3) (2) (1)		*	18. (4) (3) (2) (1)		*	33. (4) (3) (2) (1)	
4. (4) (3) (2) (1)		*	19. (4) (3) (2) (1)		*	34. (4) (3) (2) (1)	
5. (4) (3) (2) (1)		*	20. (4) (3) (2) (1)		*	35. (4) (3) (2) (1)	
6. (4) (3) (2) (1)		*	21. (4) (3) (2) (1)		*	36. (4) (3) (2) (1)	
7. (4) (3) (2) (1)		*	22. (4) (3) (2) (1)		*	37. (4) (3) (2) (1)	
8. (4) (3) (2) (1)		*	23. (4) (3) (2) (1)		*	38. (4) (3) (2) (1)	
9. (4) (3) (2) (1)		*	24. (4) (3) (2) (1)		*	39. (4) (3) (2) (1)	
10. (4) (3) (2) (1)		*	25. (4) (3) (2) (1)		*	40. (4) (3) (2) (1)	
11. (4) (3) (2) (1)		*	26. (4) (3) (2) (1)		*	41. (4) (3) (2) (1)	
12. (4) (3) (2) (1)		*	27. (4) (3) (2) (1)		*	42. (4) (3) (2) (1)	
13. (4) (3) (2) (1)		*	28. (4) (3) (2) (1)		*	43. (4) (3) (2) (1)	
14. (4) (3) (2) (1)		*	29. (4) (3) (2) (1)		*	44. (4) (3) (2) (1)	
15. (4) (3) (2) (1)		*	30. (4) (3) (2) (1)		*	45. (4) (3) (2) (1)	

Learning Styles Worksheet

Name _____ **Date** _____

Put Score from answer sheet by question number.

VISUAL LANGUAGE

5 -
13 -
21 -
29 -
37 -

Total____ x 2 = ____ (Score)

VISUAL NUMBER

9-
17 -
25 -
33 -
41 -

Total____ x 2 = ____ (Score)

AUDITORY LANGUAGE

3-
11-
19-
36-
44-

Total____ x 2 = ____ (Score)

AUDITORY NUMBER

7-
15-
23-
31-
39-

Total____ x 2 = ____ (Score)

AUDITORY/VISUAL KINESTHETIC
(Combination)

1-
18-
26-
34-
42-

Total____ x 2= ____   (Score)

INDIVIDUAL LEARNER

4-
12-
20-
28-
45-

Total____ x 2 = ____ (Score)

GROUP LEARNER

8
16
24
32
40

Total____ x 2 = ____ (Score)

EXPRESSIVENESS-ORAL

6-
14-
22-
30-
38-

Total____ x 2 = ____ (Score)

EXPRESSIVENESS-WRITTEN

2
10
27
35
43

Total____ x 2 = ____ (Score)

WICHITA PUBLIC SCHOOLS
Murdock Teacher Center
670 North Edgemoor
Wichita, Kansas 67298

Total of 24-32 in any area indicates a minor preference. Total above 32 indicates a major preference.

STUDENT LEARNING STYLES—
A SURVEY QUESTIONNAIRE

1. When I make things for my studies, I remember what I have learned better.

2. Written assignments are easy for me to do.

3. I learn better if someone reads a book to me than if I read silently to myself.

4. I get more done when I work alone.

5. I remember what I have read better than what I've heard.

6. When I answer questions, I can say the answer better than I can write it.

7. When I do math problems in my head, I say the numbers to myself.

8. If I need help in the subject, I will ask a classmate for help.

9. I understand a math problem that is written down better than one I hear.

10. I don't mind doing written assignments.

11. I remember things I hear better than the things I read.

12. I like to work by myself.

13. I would rather read a story than listen to it read.

14. I would rather show and explain how a thing works than write about how it works.

15. Saying the multiplication tables over and over helped me remember them better than writing them over and over.

16. I like to work in a group because I learn from the others in my group.

17. When the teacher says a number, I really don't understand it until I see it written down.

18. Writing a spelling word several times helps me remember it better.

19. I find it easier to remember what I have heard than what I have read.

20. I learn best when I study alone.

21. When I have a choice between listening or reading, I usually read.

22. I feel like I talk smarter than I write.

23. When I'm told the pages of my homework, I can remember them without writing them down.

24. I get more work done when I work with someone.

25. Written math problems are easier for me to do than oral ones.

**STUDENT LEARNING STYLES—
A SURVEY QUESTIONNAIRE**
(continued)

26. I like to do things like simple repairs or crafts with my hands.

27. The things I write on paper sound better than when I say them.

28. I study best when no one is around to talk or listen to.

29. I do well in classes where most of the information has to be read.

30. If homework were oral, I would do it all.

31. When I have a written math problem to do, I say it to myself to understand it better.

32. I can learn more about a subject if I am with a small group of students.

33. Seeing a number makes more sense to me than hearing a number.

34. I like to make things with my hands.

35. I like tests that call for sentence completion or written answers.

36. I understand more from a class discussion than from reading about a subject.

37. I learn better by reading than by listening.

38. I would rather tell a story than write it.

39. It makes it easier when I say the numbers of a problem to myself as I work it out.

40. I like to study with other people.

41. Seeing the price of something written down is easier for me to understand than having someone tell me the price.

42. I understand what I have learned better when I am involved in making something for the subject.

43. The things I write on paper sound better than when I say them.

44. I do well on tests if they are about things I hear in class.

45. I can't think as well when I work with someone else as when I work alone.

F

Learning Tools Inventory

Student's Name_____Date_____

Rater(s)_____

Directions: For each characteristic, rate the student(s) from 0 to 10. For assistance, refer to the Sample Behaviors Form.

0	10
Possesses none of the characteristic	**Possesses characteristic to a high degree**

1. *Tendency to establish "set"*

Enters learning situations with no idea as to what is to be learned.

Enters learning situation with a clear idea as to what is to be learned and connects prior learning to current.

0   1   2   3   4   5   6   7   8   9   10

2. *Tendency to structure information into a format which will aid learning*

Makes no attempt to structure information.

Consistently establishes a logical and useful structure.

0   1   2   3   4   5   6   7   8   9   10

3. *Ability to locate criterial information*

Cannot extract imbedded information.

Has no problem extracting embedded information.

0   1   2   3   4   5   6   7   8   9   10

4. *Tendency to generate questions regarding the material to be learned during the presentation*

Never generates questions.

Continuously generates questions.

0   1   2   3   4   5   6   7   8   9   10

5. *Tendency to check self-perceptions regarding material to be learned*

Never checks self-perceptions.   Continuously checks
self-perceptions.

0	1	2	3	4	5	6	7	8	9	10

6. *Ability to process information rapidly*

Extremely slow at all information processing.   Processes all types of information
very rapidly.

0	1	2	3	4	5	6	7	8	9	10

7. *Tendency to want to learn*

Not motivated in any learning.   Highly motivated for all
types of learning.

0	1	2	3	4	5	6	7	8	9	10

8. *Tendency to paraphrase and summarize information*

Never paraphrases or
summarizes information.   Frequently paraphrases
and summarizes information.

0	1	2	3	4	5	6	7	8	9	10

SAMPLE BEHAVIORS OF STUDENTS POSSESSING AND NOT POSSESSING LEARNING TOOLS
(Use with Learning Tools Inventory)

1. Tendency to establish "set."

   Not Possessing: Although the day's lesson (solving word problems involving percent of change) follows on the previous day's lesson (filling in a table, given two of the four components), the student is completely unaware of which topic will be covered.

   Possessing: The student expects that the day's lesson will involve use of percentages and readily applies what was learned the previous day.

2. Tendency to structure information into a format that will aid learning.

   Not Possessing: During independent study, the student does not take notes on what is read.

   Possessing: The student takes careful notes during reading and then creates an outline of the notes.

3. Ability to locate criterial information.

   Not Possessing: The class is viewing a videotape on geometric shapes in everyday life, and the student has a great deal of difficulty picking the shapes out of the background information even though he or she has no difficulty recognizing the same shapes in line drawings.

   Possessing: The student can locate the shapes even though they are part of larger and more noticeable shapes.

4. Tendency to generate questions regarding the material to be learned during the presentation.

   Not Possessing: While using a multimedia presentation on mammals, the student passively participates, not asking the teacher or anyone else any questions.

   Possessing: The student poses questions to himself or herself, such as, "It looks like mammals can be active in all types of temperatures. I wonder if that is true?"

5. Tendency to check self-perceptions regarding material to be learned.

   Not Possessing: While using the multimedia presentation on mammals, the student concludes that "bats aren't mammals because they fly." The student does not check this conclusion with anyone.

   Possessing: The student who has created a premise regarding mammals and temperature uses an on-line encyclopedia to find out more on the topic.

6. Ability to process information rapidly.

   Not Possessing: Virtually anytime this student uses a presentation that is automatically paced, he or she becomes hopelessly lost and complains that it "goes too fast."

   Possessing: Student can watch a television presentation and read at the same time.

7. Tendency to want to learn.

   Not Possessing: This student does not seem to be excited about any topic, even those that usually motivate others in his or her age group.

   Possessing: Student is excited about virtually all topics in a myriad of subject areas.

8. Tendency to summarize information after presentation.

   Not Possessing: Student finishes reading a chapter in the textbook, closes the book, and immediately goes on to the next subject assignment.

   Possessing: Student reflects a few minutes on the reading and then creates an outline of sentences that summarize the main points of the chapter.

G

Instructional Materials Evaluation Form

Title _____

Producer _____ Cost _____

Ordering Information _____

Target learners _____

Target Instructional Objective(s)

_____

_____

RATE ITEM FOR EACH CATEGORY

APPROPRIATENESS (For the learner)

If necessary, does item: Contain advanced organizers, structure the information, call attention to important information, require participation, provide feedback, proceed at a slow pace, motivate, and summarize?

Are the vocabulary, concepts, and generalizations appropriate to the instructional objective(s)?

.Not at all										*.Totally*
0	1	2	3	4	5	6	7	8	9	10

AUTHENTICITY

Factual information, styles, and portrayal of racial, ethnic, and other minority groups.

.Prevents reaching   *.No inaccuracies*
of objectives
.Severe distortions   *.No distortions*

0	1	2	3	4	5	6	7

TOPIC DEVELOPMENT

.Topic development and/or   *.Logical*
extraneous information   *.No extraneous*
prevent reaching of objectives   *information*

0	1	2	3	4	5

Instructional Materials Evaluation Form *(continued)*

ACCOMPANYING MATERIALS

Descriptive notes, user's guide, worksheets, motivational activities, and suggested pre- and post-activities

.Not adequate to reach objective | .Highly supportive of instructional objective

0   1   2   3   4   5

TECHNICAL ASPECTS

Focus, sound quality, resolution, color, smoothness of motion, and competition/redundancy of audio and visual portions of the presentation

. Technical imperfections prevent reaching objective | .No technical imperfections

0   1   2   3   4   5

PHYSICAL CHARACTERISTICS

Durability and replacement policy of distributor

.Poorly constructed
.No replacement possible | .Superior construction
.Free replacement

0   1   2   3   4   5

TOTAL _____

SUMMARY OF STRENGTHS:

SUMMARY OF WEAKNESSES:

H

Sample Unit

When someone first encounters the instructional design process, they often react by saying something like "It sounds good in theory. Let's see it in practice." This appendix provides an example of a unit designed by a team consisting of a fourth-grade teacher and a school library media specialist. There were successes and frustrations typical of the application of a systematic process of designing, implementing, and evaluating instruction at the elementary or secondary level.

For those readers who are at the lower levels of involvement in instructional consultation, the level of interaction portrayed in this example may be intimidating. Please remember that all instructional consultation is valuable, whatever the level.

Although this unit may be intimidating to some, it is far from an ideal application of the instructional design process. Whenever a process is inserted into an already existing system, the results will be a compromise between the two modes of operation. This example is no exception.

BACKGROUND OF THE PROJECT

The school library media specialist who served as instructional consultant on this project had been involved at the moderate level with this particular teacher during the previous two school years. The interaction had occurred mostly at the strategies and activities development, materials selection, and implementation steps. In-depth-level activity at these steps consisted of a project in which the teacher and the school library media specialist wrote computer programs for reading skills remediation.

The school library media specialist wanted to attempt a project in which all the steps in the instructional design process would be performed. The possibility of such an attempt seemed remote for the school year in which the project actually took place, but several factors coincided to increase the possibility.

The state tested all children in various grades, including the fourth grade, for basic competencies. The school system had tested the remaining students using standardized achievement tests. During the year in which this project took place, the achievement test was changed, and new topics were to be tested. At the fourth-grade level one of these topics was geology—specifically, crustal plate movement and its consequences. Such topics had not previously been a part of the fourth-grade curriculum at this school, and the science text that had been selected by the teachers did not contain these topics.

During a conversation with several fourth-grade teachers about these developments, the school library media specialist saw the opportunity to become part of an instructional design team that would implement all the steps in the instructional design process. The teacher who was to instruct all of the fourth-grade students on these topics agreed to join with the school library media specialist to develop the unit. Because of previous scheduling, the first of the four fourth-grade classes was due to be taught the unit in three weeks. The school library media specialist and the teacher agreed to meet twice a week after school and to work at additional times whenever possible.

During the first meeting, the school library media specialist briefly explained the instructional design process and pointed out that some of the steps would probably be emphasized more than others. The goal, the school library media specialist explained, was to design the best unit possible given the constraints under which they were operating.

STEP 1: NEEDS ASSESSMENT

The team decided to use the small-scale needs assessment procedure. Both parties agreed to collect materials on the topic of crustal plate movement for the next meeting.

Phase 1: Generate Goals

The team used several sources to generate a list of goals involving this topic. These sources included textbooks, a curriculum guide from another school system, online curriculum guides, and personal knowledge of the topic. The most useful single source of information was a fourth-grade science text that was state-approved but had not been adopted at the school. The list of goals was as follows:

1. Understand mountain-building forces.

2. Understand erosion forces.

3. Describe crustal plates.

4. Identify types of mountains.

5. Interpret diagrams.

6. Classify types of rocks.

7. Describe layers of the earth.

8. Understand consequences of crustal movement.

Phase 2: Rank Goals

The goals were ranked informally by discussing each one. The teacher expressed the belief that although it was important for the students to do well on the achievement test, it was most important that the students understand the causes of phenomena such as earthquakes. The children had seen the results of earthquakes in California, and several of them had reported that their parents had bought insurance against earthquakes that were predicted to occur nearby. There had been considerable anxiety expressed, and the teacher believed that knowledge was the best way to combat this. Therefore, the rankings were

1. Describe crustal plates.

2. Understand consequences of crustal movement.

3. Describe layers of the earth.

4. Identify types of mountains.

5. Interpret diagrams. (Many tests involve diagrams as part of the question, and the school library media specialist believed that the students should get practice in this information skill.)

6. Understand mountain-building forces.

7. Understand erosion forces.

8. Classify types of rocks.

Phase 3: Determine Extent to Which Goals Have Been Met

Because this was an initial attempt to work with a formal needs assessment procedure, and because there were very real time constraints, the school library media specialist did not press for formal testing at this point. The teacher strongly believed that the students needed instruction in all of the goal topics with the possible exception of topic 8, which had been covered in previous grades. Goals 1 through 7 were assumed to be needs.

Phase 4: Prioritize Needs

Due to time constraints (one week for instruction) and low priority, erosion forces were not selected for instruction. The other topics remained in the priority order of phase 2.

STEP 2: LEARNER ANALYSIS

The instructional team decided to use two methods of learner analysis, *Student Learning Styles—A Survey* and *Learning Tools Inventory*. The methods were used because they would provide a wide range of information and could be obtained and used within the time frame.

The teacher administered *Student Learning Styles—A Survey* two weeks before the unit was scheduled. The *Learning Tools Inventory* was used for each student. The following is a summary of the results.

Student Learning Styles—A Survey

Only the major tendencies (scores above 32) were counted.

language/visual only: seven students

language/auditory only: one student

prefers a variety of modalities: sixteen students

individual learners only: five students

group learners only: seven students

prefers oral output only: eight students

prefers written output only: four students

Learning Tools Inventory

The majority of the students were rated as needing a moderate degree of compensation in all of the learning tools. In general, establishing "set" was seen as the area needing the most support. Three students were judged to be in need of a great deal of compensation (these will be referred to as the high-compensation group). Six students were judged to possess all of the learning tools and to need little or no compensation (the no-compensation group).

STEP 3: INSTRUCTIONAL OBJECTIVES

As is very common, the instructional objectives step generated several problems. The stumbling block in this case was the establishment of a criterion for each instructional objective. Because the school library media specialist sensed that the teacher was becoming frustrated with the process, it was decided to forgo establishing detailed criteria at that point. As an alternative, percent mastery by the class on the test items relative to a specific objective was set as a target for each objective. The goals were examined and a goal-elaboration statement was created for each goal, or, in some cases, a group of goals. Primary instructional objectives were created and instructional enterprises designed. Samples of these are given in figures H.1 and H.2. (Not specified in figures H.1 and H.2 are the instructional enterprises dealing with collision of plates and spreading of plates. These include mountain building and volcanoes.) In all, twenty-four instructional objectives were identified. An overall mastery rate of 80% of the class was set for each objective.

The team decided to spend one day of instruction on layers of the earth, two days on slipping plates (earthquakes), and one day each on colliding and spreading plates (mountain building and volcanoes).

STEP 4: ASSESSMENT OF STUDENT PERFORMANCE

One test was designed as both a pretest and a posttest. The teacher believed that students at this level should have a minimum of essay questions. As a result, matching items were generated for all but one of the instructional objectives. The teacher had also been reading articles on authentic assessment and inquired about this topic to the school library media specialist. It was decided to use a project-based assessment for the plate-slipping instructional objective. For the pretest, the team decided to ask an open-ended question for the plate-slipping objective.

The average score on the pretest for all instructional objectives was 45 percent. The range was from 90 percent (for matching crust to the appropriate part of the diagram) to 0 percent (for recognizing the definition of continental drift). The students' overall test scores ranged from 28 percent to 60 percent. The high-compensation group scored an average of 34 percent. The no-compensation group averaged 53 percent. The team decided to emphasize the instructional objectives for which the lowest scores were obtained.

STEP 5: STRATEGIES AND ACTIVITIES DEVELOPMENT

The No-Compensation Group

Because all but one of the students in the no-compensation group preferred group work or had expressed no preference, the team decided to design a group project for these students. The group

Fig. H.1.

INSTRUCTIONAL ENTERPRISE

Goal: Describe the layers of the earth

Goal Elaboration Statement: The student should know the layers of the earth and their thickness. They should also know whether each layer is solid or liquid, and the relationship between depth and temperature.

Primary Instructional Objective: Given three diagrams (line drawings) of the layers of the earth, 90% of the students will choose the diagram depicting the correct relative thicknesses of the layers, will label the layers, and write the temperature of each layer on the diagram. (Concrete Concepts)

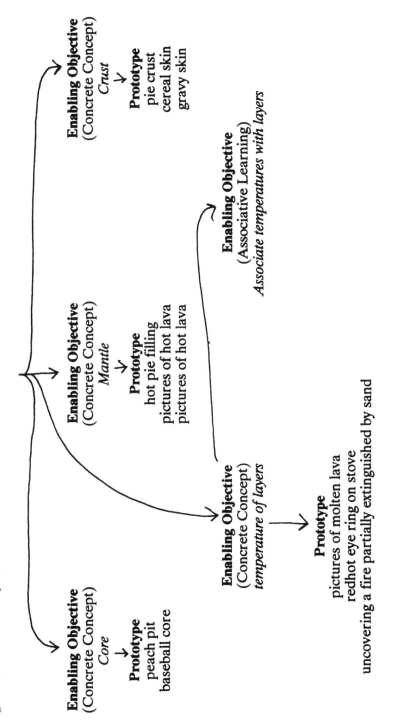

Enabling Objective
(Concrete Concept)
Crust
↓
Prototype
pie crust
cereal skin
gravy skin

Enabling Objective
(Concrete Concept)
Mantle
↓
Prototype
hot pie filling
pictures of hot lava
pictures of hot lava

Enabling Objective
(Associative Learning)
Associate temperatures with layers

Enabling Objective
(Concrete Concept)
Core
↓
Prototype
peach pit
baseball core

Enabling Objective
(Concrete Concept)
temperature of layers
↓
Prototype
pictures of molten lava
redhot eye ring on stove
uncovering a fire partially extinguished by sand

Fig. H.2.

INSTRUCTIONAL ENTERPRISE

Goal: Understand consequences of crustal movement

Goal Elaboration Statement: The student should understand what happens when crustal plates collide head-on, spread apart, slip continuously, and slip occasionally.

Primary Instructional Objective: At least 90% of the students will be able to design and carry out a project illustrating the consequences of continuous release of energy versus buildup and occasional release. They should be able to relate the outcome of their project to the results of crustal plates slipping. (Rule Learning)

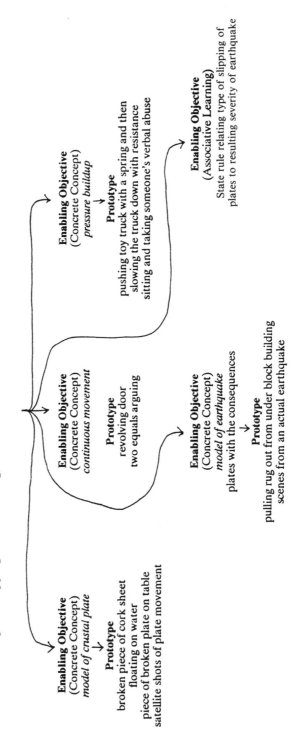

Enabling Objective
(Concrete Concept)
model of crustal plate

↓

Prototype
broken piece of cork sheet
floating on water
piece of broken plate on table
satellite shots of plate movement

Enabling Objective
(Concrete Concept)
continuous movement

↓

Prototype
revolving door
two equals arguing

Enabling Objective
(Concrete Concept)
pressure buildup

↓

Prototype
pushing toy truck with a spring and then
slowing the truck down with resistance
sitting and taking someone's verbal abuse

Enabling Objective
(Concrete Concept)
model of earthquake
plates with the consequences

↓

Prototype
pulling rug out from under block building
scenes from an actual earthquake

Enabling Objective
(Associative Learning)
State rule relating type of slipping of
plates to resulting severity of earthquake

was provided with a list of questions based upon the instructional objectives. Their assignment was to prepare materials and a report that answered the questions and to make a presentation to the rest of the class on the last day of instruction.

The members of the group who preferred oral output were to be the leaders in the presentation. Those who indicated a preference for written output were assigned the task of leading in the writing and production of the materials.

These students were provided access to the PowerPoint presentation that had been produced for the unit. A fourth-grade textbook that contained a chapter on this topic was also made available to them. The no-compensation group was included with the rest of the students when the PowerPoint presentations and several Web sites were shown. The school library media specialist assisted these students in using reference materials (traditional and Web-based) to prepare their report.

The Remaining Students

The teacher believed that the best instructional method for the remaining students, given the existing constraints, would be teacher-led lecture and demonstration. This procedure would allow the teacher the opportunity to build in compensation, especially for those students who required a high degree of compensation.

An opportunity for individual work was provided to this group by giving extra credit for projects done outside of class. The teacher provided the students with a list of topics and descriptions of sample projects. Students kept notebooks in which they drew diagrams as required in the instruction.

Kinesthetic activities were included for this group. The students simulated the forming of the various types of mountains by pretending that their hands were crustal plates colliding, spreading, or slipping.

The teacher paired each high-compensation student with a no-compensation student judged to be a positive peer leader. These pairs worked on the projects as a team; the remaining students were given a choice whether to pair up for the projects.

STEP 6: MATERIALS SELECTION

Because of the time constraints, the search for appropriate materials was limited to local sources, including the school, the local public library, and the school system's media center. Resources were available for the production of transparencies and the PowerPoint presentation.

The learner analysis results indicated that a variety of modalities were required. Because both group and individual learning would be involved, materials to match these requirements were sought. Materials that presented the information in diagrammatic as well as a pictorial form were sought, as well as a medium that could show the movement of crustal plates.

Very few appropriate materials were located. A videotape on earthquakes and volcanoes was available from the district, but the vocabulary and pacing were judged beyond all but the no-compensation group. The school library media specialist also found NASA-related Web sites that contained satellite photographs showing slippage locations.

A PowerPoint presentation was produced to complement the commercial materials. The following is a sample of instructional objectives and the materials acquired or produced for each.

Instructional Objectives Pertaining to Identifying the Layers of the Earth on a Diagram

PowerPoint presentation: shot of an apple; shot of an apple with one quarter of it removed; shot of earth from space; shot of a drawing of earth with one quarter removed (illustrating the layers).

Fig. H.3.

LAYERS OF THE EARTH

CRUST: *Very thin*

MANTLE: *Largest part*

CORE: *Center part (small)*

TEMPERATURE INSIDE THE EARTH

Deeper---Hotter
Rock is often melted

Transparencies: a "structuring" transparency listing the main points to be covered (see fig. H.3); a diagram of the earth with one quarter removed (the labels for the layers were separate and could be placed on and taken off of the transparency).

Illustrations: an illustration from *Journey to the Center of the Earth.*

Instructional Objective Pertaining to Fault-Block Mountains

PowerPoint presentation: full-color shots of examples; shots of diagrams of examples; reduced-detail photographs of plates colliding; shot of a student's hands moving together and forming an approximation of a fault-block mountain (see fig. H.4).

Transparencies: a "structuring" transparency; a diagram of a fault-block mountain with an overlay of the name.

Videotape: a portion of the videotape animating the collision of plates and the forming of a fault-block mountain; a portion of the videotape showing an example of a fault-block mountain with photographs of a highway cut through such a mountain.

Web-based materials: several satellite photographs of locations of slippage.

Fig. H.4. Student's hands illustrating a fault-block mountain

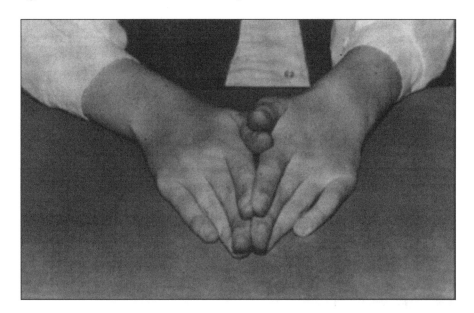

STEP 7: IMPLEMENTATION

The learner analysis had indicated that all the students in the teacher-led group required at least a moderate amount of compensation. The team decided to use the structuring transparencies as the core of this effort. At the start of each lesson, the teacher used the transparency to "set" what was to be covered in that lesson. For each lesson after the first, the major topics that had been covered previously were reviewed at the beginning of the lesson.

The teacher tried to consistently call attention to the criterial information in the visuals used. This was done both verbally and through pointing to the information. (For example, because the videotape was particularly complex visually, the teacher stood beside the screen and pointed to the folded rocks, the lava, etc.) The students were required to participate throughout the instruction through the use of kinesthetic activities, oral questioning, and other techniques.

Special attention was paid to those students who required a great deal of compensation. The teacher directed questions to these students, made sure that they were drawing diagrams correctly, and made certain that their answers to questions were correct before moving on.

Lesson Plan for Day 1

PRIMARY INSTRUCTIONAL OBJECTIVE

Given three diagrams of line drawings of the layers of the earth, 90 percent of the students will: choose the diagram depicting the correct relative thickness of the layers; label the layers correctly; and write the approximate temperature of each layer on the diagram.

ENABLING OBJECTIVES

1. Identify the core on a diagram. (Concrete Concept Learning)

2. Identify the mantle on a diagram. (Concrete Concept Learning)

3. Identify the crust on a diagram. (Concrete Concept Learning)

4. Select from various diagrams the one that best represents the relative thickness of the layers. (Concrete Concept Learning)

5. Recall the approximate temperature of each of the layers. (Associative Learning)

LEARNER GROUP

Students prefer mixed modalities. Need moderate to high degree of compensation, especially "set."

PRETEST RESULTS FOR ENABLING OBJECTIVES

1. 70%

2. 76%

3. 90%

4. 19%

5. 25%

MOTIVATING ACTIVITY

Because this was the first lesson in the unit, the team decided to use a motivating activity that would apply to the whole unit and make what they were about to study relevant to the personal life of each student. The students were paired and each given a list of personal statements referring to the other's appearance, intelligence, and other traits. In part 1 of the exercise, the students took turns reading the statements to each other and responding. In part 2, Student 1 read each statement, and the other student was not allowed to respond at all. Then, Student 2 assumed the role of the "taunter."

This exchange was followed by a general class discussion regarding how the students felt when they had to "sit and take it" versus being able to respond. The teacher pointed out that there are forces in the earth that, if not allowed release, build up with devastating effects.

DESCRIPTION OF PRESENTATION

What shape is the earth? (digital photograph)

Shaped like an apple. (digital photograph)

We can cut out a section of the apple to see what is inside. (digital photograph)

Pretend that you are a worm on the apple. Dig through skin, flesh, core.

If we could cut out a section of the earth, scientists believe that it would have similar sections. (digital photograph) Point out layers.

Point out layers on transparency. (digital photograph) Students come up and place labels on photograph. Students copy diagram of layers.

Compare thickness of parts of the apple to parts of the earth. *Emphasize this.* What would really happen if you tried to journey to the center of the earth? It is so hot deep in the earth that rocks are melted. (digital photograph)

Place labels with temperatures on the photograph and have the students predict which layer each is associated with.

Review (concentrate on relative thickness).

PROVISIONS FOR PARTICIPATION

Have J____, R____, and M____ (the high-compensation students) come up and place labels on the photographs.

Each student draws and labels diagram.

Check diagrams.

Question correspondence between layers of the apple and layers of the earth.

POSTTEST

Use pretest.

Summary of the Instruction

Several logistical problems arose during the instructional period. The teacher became ill shortly before the week of instruction and lost the ability to speak for a time. Although she managed to be present for all of the instruction, her performance was no doubt affected.

Several of the students were absent during the week. One was suspended for four days for threatening another teacher. Finally, the instruction and testing took place during the week before Christmas vacation. The teacher reported that several of the students seemed distracted by the upcoming vacation.

STEP 8: EVALUATION

The same test was used for the pretest and posttest. The students scored an average of 80 percent on the posttest. The no-compensation group averaged 89 percent. The high-compensation

Fig. H.5. Results of resisting tectonic plate slipping

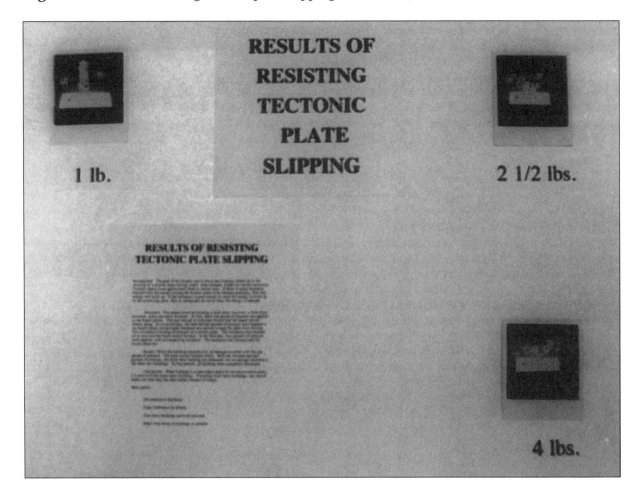

group averaged 80 percent. The results of the projects were very encouraging. Students were very creative in finding ways to demonstrate the impact of plate slippage. One particularly impressive project demonstrated the effect of different amounts of sudden force on structures built of dominoes. (See figure H.5.)

EVALUATION OF THE STEPS IN THE INSTRUCTIONAL DESIGN PROCESS

Needs Assessment

Preparation for citywide achievement tests was the driving force behind the selection of topics for this unit. Various sources were consulted in conducting the needs assessment. The instructional goals could have been stated more specifically.

The greatest weakness of the implementation of this procedure was the reliance on intuition to determine what the students already knew of the topics selected. Instruction was altered on the basis of the pretest results, but an awareness that many of the students had already mastered several of the enabling objectives could have helped redirect the resources earlier.

The teacher agreed to attempt to determine the extent of pre-knowledge through other methods in subsequent design attempts. These could include informal questioning and spot testing.

Learner Analysis

The methods of learner analysis chosen were judged adequate for separating the students into groups for which materials and activities could be selected. The teacher believed that the process of completing the instrument in *Student Learning Styles—A Survey* benefited the students because they had not previously participated in a formal learner analysis. However, the teacher added that the scale used might have caused some difficulty for the students.

No attempt was made to determine and account for environmental preferences. Instruction was not varied for individual students on the basis of the information from the pretest. The team decided that in future unit design an attempt would be made to use pretest information to vary instruction individually for each student.

Instructional Objectives

Goal-elaboration statements were created from the instructional goals, and primary and secondary instructional objectives were derived from these. An instructional enterprise was formulated tying the objectives and schema clusters together.

The instructional objectives could have been more specific in terms of learner description and criteria. The school library media specialist thought that they were as specific as available resources allowed. The teacher believed that several of the objectives were at too high a level for the limited time available. It was decided that in future redesigns of this unit, entrance skills would be stated more clearly and a stronger attempt made to determine if the students possessed these skills.

Assessment of Student Performance

Probably the greatest strength of the test used was that it was derived directly from the instructional objectives and provided an indication as to whether the objectives had been met. The team also attempted to include some authentic assessment of the instructional objectives, and this turned out to be a very positive aspect of the unit. Although the test was judged adequate, several concerns were raised by the team.

Suggestions for improvement included grouping similar items together—for example, all questions about the diagrams. Scrutiny of the items raised several concerns about reliability and validity. As an example, the students were required to select *seismograph* from a list of words as matching the definition "a machine that measures the strength of an earthquake." *Seismograph* was clearly the only word in the list that could be a machine.

The teacher was very pleased with the project results. These were used in a presentation at the state education association meeting. The teacher has become an advocate for a variety of assessment techniques.

Strategies and Activities Development

Strategies and activities were selected on the basis of the learner analyses and instructional objectives. A learning tool was included in the needs assessment results (using diagrams). In addition, the team modeled and encouraged the use of learning tools. The team believed that for most of the students, the strategies and activities used were appropriate, as most of the students appeared to be on-task the majority of the time. An exception was one student in the no-compensation group who indicated a preference for individual work but was put in a group. This student, who had a score of 56 percent on the pretest, had a score of only 76 percent on the posttest. The teacher believed that this student would have done better if allowed to work individually.

Materials Selection

The team believed, given the time constraints, that the materials obtained were more than adequate. The materials were selected on the basis of the instructional objectives and the students' characteristics.

Time constraints prevented one-to-one or small-group testing of the materials. However, several of the materials were revised following their use with this unit. Many of the digital photographs had been slightly underexposed and were redone.

The team decided to conduct a search for more and better Web-based materials for this unit as a long-range project. The library media supervisor in the district was made aware of the topics, and assistance was requested.

Implementation

Probably the strongest aspect of the instruction was the teacher's ability to compensate for deficiencies in the learning tools. This was done both during instructor-presented and packaged instruction. The teacher maintained excellent classroom control. No major discipline problems occurred. Because mastery of much of the subject matter was dependent upon previous mastery, several of the students who missed two or more days were at a severe disadvantage. The teacher could not provide remediation to bring these students up-to-date with the class because resources were not available for this effort.

The teacher observed that the next time this unit was taught, an effort would be made to question a larger percentage of students to ascertain readiness for the next topic. A method of keeping track of whom had been questioned and whether a correct answer had been given would be considered.

SUMMARY

The major accomplishment of this unit, most likely a direct result of the participation by the school library media specialist as a member of the instructional design consultation team, was the success of the high-compensation group. These students, who had consistently scored at the bottom of the class, achieved mastery of many of the objectives. Furthermore, the teacher observed a marked change in attitude following the unit. One of the students requested more study of "mountains and stuff."

The 80 percent mastery goal was not met for five of the twenty-four instructional objectives tested. However, solid gains were observed for four out of five of the objectives for which the 80 percent goal was not reached (as an example, from 0 percent to 75 percent for the item testing the objective of continuous movement of crustal plates). Moreover, an overall average of 80 percent was achieved despite logistical impediments. Finally, the team members agreed that the instructional design process provided the tools to alter instruction to improve the percentage of mastery the next time the unit was presented.

INDEX